Hate in Precarious Times

Hate in Precarious Times

*Mobilizing Anxiety from the
Alt-Right to Brexit*

Neal Curtis

I.B. TAURIS
LONDON • NEW YORK • OXFORD • NEW DELHI • SYDNEY

I.B. TAURIS

Bloomsbury Publishing Plc

50 Bedford Square, London, WC1B 3DP, UK

1385 Broadway, New York, NY 10018, USA

29 Earlsfort Terrace, Dublin 2, Ireland

BLOOMSBURY, I.B. TAURIS and the I.B. Tauris logo are trademarks of
Bloomsbury Publishing Plc

First published in Great Britain 2021

Cover design: Charlotte Daniels

A catalogue record for this book is available from the British Library.

A catalog record for this book is available from the Library of Congress.

ISBN: HB: 978-0-7556-0303-9
PB: 978-0-7556-0304-6
ePDF: 978-0-7556-0306-0
eBook: 978-0-7556-0307-7

Typeset by Deanta Global Publishing Services, Chennai, India

To find out more about our authors and books visit www.bloomsbury.com and
sign up for our newsletters

To Dorice Mary Curtis (1937–2019) and Henry Kenneth Curtis (1935–2019)
who taught me a lot about love.

I think the logic we're enjoined to adopt is, basically, it's only definitely fascism once it's definitely too late.

– @kerlarsenickoff

Contents

Acknowledgements

I would like to thank my wife, Amber Walls, and my son, Noah Curtis. They have both given me a huge amount of support during the writing of this book. While my wife works hard every day to improve the life of young people in the present, I know my son will have to work hard to improve the life of people in the future. He is growing up in a world far more precarious than the one I knew. I would also like to thank Jenny Stümer, who has talked to me about many of the issues discussed here and commented on other pieces of work that later found a home in this book. Gratitude is also due to Lillian Hanly for enlightening me on numerous issues relevant to the themes presented here. I am also grateful to the anonymous reviewers for their comments on the proposal and earlier draft. Additional thanks should also go to Nabeel Zuberi and Avril Bell for pointing me in the direction of some helpful reading material. In addition, thanks go to all my colleagues in Media and Communication at the University of Auckland who work hard to give each other time to write up larger projects such as this. In difficult times, their solidarity is appreciated. I would also like to say thank you to Tomasz Hoskins and Nayiri Kendir at Bloomsbury for making this book possible. Finally, I would like to acknowledge all those struggling for recognition, equality and justice whose voices continue to educate me. I would also like to acknowledge all indigenous people still affected by the legacy of colonialism, especially the *Tangata Whenua* of *Aotearoa*.

Introduction

Towards the end of high school, I read *Biedermann und die Brandstifter* (Biedermann and the arsonists) by Max Frisch. It was a compulsory text for our German class and a book that has stayed with me all my life. Primarily, I think, because at some fundamental level, it terrified me, articulating a basic truth about our capacity to blindly walk into a catastrophe. Despite our intelligence and ingenuity, reasoning and rational calculation, fantastic imaginings and foresight, the play shows just how reluctant we are to acknowledge what is readily apparent if it challenges what we want to believe. Written in 1958, the play centres on the activities of two arsonists disguised as itinerant salesmen who convince people to let them stay in their house only to burn it down. In the play, Biedermann is fully aware of the arsonists. He sits down to breakfast and obsessively reads reports about them in the local newspaper; yet, when they knock on his door, he can't bring himself to think that the cordial Schmitz and, later, the candid Eisenring are the criminals his town is being terrorized by. Consequently, he lets them in.

As Schmitz and Eisenring make their preparations to burn down Biedermann's house, he watches them take barrels of gasoline up the stairs. When Biedermann asks what they are doing, they tell him they're going to burn down his house. He laughs, still unable to believe the two 'salesmen' are really going to do what they are so clearly now doing. Finally, he even helps measure the fuse and then gives them the matches to start the fire. Frisch was, of course, at pains to make it clear that Biedermann was not unique in his inability to see what was really happening. The German word *bieder* means ordinary or conventional but also has connotations of conservative and upright. Biedermann is, thus, the worthy everyman who believes his own sense of propriety makes him immune. Among the many interpretations of this story, the most popular is as an allegory for the ease with which the German people enabled the rise of Nazism. In our current political context, it is therefore an especially relevant literary work given the current resurgence of populist nationalism, neo-fascism and white supremacism that is threatening to overturn the international, liberal democratic consensus.

The threat is most evident in the rise of Donald Trump, a man with deep authoritarian tendencies who loves strong leaders like Putin, Erdogan and Duterte; he boasted that he'd like the American people to listen to him in the way the North Koreans listen to Kim-Jong Un and constantly refers to mainstream media as 'the enemy of the people'. Aside from these dictatorial aspirations, Trump exemplifies the problem because he rose to power on a racist, white nationalist ticket that included the demonization of Muslims and Mexicans. This agenda was signalled prior to the election through Trump's promotion of Birtherism, the racist conspiracy theory about President Obama's place of birth, and then confirmed by early nominations to his administration that included Jeff Sessions as the attorney general. This is a man known for his attempted prosecution of civil rights activists known as the Marion Three and whose last act as the attorney general was 'to sabotage the legal instruments of federal civil rights enforcement', which will have a disproportionate effect on black communities across the United States (Bennett and Takei 2018). There was also the short-lived appointment of Michael Flynn as the National Security Adviser, who proposed that 'fear of Muslims is rational', and Stephen Miller, whose portfolio includes the Muslim ban and the policy separating migrant children from their parents. This politics was also signalled through the appointment of Sebastian Gorka as a security adviser and a man fond of wearing medals with a connection to Hungarian Nazis.

It was also evident in Trump's inability to condemn the neo-Nazis who marched through Charlottesville at the murderous 'Unite the Right' rally, preferring instead to call them 'very fine people'. He also pandered to this strain of politics early on by pardoning Joe Appaio, who was charged and found guilty of maltreating Latino prisoners under his supervision, and by giving his support to Roy Moore, who thinks the United States should do away with constitutional amendments after the tenth – which includes amendment 13 abolishing slavery, amendment 15 giving all races voting rights and amendment 19 giving the vote to women. More recently, his divisive politics were epitomized in the executive order that announced a 'Garden of National Heroes' on 4 July 2020. This was designed to explicitly counter the upsurge in anti-racism and demands to take down statues celebrating the Confederacy, slave owners and colonialism that followed the killing of George Floyd. The location for his speech was itself an affront to the anti-racism movement. It was delivered at the site of the Six Grandfathers in the Black Hills, a place sacred to the Lakota that was vandalized in 1927 to create what is now called Mount Rushmore. This politics was then made explicit in September 2020 when he expressed his desire to end Federal anti-racism training.

Trump's early agenda was most explicit in the choice of Steve Bannon as his chief strategist. Bannon has a varied biography, which in August 2020 included being charged with fraud in relation to a border wall fundraising scheme, but is best known as the one-time CEO of the far-right media outlet, *Breitbart*. In 2016, Bannon declared the media outlet was a platform for a political movement that called itself the Alt-Right, the name that neo-Nazis, white supremacists and white nationalists now prefer to use. He later tried to distance himself when the association seemed less expedient (Nguyen 2017). Primarily, the Alt-Right is a new name for an array of old and especially unpleasant far-right groups who respond with extreme prejudice – but without any sense of irony – to each and every progressive advance made under the umbrella of 'identity politics'. Bannon is also a hard-line, conservative Catholic, and in a speech at the Vatican in 2014, he called for the 'Church militant' to fight against the 'barbarity' now challenging the Judeo-Christian foundations of the West. In March 2018, he also told a far-right audience in France: 'Let them call you racist. Let them call you xenophobes. Let them call you nativists. Wear it as a badge of honor. Because every day, we get stronger and they get weaker.'

Most recently, as reported by the Southern Poverty Law Center (Hayden 2019), Stephen Miller's white nationalism was revealed through the leak of emails to Breitbart, in which he recommended articles from white supremacist websites *VDARE* and *American Renaissance*. Miller also suggested *Breitbart* run a story promoting the deeply racist French novel, *Camp of Saints*. As Hayden (2019) reports,

> The novel's apocalyptic plot centers on a flotilla of Indian people who invade France, led by a nonwhite Indian-born antagonist referred to as the 'turd eater' – a character who literally eats human feces. In one section, a white woman is raped to death by brown-skinned refugees. In another, a nationalist character shoots and kills a pro-refugee leftist over his support of race mixing. The white nationalist Social Contract Press plucked the 1973 book from relative obscurity and distributed it in the United States. (np)

Bannon has on many occasions also expressed his admiration for *Camp of Saints*, and when Miller was asked about these emails, he simply evaded the question pointing out his recommendations were 'pro-American'. This is a phrase, like the choice of 'America First' as Trump's campaign slogan, that has a prominent history in the pre-war politics of American neo-Nazis and white supremacists.[1] However, the Alt-Right's politics has increasingly found a home in the conservative mainstream that is increasingly shifting away from the multiculturalism and equality that twentieth-century democracy espoused. As such, this is a phenomenon that is not reducible to Trump. Rather, Bannon's genius was to make him the lightning rod for a broader resentment towards the 'establishment', representing a cultural shift we will need to address for many years to come.

The reason I say this is because the United States is not an isolated case. The threat to the liberal democratic consensus can also be seen in the rise of nationalist, often white nationalist movements across Europe. In the UK, the governing Conservative Party had effectively been hijacked by the UK Independence Party (UKIP) led by Nigel Farage – an organization well known for its hostility to multiculturalism and its focus on anti-immigration policies. UKIP's very existence was premised upon the attempt to secure the UK's exit from the EU, which it incorrectly blamed for a host of problems not least the dilution of British culture through 'waves' of migration.[2] With the Conservative Party having appropriated UKIP's hard right position – exemplified in the Brexit fiasco and Theresa May's creation of a 'hostile environment' for immigrants – the reason for UKIP's existence became less clear. To this effect, it shifted towards an identity it had formerly tried to hide – when in 2018 Tommy Robinson was made an adviser to the party by the then leader, Gerard Batten. Robinson, whose real name is Stephen Yaxley-Lennon, is the founder of the far-right group known as the English Defence League and a long-time proponent of Islamophobia and anti-Muslim propaganda, as well as anti-EU rhetoric. Since then, Nigel Farage made a brief return to politics by starting the Brexit Party, a vehicle simply designed to force the hand of the Conservative Party when he thought it may might not deliver on the vote for the UK to leave the EU.

Under Boris Johnson, the party has even more vociferously committed itself to a nationalist, anti-immigration stance, with significant members such as Jacob Rees-Mogg happy to see Steve Bannon as an ally and Bannon himself claiming to mentor Johnson. While there has been a long-standing political shift to the right in Western democracies that began with the policies of Margaret Thatcher and Ronald Reagan, this recent 'populist' lurch further rightwards in the UK has its roots, I believe, in the economic and social pressures that resulted from the failures of the neoliberal dogma Thatcher introduced, an issue I focus on in Chapter 6. The precarity that followed the Financial Crisis of 2008 and was exacerbated by the politics of 'austerity' was redirected into a generalized xenophobia that was mobilized by nationalists to secure the Leave vote in the referendum and Johnson's later landslide election victory in 2019. Both were sold to the British people using a media environment dominated by a virulently right-wing press and a BBC seemingly in thrall to the Conservative Party. As the current economic system continues to deliver material inequality and insecurity, this politics of romanticized nationalism in the face of a clearly defined enemy, distributed through a compliant media and unregulated social media has become the new strategy for securing power in many countries. It is also a perfect example of what Lauren Berlant (2006) calls 'cruel optimism'. This is a 'condition of maintaining an attachment to a problematic object' such that the attachment actually 'contributes to the attrition of the very thriving that is supposed to be made possible in the work of attachment in the first place' (21). In other words, by attaching ourselves to a romantic and exclusive nationalism not only will we not thrive and receive the security we desire, but we will actively undermine it.

This political shift would be very troubling if it were only the United States and the United Kingdom that had succumbed to hard-line nationalist agendas, but the problem is compounded by a dangerous shift to far-right and fascist affiliations across Europe. I will return to this in Chapter 1, but, like Michael Mann, I tend to think of fascism as the name for a more 'general phenomenon' (2004: 9) to which Nazism and other forms of belligerent ethno-nationalism are linked. This type of politics has made significant advances in France where the Front Nationale (now known as National Rally) came second in the 2017 election, while in 2018 the neo-Nazi party known as Alternative for Germany (AfD) became the third largest group in the Bundestag. Like all of these groups, the AfD leader, Georg Pazderski, talked of providing 'a real opposition' to the bogeyman these parties uniformly refer to as the 'establishment' or the 'elite'. This racist populism is also ascendant in Austria where the coalition government included the far-right Freedom Party until scandal brought what is surely just a temporary setback. In the Netherlands, their own far-right were narrowly 'defeated' in the spring of 2017 only by the governing parties embracing many of the Party for Freedom's policies.

The standard for many of these groups is the success of Viktor Orbán in Hungary – a country with a strong fascist history (Mann 2004: 237) – and his self-declared 'illiberal' revolution that has included attacks on the press and universities as well as populist legislation against Hungary's Muslim and LGBTQ communities. This approach is summed up in his declaration that 'Today Europe is as fragile, weak and sickly as a flower being eaten away by a hidden worm [. . .] the masses arriving from other civilisations endanger our way of life, our culture, our customs and our Christian traditions'. These traditions, of course, include a very strong patriarchal society, leading him to table legislation to outlaw gender studies from Hungarian universities. In many respects, this speech epitomizes one of the central causes of fascism identified by Mann, that of 'civilizational contradiction and decay' (2004: 23). It is also central to the rhetoric of Bannon for which Trump has become such an excellent mouthpiece. Orbán's nativist agenda is also evident in the growth of far-right politics in Poland where the governing Law and Justice Party described the fascist takeover of the country's Independence Day march in November 2017 as a 'beautiful sight'.

To this, we can add the white nationalist Identitarian Movement that originated in France but has spread across Northern Europe. Further evidence is the resurgence of far-right sentiment in Spain and Italy, who have, of course, strong historical connections to fascism; and all this time, Steve Bannon tours Europe stirring up nationalist and nativist extremism with the intention of fundamentally transforming, if not completely dismantling, European liberalism. Further afield the signs of authoritarian nationalism can be found in India under Narendra Modi and his Bharatiya Janata Party (BJP), which has historical links with Indian fascism and the Hindutva movement, and in Turkey under Recep Erdogan. More recently, it has surfaced in Brazil with the election of Jair Bolsonaro – who idolizes Trump so much he live-streamed himself on Facebook watching his hero's post-impeachment speech – and, of course, it has been the basis of Vladimir Putin's leadership in Russia, who has rather disturbingly become an idol for this political movement. And yet, like Biedermann, we still can't believe this means anything because we refuse to accept these groups can or even want to burn down our house.

The politics of hate, which I believe has come to define this movement and our political moment, has a very long history (Anderson 2017). If we are to understand the current situation, we must acknowledge the history that informs it and from which it takes inspiration. As I have noted, the current manifestation of this politics is synonymous with the movement known as the Alt-Right, of which there have been some very good and detailed studies to date (Neiwert 2017; Wendling 2018; Hawley 2019; Marantz 2019). It is a quintessentially American movement that has also acted as an accelerant and signal booster for far-right groups in the UK and across Europe in a rather perverse iteration of US soft power. In May 2020, the influence of this movement on mainstream politics even further afield was evident when the new leader of the New Zealand National Party, which had formed the government for nine years from 2008 to 2017, was interviewed about the reason he proudly displayed one of Trump's Make America Great Again hats in his office. In response, he claimed he also had memorabilia from Hillary Clinton's campaign and that he was just interested in American politics. A hat is just a hat; we were told. The fact this hat had become so closely associated with white supremacy seemed of little concern to a man seeking to be the prime minister of a country with a colonial history that is still riven by racial prejudice and ethnically marked inequality. He then announced an opposition cabinet that was remarkably white; when questioned about it, Judith Collins MP, echoing a now infamous Alt-Right meme, asked, 'Is there something wrong with me being white?'

Hence, as I will argue throughout the chapters here, this book is not simply an expression of concern about politics at the margins because it is increasingly infiltrating the centre. To this effect, I will sometimes use the term 'radical right' when referring to the aims, interests and discourses that the far-right now share with supposedly more traditional forms of conservatism. The 'radical right' is not only epitomized in the transformation of the US Republican Party into a Trump cult built on white anxiety and the accompanying sense of white entitlement, but it can also be seen in the UK and the Brexit referendum where a divisive neo-nationalism has taken hold of the country. Here, traditional conservatism retains the belief that the 'Great' of Great Britain does not simply refer to the federation of countries that comprise the British Isles but signals the nation's moral superiority and the legitimacy of its empire. This has been mobilized to appeal to the explicitly racist politics of those supporting far-right groups like the English Defence League and Britain First but is also deployed to conjure up nostalgia for a 'Great' Britain that regular 'patriots' believe has been lost. At the same time, a vitriolic and xenophobic press has enabled this alliance of elitism and crude bigotry to become a broad 'populist' movement. The fact that successive UK Conservative governments have consistently heightened racial tension and used immigration to garner support created a culture in which far-right sentiment could bloom and believe itself justified. On 13 June 2020, the absurdity of this alliance was put on display when, amid Black Lives Matter protests and demonstrations against imperial statues, a call was put out on social media to protect them. Far-right counter-protestors assembled in Central London, attacked the police and openly displayed Nazi salutes not far from the Cenotaph. What followed was UK prime minister, Boris Johnson, well known himself for regular racist outbursts, going on TV to denounce the 'thuggery'. At the same time, the right-wing tabloid, *The Mail on Sunday* (which together with The *Daily Mail* has been an important conduit for racial animosity), ran a front page headline asking, 'What HAS become of the tolerant Britain we love?' As Richard Littler commented on Twitter, this might as well read: '"Who ate all the chickens?" Asks the fox with feathers in its mouth.'

As noted earlier, though, while the UK Conservative Party has cut off any threat to its right flank by courting far-right support (albeit while performing contortions to publicly decry it) and has purposefully played on the racial anxieties of post-imperial Britain, the radical right in the UK has been very much influenced by what has happened 'across the pond' with the political success of the Alt-Right. The origin of the term Alt-Right is said to have been Paul Gottfried's speech to the H. L. Mencken Club in 2008 titled 'The Decline and Rise of the Alternative Right', a name that was then used by Gottfried's protégé and neo-Nazi activist, Richard Spencer, for the *AlternativeRight* website he founded in 2010. Gottfried has described himself as a 'paleoconservative', a strain of conservatism that has Pat Buchanan as its most celebrated advocate. According to Mike Wendling, 'Paleos dislike immigration and multiculturalism. In contrast to neoconservatives, they are sceptical of free trade and foreign military adventures. They look to the past and are strict traditionalists when it comes to gender, ethnicity, race and social order' (2018: 17–18). However, as Wendling also notes, the Alt-Right is a 'Frankenstein of a political group' (223) and hence evades easy categorization. That said, although the Paleo description fits, perhaps the most defining element in this group's philosophy is the doctrine of white supremacy and the politics of illiberal, white nationalism it espouses.

To this effect, this movement readily taps into deep-seated prejudices that were instrumental in the colonial projects that defined various modern European nations and the attitudes and practices of the British Empire that helped position that small nation on the 'top table' of international politics. British and European imperialism led to the creation of a number of countries built on the dereliction of indigenous peoples, the dispossession of their resources and the accrual of vast wealth through the system of slavery. Although these countries are now regarded as defenders of democracy and advocates of equality and multiculturalism, the racist disposition that enabled and supposedly justified colonial expansion remains just beneath the surface today, readily accessible to anyone willing to exploit it. This is why it is so concerning when George Hawley, in his otherwise very good introduction to the Alt-Right, claims, 'the number of people who support the Alt-Right's radical agenda remains small' (2019: 6). Given the propensity for the rhetoric and ideology of the Alt-Right to tap into latent myths of racial and/or cultural supremacy, *explicit* support for the Alt-Right is not the issue. The fact they can become a lightning rod for a range of other discriminatory forms of politics, especially under the conditions of precarity I will describe in this book, ought to be our primary concern.

Although the racial prejudices of the Alt-Right date back to the Crusades and the later colonization of the 'New World' – and, in the case of the Alt-Right's misogyny, their prejudices are as old as *hist*ory itself – as a right-wing phenomenon, the movement has significant precursors. The most proximate is the white power movement that began in the wake of the Vietnam War and grew throughout the 1980s and 1990s until one of the movement's adherents, Timothy McVeigh, bombed the Alfred P. Murrah Federal Building in Oklahoma in 1995, and the white power movement went into something of a hiatus. I will return to this in Chapters 2 and 4 through the important work of Kathleen Belew (2018), but the Alt-Right has another progenitor in the American Right that Richard Hofstadter wrote about in *Harper's Magazine* in

1964 under the title 'The Paranoid Style in American Politics'. Although this essay is now more than fifty-five years old, it is strikingly resonant with the attitudes of the Alt-Right today and of the Trump supporters who wanted to Make America Great Again. In that article, after tracing the style all the way back to the nineteenth century, Hofstadter wrote:

> The spokesmen of those earlier movements felt that they stood for causes and personal types that were still in possession of their country – that they were fending off threats to a still established way of life. But the modern right wing, as Daniel Bell has put it, feels dispossessed: America has been largely taken away from them and their kind, though they are determined to try to repossess it and to prevent the final destructive act of subversion. The old American virtues have already been eaten away by cosmopolitans and intellectuals; the old competitive capitalism has been gradually undermined by socialistic and communistic schemers; the old national security and independence have been destroyed by treasonous plots, having as their most powerful agents not merely outsiders and foreigners as of old but major statesmen who are at the very centers of American power. (4)

Of course, it is important to be aware of what makes the Alt-Right specific as an early twenty-first-century political movement but to separate it from the history of racism, colonialism and the long tradition of the white man's many chauvinisms, and, indeed, paranoia, is a failure. It is imperative we recognize how it can still appeal to and activate attitudes that are disavowed but remain dominant despite our overtures to equality and democracy. In addition, we need to be more honest about the historical prevalence of fascism. Like all things that are hard to own up to, remember or reflect upon, we tend to diminish or completely repress them. This is certainly the case with fascism. Popular history tells us this was some sort of political perversion, that it was peculiar to Germany and perhaps Italy. Some people might also include Spain, but very rarely do people easily include Austria, Latvia, Bulgaria, Hungary, Romania, Croatia, Norway and Greece. In the UK in particular, the narrative comfortably sets fascism outside, allowing the UK to become the source of virtue; yet, we know Oswald Mosley and his Brown Shirts did not lack support in Britain. Even the connection between this repugnant ideology and the British royal family is now well known, thanks to the episode on the Marburg Files in the second series of Netflix's popular series *The Crown*. The fact that Edward VIII had strong ideological links to Nazism is an indication of just how widespread and acceptable its aristocratic vision of white supremacy and imperial mission was.

The resurgence of far-right politics in conjunction with the waning of the post-war social democratic consensus is, then, the defining feature of our current situation, but this threat is only a symptom of a much deeper problem. While the emboldening of nationalist and fascist ideologies and a range of other discriminatory chauvinisms are finding more support within the corridors of power, they are given sustenance by a constellation of conditions that have contributed to people's heightened sense of vulnerability and the anxiety that accompanies it. In other words, while democratic society is at its most precarious since 1939, it is a more pervasive sense of precarity that is feeding this. As such, this book attempts to set out the nature of this precarity and show how the uncertainties of our time make far-right politics especially attractive. There exists a set of ontological, existential, economic, social and epistemological vulnerabilities that make inward-looking, exclusive, discriminatory and, ultimately, hateful creeds especially attractive. They also make our ability to resist them increasingly less robust. The structure of the book, therefore, begins with a more developed consideration of contemporary politics and the hate that defines it before setting out the specific forms of precarity that fuel such politics.

As I will explain in Chapter 2, hate is an especially empowering emotion, and that empowerment produces an immediate effect. While love can be the source of great support, stability, joy and fulfilment, it also places the lover in a relationship of dependence, one that is marked by vulnerability and risk. I am sure I do not need to expand on the fragility of love. We have a history of literature for that. By contrast, hate, while needing an object to hate, is quite immune to changes in that object. It doesn't really matter what the object does (or doesn't do). If the desire to hate it remains, the emotion can continue to find its target. Because of this, hate can more easily 'fill up' and satisfy us. It also comes with important narrative and cognitive aspects that place the object of hate in a position of inferiority to the person doing the hating. Where the object of love is often exalted, the object of hate is regularly demeaned.

In our current situation, which for the vast majority of us comprises a range of precarities marked by concerns over our 'way of life', physical threats from terrorists, uncertainties over the global economy, fears about our social status and increasing uncertainty about what we can believe is true, a politics that immediately emboldens us and shores up our identity, our place, our sense of entitlement and the legitimacy of our prejudice becomes very attractive. As such, the purpose of the book is to explain how we arrived at this historical moment where an illiberal and anti-democratic politics, rooted in very old chauvinisms, has become resurgent in the international political arena. This is not a book of prediction, even if it extrapolates from our current condition to present a warning. What it does propose, however, is that irrespective of the ebb and flow of political fortunes of those now ascendant, the precarity outlined here is unlikely to go away and will remain the source for the projection of deeply divisive and potentially authoritarian politics long into the future. Only by recognizing and understanding the constellation of precarities that exist, as well as the sociopolitical dangers they harbour, can we hope to overcome the difficulties we face and build a more equitable, just, peaceful and sustainable future.

On that last note, the one precarity I do not talk about here is the environmental precarity of climate change. This is not to diminish its importance. In fact, I think it is the most important issue for this generation. However, while the denial of climate science has been an important theme that unites the radical right, I do not believe it has (yet) been instrumental in the formation of that politics and its subsequent infiltration of the mainstream. All the other examples of precarity I do discuss are ones I believe have made a direct contribution to the resurgence of far-right thought and exclusionary forms of nationalism. Having said that, climate change will certainly exacerbate the constellation of precarities I present here. Resource depletion, pollution, extreme weather (including flooding and droughts), rising sea levels and the inability of arable land to continue to produce food or the shifting of production to match changing ecological conditions will all contribute to greater competition among states, put severe strain on already weakened public institutions and services and, no doubt, increase the global movement of people. What is most troubling is the sense that the planetary cooperation needed to solve these problems is being abandoned in favour of isolationist and belligerent nationalisms. Again, these might be passing (even if extended) political anomalies, but I find it unlikely that the attitudes underpinning both the Trump and Brexit phenomena will simply evaporate even if their architects move on.

Another precarity that emerged during the writing of this book was the COVID-19 pandemic. As much as this was a natural disaster where a virus that evolved in wet markets in Wuhan, China, quickly moved through the vectors of international air travel infecting every part of the globe, it was also a social disaster. It was exacerbated by underfunding in national health services, government incompetence, a cynical corporate sector willing to sacrifice millions on the altar of 'the economy' and a not insignificant indifference to that scale of death from certain sections of national populations. While a UK government with an interest in eugenics – an issue that itself registers the resurgence of far-right thinking – proposed Britons 'take it on the chin' to achieve 'herd immunity', protestors against the lockdown in the United States were happy to parade banners declaring 'I will not trade my freedom for your safety' or demand that we 'sacrifice the weak'. It is impossible to know what the full effects of the pandemic will be beyond a deep and prolonged recession, if not an economic depression, so this is also not something that receives attention in this book. However, what is interesting about the pandemic is how it became a lens through which the precarities I do speak about came clearly into view.

In the first place, it revealed our ontological precarity by showing how fragile our 'way of life' is. It also showed how intransigent people could be when their 'world' is threatened. The pandemic gave us ample evidence of people whose sense of 'freedom' is divorced from any and every sense of limit, even if that limit is the simple and valid request to make every attempt not to be a means for the virus to spread. Here, one interpretation of the world based in spurious philosophical thinking about absolute individual sovereignty usurped the scientific interpretation of the world as a collection of myriad paths for infection. The desire to commit even more fiercely to the former fabulation in response to the facts of the second speaks volumes about our sense of identity and how confrontational we become if it is challenged. The pandemic also exposed us to the physical and existential threat of illness and death, and – like many of these situations – it, too, became the vehicle for quite pronounced racism, in this instance, towards Chinese people.

Economically, aside from the push from corporate-aligned conservatives to let millions die as a tribute to Mammon, the virus also showed how fragile the socio-economic structure is that we have built. It immediately became clear how a lack of labour rights including sick pay and holidays, as well as access to healthcare was exposing people to far greater risk. As in 2008, the wonders of free-market capitalism could only be rescued by a deep and prolonged dose of socialism where the state stepped in to protect its citizens. In this, it became clear how much the mercantilist doctrine that the sole legitimacy of the state is the protection of property had usurped the original legitimacy of the state based on the preservation of life and maintenance of peaceful order. Following on from this, the pandemic clearly highlighted areas of social privilege where those with sufficient funds and properties could sit out the lockdown in relative comfort, as low-income workers were more likely to have to face infection by staying at work. In the United States, the sacking of Amazon's workers for protesting about insufficient protective gear was a perfect example of this.

There was also the evidence from the UK relating to the disproportionate effect the pandemic was having on Black, Asian and minority ethnic (BAME) groups where a higher toll seemed to expose already existing health and income inequalities. Echoing this, Adam Serwer (2020) argued that high cases of coronavirus infection in African American communities reflected the United States' long-standing 'racial contract'. In addition, the widespread disinformation emanating from the UK government over infection rates, death tolls and their policy regarding the protection of care homes, plus the utter insanity of a US president proposing to inject people with disinfectant, all amid conspiracy theories about 5G-technology spreading it is indicative of our epistemological precarity in an era of post-truth.

So, after describing the hateful politics that I believe represents a significant threat to democracy, Part Two of the book explores these precarities in five chapter-length studies. The first considers the ontological issues faced by people whose identities are tied to the old forms of racial supremacy that shaped imperialism. It analyses how important a particular view of the world is for the construction and maintenance of the self and how the resurgence of far-right politics stems from the threat posed to their world by the liberal multiculturalism of the post-colonial age. The second precarity is devoted to the supposedly existential threat of radical Islamism and the War on Terror. It argues that neoconservative rhetoric mobilized the racism, Islamophobia and xenophobia that are central to the politics of the radical right today. It also shows how this war was imbued with age-old fantasies of apocalypse that have, in turn, fed Trump's racist policies at the southern border. The third precarity is economic and addresses the failures of neoliberalism and the ongoing austerity supposedly made imperative by the Financial Crisis of 2008. It proposes that intensifying significant material precarity and instability for working people makes racist and xenophobic politics more attractive and opens up the possibility for charismatic leaders to scapegoat individuals or social institutions as the locus of blame. The fourth type of precarity is social and looks at how advances made by civil rights movements, the feminist movement and the LGBTQ community have made significant inroads into the advantages of the white, straight man and proposes that the radical right's assault on 'PC culture' is evidence of a concerted effort to push back against these progressive politics. Finally, the fifth precarity considers our epistemological precarity in the age of 'post-truth', 'fake news' and 'alternative facts'. In an age when science is being consistently undermined because it doesn't fit with the beliefs of powerful people, and social media seems to have been designed to distribute disinformation on an industrial scale, how do we defend democratic norms? These chapters are also designed to be historically and theoretically self-sufficient so that reading only one should provide a reasonable introduction to the problem.

As I said earlier, though, this book does not claim we are about to succumb to global fascism. What it does, however, is set out the signs that a deeply illiberal, discriminatory and authoritarian politics is emerging in many countries that we have for some time considered democratic. The book also seeks to outline the various causes for this, all of which need to be thought together and be rigorously countered if far-right politics is not to find an even firmer foothold. Despite concerns that we are not sufficiently focused on what has been happening and are potentially inviting the arsonists into our house, I remain optimistic that countering the resurgence of far-right politics is possible. The COVID-19 pandemic showed that there still is such a thing as society and that solidarity with unknown others is still central to the way many people think. It also confirmed the importance of scientists, specialists and experts, as well as the need to elect competent officials and ensure they are scrutinized and accountable.

During this time, we also saw the incredible protests in response to the killing of George Floyd. These were tied to the Black Lives Matter movement that has been in existence since the acquittal of George Zimmerman in 2013. The protests were given a particular intensity in the United States by the actions of the police, not to say the president. Tensions were also heightened by the activities of far-right provocateurs and the many strains of the 'Boogaloo bois' (Macnab 2020) looking to induce rioting and looting. What was extraordinary, though, was the way this quickly evolved into widespread protests and significant reflection on colonialism and the crimes of empire around the world. For me, it confirmed we really are living in the age of necropolitics where the dying ideologies of patriarchy, white supremacy, colonialism and capitalism, among others, are in their last death throes. Antonio Gramsci's famous maxim that 'the crisis consists precisely in the fact that the old is dying and the new cannot be born' (1971: 276) seems to be increasingly apposite; yet, the protests were so powerful that I genuinely believe we can still bring about something new, something that isn't beholden to the old chauvinisms and prejudices and move beyond this necropolitical moment.

Part 1

Hate

1

The politics of hate

One of the reasons the far-right has become resurgent is because, in true Biedermann style, we cannot accept that what walks like fascism and talks like fascism might actually be fascism or some nascent variety thereof. Although a number of far-right, ethno-nationalists have come to power in recent years, our media still platforms opinion that normalizes such politics because, as Sinclair Lewis put it way back in 1935, we believe it can't happen here. While we find it almost impossible to countenance what has been taking place, we have the additional problem of believing fascism has always been a marginal political affiliation and will always remain so. However, as Michael Mann (2004) has convincingly argued,

> Fascism was not a mere sideshow in the development of modern society. [. . .] Alongside environmentalism, it was the major political doctrine of world-historical significance created during the twentieth century. There is a chance that something quite like it, though almost certainly under another name, will play an important role in the twenty-first century. Fascists have been at the heart of modernity. (1)

This is the first of seven reasons Mann gives for the persistent dangers of fascism. The second is that fascism was not 'set apart' as a form of politics, rather it 'only embraced more fervently than anyone else the central political icon of our time, the nation state, together with its ideologies and pathologies' (1). This comprised the second feature, namely, the specific development of an exclusionary idea of a nation based on a nativist sense of 'the people' against foreigners both domestic and abroad. This is patently happening today in a number of countries. It also involved the development of a state as the 'bearer of a moral project' (2). Fascism for Mann was therefore the accentuation and acceleration of the *dominant* political ideology.

Third, 'fascists did offer plausible solutions to modern social problems' (2) and convinced people 'it could bring about a more harmonious order' (3). Unfortunately, the leaders of numerous nation states today are offering 'plausible solutions' – or at least plausible to their audience – in which a form of ethno-nationalism and its accompanying identity politics are the answer to all our ills. This is possible because of Mann's fourth reason, namely, that the nation state remains a 'sacred icon' and people retain especially 'close relations' to it (4). This can be seen when members of the British public wave flags and cheer for their monarch. It is an attitude carefully cultivated and maintained through various rituals including royal weddings, the queen's Christmas speech, royal attendance at sporting events and media spectacles like the Royal Variety Performance. This is all reinforced in the ubiquity and banality of royal palace tea towels, commemorative plates, celebrity royal stories and enforced pilgrimages to Buckingham Palace as a child. This is what Michael Billig (1995) calls 'banal nationalism'. However, while it might manifest in the quotidian cushion cover or the kitchen apron, it should not, according to Billig, be thought of as benign or harmless because it is an important element in the functioning of power. For him, it unconsciously readies or primes people (7) to take part in and support the exercise of more violent expressions of power such as war and emerging forms of belligerent nationalism.

For Mann, the fifth and sixth reasons why we should still take fascism seriously is that as hierarchical movements they gave young men a purpose and a sense of position – an especially important issue in our precarious age – which then enabled their 'capacity to commit evil' (2004: 3). Mann's seventh and final point is particularly resonant. Understanding how the supposedly benign processes of capitalist globalization continue practices of dispossession and violence, Mann notes that 'given time for a supposedly stateless neoliberalism' to continue to do damage, the 'rejection of the powerful state will probably fade. Then extreme statist values might be harnessed again to extreme paramilitary nationalism in movements resembling fascism' (4).[1] I doubt Mann was thinking of the United Kingdom, the United States or European nations here, but the language of a culture-destroying globalism is now centre stage in the mainstream politics of many of these countries. In an attempt to understand what is happening, I will first offer a more detailed description of what the Alt-Right stands for, before showing how, despite its antagonism to traditional forms of conservatism, its core beliefs have still managed to find a foothold there.

The Alt-Right and white nationalism

Since their arrival on the scene, the Alt-Right and its members have been the subject of numerous puff pieces in newspapers intrigued by their style and somehow surprised that not all modern-day Nazis wear jackboots or model themselves on the swastika-tattooed skinhead. In May 2018, the *Sunday Times* in the UK ran a piece on the European version of the Alt-Right known as Generation Identity. In a piece titled 'Heil Hipsters', Andrew Gilligan noted how the new brand of the far-right were 'Middle class and well-spoken, dressed in skinny jeans and New Balance trainers rather than bomber jackets and boots'. This trend was kicked off by the 2016 *Mother Jones* article on Richard Spencer titled 'Meet the dapper white nationalist' (an article that has since lost the word 'dapper' from the title).[2] It was published just one month prior to Spencer's 'Hail Trump, hail our people, hail victory' speech, given at the National Policy Institute (NPI) conference at the Ronald Reagan Building in Washington. The NPI is a far-right think tank of which Spencer is president and has played an important role coordinating with far-right groups across Europe.

The sharp style, however, masks very dull racism. Central to the movement is the belief in 'human biodiversity' (HBD). This sounds like it might lend itself to a rather cosmopolitan outlook but is very much removed from that. According to Mike Wendling, HBD 'argues that because different people have different traits, and some of these traits are linked to genetics, genes [. . .] are determinative' (2018: 22). This is little more than the widely discredited race science that deems black people are both physically and cognitively inferior, but it is nevertheless used to support the Alt-Right's belief in the need for ethnically based nation states and what Spencer calls 'peaceful ethnic cleansing' (Wendling 2018: 22). This is modelled on the post-war settlement of 1919 that created new nations out of collapsed empires (23). Ultimately, though, this race science also includes the implicit belief that the biological superiority of white people necessarily produces the better culture. This leads to Spencer's additional desire to create a 'bigger civilizational, hegemonic domain' (25) for white people in which a putative 'European' culture, described as Greco-Roman and/or Judeo-Christian might be defended. Again, a version of this rhetoric, albeit diluted, has become readily evident in the policy statements of a range of traditional conservative parties around the globe.

As a result, the Alt-Right has also adopted the 'one drop' mantra of the nineteenth-century white supremacists that argues 'any non-white ancestor fundamentally alters all lineal descendants forevermore' (Wendling 2018: 44). Despite the near certainty that none of them would pass a DNA test screening for such Aryan purity, they persist with the fantasy. In keeping with their bid to prevent any further contamination to either biology or culture, they also believe 'diversity is code for white genocide', a key point that had put them at odds with traditional conservatism. As George Hawley notes, 'The Alt-Right hates the conservative movement [for their] hesitancy to engage directly with the issue of race. According to the Alt-Right, conservatives obsess over tax cuts, deregulation and other small bourgeois concerns, but they fear tackling demographic questions, which the Alt-Right consider existential' (Hawley 2019: 164). However, traditional conservatism has become increasingly less reluctant to make race an issue, as can be seen in Trump's 2016 victory and the rhetoric of the Brexit campaign.

The centrality of race means there is a strong connection between the Alt-Right and the early white power movement, which Kathleen Belew argues was 'thrown together by tectonic shifts in the cultural and political landscape' (2018: 1) in the 1970s. Similarly, the Alt-Right also emerged at a time when the economic and political failures of neoliberalism were most pronounced, and the US diversity index had doubled in the period 2000–15 (Neiwert 2017: 323). Although the Alt-Right disparagingly refer to the earlier movement as 'white Nationalism 1.0' (Hawley 2019: 31) due to their perceived lack of success, the earlier movement did manage to bring their ideology into the mainstream of US Conservatism when the Tea Party became the 'conduit for a revival of the Patriot movement and its militias' (Neiwert 2017: 139). This mainstreaming of the movement was significant given that the various white supremacist groups in the United States that had come together to form the white power movement in 1979 declared revolutionary war on the US Federal Government in 1983, with one particular white power group, The Posse, recognizing no higher authority than the local sheriff (Belew 2018: 119). Given the Tea Party was crucial to the evolution of the Alt-Right, it is possible to argue there is greater continuity between the two movements than some members of the Alt-Right acknowledge and that the seeds of Trumpism were flowering long before Trump descended that escalator and declared his candidacy.

As Belew notes, the declaration of war on the federal government in 1983 was significant because 'white supremacy undergirded state power throughout US history' (2018: 106) and the power of the state had traditionally supported white supremacy (Anderson 2017). The key to understanding this is the publication of Louis Beam's *Essays of a Klansman* that same year. Having returned from Vietnam he 'urged activists to continue fighting the Vietnam War on American soil' (Belew 2018: 3). In step with much of the anti-globalist rhetoric of Trump and the Alt-Right today, Beam and other members of the white power movement felt under threat from what they called the Zionist Occupational Government (ZOG), which later became the New World Order. According to Belew, 'white power activists believed that the Jewish-led ZOG controlled the United Nations, the US federal government, and the banks, and that ZOG used people of color, communists, liberals, journalists, academics, and other enemies of the movement as puppets in a conspiracy to eradicate the white race and its economic, social, and cultural accomplishments' (7).

In 1984, Louis Beam set up the bulletin board, Liberty Net, that listed anti-Klan names and targets (Belew 2018: 121). This was a precursor to much of the Alt-Right's online activity. Echoing the later language of Trump, Belew explains how Beam 'understood the Vietnam War as the catalyst for American decline' (30), and in keeping with the language of the Alt-Right who try to play down the genocidal aspects of Nazism by referring to themselves as separatists, they sought a revolution that would deliver 'a racial utopian nation' (5). One especially dramatic vision for securing such a nation was Beam's plan to take advantage of the Cold War and the nuclear conflict he considered inevitable. Believing the US military would be depleted and incapacitated, he argued a white separatist army 'could take control of the United States – or at least Texas – expelling all non-white people to create a white homeland' (40).

Some of the other figures and organizations that would support a version of this cause at different times were Robert Shelton and his United Klans of America, which was infamously responsible for directing the bombing of the Sixteenth Street Baptist Church in Birmingham, Alabama, in 1963; an organization called The Covenant, the Sword, and the Arm of the Lord (CSA), a Christian Identity movement formed in 1971 that provided paramilitary training to other white supremacist groups; Tom Metzger's Confederate Knights of the Ku Klux Klan that was renamed White Aryan Resistance (WAR) in 1983; Richard Butler's Aryan Nations that was involved in the harassment of Vietnamese immigrants in 1980 and the short-lived but important group known as The Order founded by Bob Matthews.[3] It was another member of The Order, David Lane, that coined the 'Fourteen words' (Hawley 2019: 44) that became the white supremacist rallying cry: 'We must secure the existence of our people and a future for white children.' This remains an integral part of Alt-Right discourse and can be seen in the use of the number 1488, which adds the numerical value of HH (Heil Hitler) to the fourteen words to produce a shorthand or code of identification. Most disconcertingly, echoes of the fourteen words were found in a US Department of Homeland Security press release from February 2020 that read: 'We Must Secure The Border And Build The Wall to Make America Safe Again.'[4]

Remaining in the present, aside from Richard Spencer, other key figures in the Alt-Right's theory of race include Don Black who founded the website *Stormfront* in 1995, and the earlier bulletin board in 1990, for which Louis Beam's *Liberty Net* in 1984 was a precursor. Another major figure is Andrew Anglin, founder of the white nationalist website *Daily Stormer*. Anglin, in turn, has also commented on the important role played in this area by

Jared Taylor who founded the think tank, the New Century Foundation in the 1990s and its influential magazine *American Renaissance*; Matthew Heimbach, who formed the Traditionalist Youth Network and its political wing the Traditionalist Workers Party in 2015; Brad Griffin, founder of *Occidental Dissent*; Taki Theodoracopulos, publisher of *Taki's Magazine*, a paleoconservative website popular with the radical right and a columnist for *The Spectator* in the UK censured for racism while Boris Johnson was editor and Peter Brimelow, the British author of Alien *Nation* and founder of the white nationalist website *VDARE* in 1998.

This centrality of race for the Alt-Right came to a head when other affiliates to the movement, Milo Yiannopoulos and Allum Bokhari, published an essay in March 2016 for *Breitbart* called 'An Establishment Conservative's Guide to the Alt-Right' that denounced neo-Nazis. Yiannopoulos, for a brief time, cultivated some far-right celebrity, but he was little more than an opportunist who made money from trading in online abuse, especially of women, and has since disappeared into relative obscurity following social media bans. Nevertheless, the essay did provoke a response from Anglin who 'set out to correct the record' (Neiwert 2017: 250) with his own take titled 'A Normie's Guide to the Alt-Right' in which he wrote: 'The core concept of the movement, upon which all else is based, is that Whites are undergoing extermination, via mass immigration into White countries which was enabled by a corrosive liberal ideology of White self-hatred, and that the Jews are at the center of this agenda' (250).[5] However, as Neiwert notes, Spencer has a shorter name for this, preferring to call it 'white Zionism' (238).

Interestingly, though, in November 2019, Yiannopoulos's ongoing spat with the neo-Nazi branch of the Alt-Right resulted in him leaking a recording of Richard Spencer from a meeting on 13 August 2017, the day after the 'Unite the Right' march in Charlottesville where a white supremacist injured nineteen people and killed Heather Heyer by driving a car into a group of anti-fascist protestors.[6] In the recording, the glamour of 'fashy' style succumbs to the ugliness of Spencer's hostility and hate. In a screaming rant, he shouts:

> We are coming back here like a hundred fucking times. I am so mad. I am so fucking mad at these people. They don't do this to fucking me. We are going to fucking ritualistically humiliate them. I am coming back here every fucking weekend if I have to. Like this is never over. I win! They fucking lose! That's how the world fucking works. Little fucking kikes. They get ruled by people like me. Little fucking octoroons . . . I fucking . . . my ancestors fucking enslaved those little pieces of fucking shit. I rule the fucking world. Those pieces of fucking shit get ruled by people like

me. They look up and see a face like mine looking down at them. That's
how the fucking world works. We are going to destroy this fucking town.

While the Alt-Right claims it opposes identity politics – especially those
based on race, sexuality or gender – the movement is clearly committed to
white identity which they claim multiculturalism undermines. Wendling
drew this out in an interview with another very important Alt-Right figure
Theodore Beale who is best known by his pen name, Vox Day. Asking about
this potential contradiction, Day replied: 'The alt-right has never railed
against identity politics. You are confusing us with conservatives' (46). A
politics of white identity is necessary, he claims, as a bulwark against the
'oppressive forces of equality forming a dissent-crushing monolith' (29). Vox
Day has also produced one of the earliest Alt-Right manifestos containing
his sixteen points detailing 'What the Alternative Right Is'.[7] In it, he describes
its difference from conservatism and the centrality of white nationalism,
expressing a supposed separatist pacifism in which nationalists mutually
recognize the right for all nations to exist – a rather ludicrous piece of utopian
thinking that will no doubt be thrown out of the window when capitalist
competition over the depletion of resources kicks in. Under point fourteen,
he appropriately repeats Lane's fourteen words, and yet, under point sixteen,
he breaks with the supremacist orthodoxy to argue that 'The Alt-Right does
not believe in the general supremacy of any race, nation, people, or subspecies' despite point four having already awarded supremacy to 'Western
civilization'.

An earlier essay by Day from 2015 titled 'The Bitter Harvest of Feminism'
introduces another major feature of the Alt-Right and those more readily
known as Alt-Lite (Hawley 2019: 185), namely, their hostility to the women's
movement. First, the Alt-Lite includes a range of people who are also critical
of traditional conservatism, and staunchly nationalistic, and yet they disavow
the explicit racism and white supremacy of the Alt-Right. The Alt-Lite is
probably the best place to situate Milo Yiannopoulos, and it includes people
as diverse as Mike Cernovich, author of *Gorilla Mindset*, 'a self-help book
for aspiring alpha males' (Marantz 2019: 13); the torture promoting legal
professor, Alan Dershowitz; the billionaire entrepreneur and founder of
PayPal, Peter Thiel and Cassandra Fairbanks, organizer of the 'DeploraBall', a
gathering of all the glitterati that self-identified as the people Hilary Clinton
disastrously referred to as 'deplorables'. We might also add a variety of Fox
anchors including Tucker Carlson, Sean Hannity, Tomi Lahren and Laura
Ingraham although the overt racism and explicit nativism they express while
on air show that the dividing line between Alt-Right and Alt-Lite is somewhat
porous and malleable.

Their attitude to gender is encapsulated in Yiannopoulos's brief celebrity that was largely created via relentlessly abusive social media campaigns against any woman advocating even the most mainstream of feminist positions. His Twitter poll that asked 'I'd rather my child had a) feminism or b) cancer?' epitomizes Alt-Right/Alt-Lite tactics. Generally, the attitude towards gender, like race, is based on 'sex realism' or the idea that 'men and women have different cognitive characteristics, which are rooted in biology rather than socialization' (Hawley 2019: 103), and that biology should therefore determine social roles. Also, such roles should not aspire to equality because nature or biology does not. Most of this thinking coagulates in the 'manosphere', a region of the internet where meninists and Mens' Rights Advocates (MRAs) argue against what they see as the overturning of natural gender relations, and promote traditional conceptions of 'alpha masculinity', or what another popular blogger and internet troll, Daryush Valizadeh, aka Roosh V, calls 'neomasculinity'. The sort of attitude and language of the 'manosphere' can be seen in Mike Cernovich's regular contributions. Admittedly, much of this will be done simply to 'trigger' or 'own the libs' and generate publicity for his book, but it is revealing of the general ethos. His Twitter feed has been especially instructive. In August 2012, he wrote, 'Have you guys ever tried "raping" a girl without using force? Try it. It's basically impossible. Date rape does not exist.' In September 2013, he posted: 'Rape via an alpha male is different from other forms of rape. We can't really understand this, as our culture is too detached from instinct.' In March 2016, he added a good dollop of racism (also a regular feature) when he claimed, 'The only rape culture is Muslim rape culture.'[8]

However, these attitudes are not new in far-right or radical right circles. As Belew has demonstrated, they were integral to the white power movement that emerged after the Vietnam War, which was itself seen as a form of emasculation that required the 'remasculinization of America' (2018: 7). In keeping with Lane's 'fourteen words', the white power movement also saw women as bearers of white children and saviours of the race from annihilation (8), and childbirth was 'intimately tied to the battle at hand' (160). They also believed in male supremacy as set out in William Pierce's 1974 novel, *The Turner Diaries* (110), which has been even more influential on the ideology of a race war than Beam's *Essays of a Klansman*.

As Belew recounts, when white power members, including Beam plus members of The Order and CSA were put on trial in 1987 for seditious conspiracy, they successfully used the 'invocation of a primal American story about defending white women' (157) as their justification. As Belew goes on to note, 'Protecting white female bodies [. . .] from miscegenation, racial pollution, and other dangers continues to structure the worldview not only of white power movement activists but also of several jurors as well as the mainstream media' (157). Rather incredibly, 'the war on the state would be told as a love story' (157). Back then, it was ZOG that wanted to abort white babies and allow black men to rape white women (159), and the myth of the black rapist continues to be central to the movement's world view.[9] It was even expressed by Dylan Roof prior to him murdering members of a black congregation: 'You've raped our women' (Neiwert 2017: 19), he is reported to have said. This myth has, of course, morphed and generated variations, especially around the Muslim man as a rapist or paedophile, but the combination of race and gender has perhaps most clearly coalesced in the term 'Rapeugee' (Wendling 2018: 98) that is regularly seen in Alt-Right online discourse.

This desire to protect is also a central aspect in the contemporary movement's obsession with virility, a matter summed up in their go-to insult of 'cuck'. This abbreviation of cuckold, the antiquated term that describes a man who has been cheated on by his wife is thrown at any person who criticizes their ideology or who doesn't parrot their liturgy of doctrinal chauvinisms. This includes traditional conservatives or 'cuckservatives'. In contrast to the dominance of the alpha male, however, the Alt-Right has also spawned a subspecies of 'betas', a group of socially dysfunctional men who have also come to describe themselves as 'incels', or men who are 'involuntarily celibate'. This position is based on a belief popularized by Alt-Lite thinkers like Jordan Peterson who in a talk on 13 June 2017 used hypergamy – in his words, the belief that 'women mate across and up dominance hierarchies' – to explain heterosexual relations in humans. This has, in turn, been used by 'incels' to claim it is the fault of women who always seek out powerful men that they have been left without sexual partners.

After a terrorist incident in which an 'incel' named Alek Minassian killed ten in Toronto, eight of whom were women, he explained how he had been radicalized via a message board on Reddit and expressed his admiration for another 'incel', Elliot Rodger, who went on a killing spree in Isla Vista in 2014. The Isla Vista attack, in which Rodger killed six people and injured a further fourteen, was defined by the video he posted on YouTube, the full transcript of which was published by the *Los Angeles Times* on 24 May 2014. An excerpt reads as follows:

> For the last eight years of my life, since I hit puberty, I've been forced to endure an existence of loneliness, rejection and unfulfilled desires, all because girls have never been attracted to me. Girls gave their affection and sex and love to other men, never to me. I'm 22 years old and still a virgin, never even kissed a girl. [. . .] On the day of retribution, I am

going to enter the hottest sorority house at UCSB and I will slaughter every single spoiled, stuck-up, blond slut I see inside there. All those girls I've desired so much. They have all rejected me and looked down on me as an inferior man if I ever made a sexual advance toward them, while they throw themselves at these obnoxious brutes. I take great pleasure in slaughtering all of you. You will finally see that I am, in truth, the superior one; the true alpha male.

Among his ravings, Rodger spoke about feeling 'invisible' and the need to display his 'magnificence and power'. Such an attitude was also evident when Chris Harper-Mercer killed ten and injured another seven people at Umpqua Community College in 2015. In keeping with Rodger's jealousy of alpha males and hatred for the women that liked them, Harper-Mercer's killing spree was an attack born of perceived inadequacy. The FBI investigation into the attack linked it to a message board on 4Chan, /r9k/, that was calling for a 'Beta Uprising' or 'Beta Rebellion'. The attack at Umpqua Community College was supposed to be the first of many such attacks in which inadequate men were to prove themselves adequate by murdering people, especially women. The message board promised attacks at Temple University and the University of Pennsylvania, among other colleges, that fortunately did not transpire.

In response to the mass murder in Toronto, a conservative Canadian economist decided that the remedy could be to redistribute sex:

> One might plausibly argue that those with much less access to sex suffer to a similar degree as those with low income, and might similarly hope to gain from organizing around this identity, to lobby for redistribution along this axis and to at least implicitly threaten violence if their demands are not met. As with income inequality, most folks concerned about sex inequality might explicitly reject violence as a method, at least for now, and yet still be encouraged privately when the possibility of violence helps move others to support their policies. (Sex could be directly redistributed, or cash might be redistributed in compensation.)

Unsurprisingly, this was roundly condemned, but that hasn't stopped it from becoming part of accepted opinion among the 'incel' community who widely advocate for some form of sex redistribution or at a minimum what Jordan Peterson calls 'socially enforced monogamy'.[10] Now, while this might appear to be an extremist position that you would hope only exists in the margins, an indication this philosophy is entering the mainstream can be seen in Todd Phillips's 2019 movie *Joker*, a film about the origins of Batman's infamous arch-enemy, but one that is also a paean to white victimhood, the injustice of 'incel' experience and an exercise in misogynoir (Curtis 2019). It is therefore very disturbing that it won a nomination for best picture at the 2020 Oscars. More broadly, though, the overall focus of attacks from both Alt-Right and Alt-Lite is the democratic language of equality, which they refer to as 'politically correct' or simply 'PC', a term that first appeared in July 1998 in a speech called 'The Origins of Political Correctness' delivered by paleoconservative William Lind (Neiwert 2017: 224). This is also linked to the use of the term Cultural Marxism that was popularized by the white supremacist Kevin MacDonald and stood in for the left-wing thought of the Jewish intellectuals who were part of the Frankfurt School of critical theory. They are also very fond of attacking the idea of safe spaces that, for obvious reasons, various minority groups try to create. If you are a trans person, for example, it is understandable that you would appreciate a space where you feel relatively protected from the hostility targeted at you on a daily basis. Yet despite their criticism of 'safe spaces', all the Alt-Right and their affiliated groups in the radical right really want is to protect their own 'safe space' of white, male, heterosexual, Christian privilege. In fact, Alt-Right predecessors in the United States were the originators of the 'safe space'. During segregation, their Jim Crow laws designated a range of spaces 'safe', such as drinking fountains, diners, bars, benches, buses, schools and universities. Inside movie theatres and sports stadiums, they also created 'safe spaces' where their assumed supremacy could not be challenged.

The traditional right

Having said all this, the efficacy and political potential of the Alt-Right/Lite is up for debate. At one level, this loosely organized and often internally conflicted group seems to offer little that might impact wider politics. Hawley, for example, thinks 'rather than becoming a permanent fixture of American political life, the Alt-Right may be remembered as just one more oddity of the Trump era, ultimately signifying very little' (2019: 216). As he goes on to say, we need to also note that, since their high point in 2016, the Alt-Right is declining (213). Perhaps, as Mark S. Hamm argued in an earlier study of US far-right groups, 'the specific ideological force field' (2009: 95) that inflects each faction has grown too much. In terms of their efficacy, Hawley also believes that the connection between Trump and the Alt-Right is 'overstated' (2019: 5). He claims there has only ever been one Alt-Right politician, namely, Paul Nehlen (147), and yet representatives like Steve King and Matt Gaetz do a very good impersonation, as do numerous other US politicians that parrot Alt-Right language.[11] In fact, the Alt-Right has done exceedingly well to shift the 'Overton Window' or the frame of acceptable discourse, and so, in this regard, Hawley's dismissal of them smacks of the Biedermann syndrome I find so disconcerting.

It is probably better to acknowledge changes in Alt-Right activity and presence by saying, along with Wendling, that 'the movement's first phase is over' (2018: 222) and that phase two is only just beginning to evolve. Having managed to bring their agenda to the front and centre of our politics, it would be foolish to think their future is as incidental bit players, especially when they have very wealthy backers. As Wendling points out, the Alt-Right's claim that they are part of the counterculture 'rings hollow' (9) given the support their views on race, migration, women's rights and American nationalism get in mainstream media outlets like Fox News and even on occasions the American broadsheets. We know there are clear links between Trump and the Alt-Right. He infamously used #WhiteGenocide in a tweet dated 22 November 2015 (Neiwert 2017: 278), and in September 2016, Spencer called Trump's comments on illegal immigrants 'Our Big, Fat, Beautiful Dog Whistle' (272). There was then all the commotion in June 2020 when Trump retweeted a video of his supporters in Florida shouting 'white power' at anti-Trump protestors. Neiwert also notes that mid-level figures in Patriot hierarchy were involved in the Trump campaign (309) and closes his book by arguing that while 'Trump may not be a fascist, [. . .] he is an authoritarian who, intentionally or not, is empowering the existing proto-fascist elements in American society' (369). This became disturbingly evident in his response to the renewed Black Lives Matter protests after the killing of George Floyd in June 2020 that included a tweet repeating the infamous words of Miami's Police Chief Walter E. Headley whose response to the 1967 'race riots' was to proclaim in a local newspaper that 'when the looting starts the shooting starts'. Such proto-fascist elements also become really clear when we recognize how readily available the primary chauvinisms of the Alt-Right are to any mainstream politician who chooses to deploy them.

As such, while we absolutely must worry about the type of politics the Alt-Right advocate and clearly need to understand who they are and what they represent in order that we might counter it, it is not this movement itself that we should be primarily concerned about. The main issue is how their nativist, nationalist, supremacist and anti-democratic rhetoric appeals to already established forms of mainstream politics on the right despite their hostility towards 'the establishment'. As I noted in the introduction, a range of more traditional far-right and mainstream conservative parties have for some time been pushing racism, xenophobia and the 'defence of the West' as solutions to the precarity that plagues various countries. They are also deeply committed to broadly supremacist beliefs rooted in European-Christianity, patriarchy and aristocracy. Such attitudes, while they can represent a particular ideology tied to a specific group or movement, also take the form of a more generalized ideology that becomes part of the deep-rooted mythology of a culture. We absolutely must understand that it is not possible to live in a European country that formerly held colonies or live in one of these colonies that is now dominated by European settlement (United States, Canada, Australia or New Zealand) without belonging to a country where white supremacy is written into its institutions and is part of its cultural make-up. We can deny this all we want, but these attitudes are there and remain readily accessible.

Traditional conservative philosophy and politics is also ingrained with supremacist beliefs of the aristocratic kind that resonate very strongly with attitudes among the Alt-Right and other contemporary far-right groups. This is why there has been a renewed interest in eugenics among today's radical right. Indicative of this is an article published in *The Spectator* and written by its editor Fraser Nelson (2016). In it, he argues that one advantage of eugenics is that it would allow us to get rid of 'those disposed to a life on welfare as a result of genetic predispositions', which make them resistant to employment. While misunderstanding a social problem as a natural one, this also further underlines the very old conservative view that certain people (or a certain group) are naturally better than others and therefore more suited to rule. It also includes the belief that society, in this case the welfare state, actually interferes with natural processes that really should be allowed to run their course.

In a study of earlier examples of white supremacism in Europe in 1980, Thomas Sheehan found that this philosophy was very prominent to their world view. Here, the view that society is artificial gave a very particular meaning to their conception of violence. He writes:

> Aristotle saw everything as possessed of an intrinsic nature or finality (*telos*), and all movement or becoming that tended toward the fulfilment of that finality was 'teleological' or in accord with the thing's essential nature (*kata physin*). In this straightforward view of reality, true development is movement toward the essential (*genesis heneka ousias*), and violence is movement against the essential. And for today's terrorist it is the same – except that he disagrees with society about what is politically natural and essential (*physis, ousia*) and hence about what constitutes violence. In his inverted world [. . .] society as it stands is 'unnatural' and therefore violent; and what society calls violence is for him either *self-defence* (resistance against the unnatural) or *therapeutic* (restoration of the essential) or *maieutic* (helping give birth to the natural and essential). (1981: 48)

My point is that while far-right groups like the Alt-Right might seem to exist at some remove from the UK Conservative Party they share a range of supremacist beliefs (racial, ethnic, social and civilizational) that make them far more closely aligned.

Consequently, while we should worry about the Alt-Right, what should be of more concern is a phenomenon referred to as the 'Bannonization' of Europe (Thompson 2018). This perhaps overstates his significance, but it is nevertheless suggestive of the networking taking place among new and traditional far-right groups as well as established conservative parties. Having used, promoted and aligned himself with the Alt-Right, Bannon distanced himself from them after exiting his role as the chief strategist in Trump's White House. Although Hawley notes Bannon declared himself an economic nationalist rather than a racial nationalist (2019: 191), this is not supported by his consistently racist and white supremacist views; and as a man well versed in political strategy, media management and public relations, we should be highly sceptical of his attempt to distance himself from the Alt-Right. Ever since he has gained what Jeffrey Alexander calls 'perplexing symbolic power' (2019: 138), he has used it to tour Europe seeking to strengthen an already existing European network of nationalist and far-right parties and think tanks – a tactic that itself has a long history (Fronczak 2018). In this regard, he began The Movement with Belgian far-right politician Mischaël Modrikamen, leader of the Belgian far-right People's Party. The success of this group remains a little vague, as Bannon himself has explained they do not want to contravene national election laws and are hence running a low profile, but we ignore these groups at our peril.

He has also visited Sweden and developed relations with the far-right Sweden Democrats that recently became the country's third largest party and whose rhetoric includes Trumpisms such as 'drain the swamp' and outright Nazi slogans regarding Sweden's need to create 'breathing room'. Bannon has also been meeting with the *Dignitatis Humanae Institute* in Italy, a right-wing Catholic organization for whom he has reportedly drafted curricula (Hosenball 2018), as well as fraternizing with members of both the Five Star Movement and the far-right group the Northern League, which together formed a government in Italy in 2018. The Five Star Movement is a party that defies easy categorization due to its commitment to public services and environmentalism while also being anti-immigration, anti-globalist, Eurosceptic populists. The League was ousted from the coalition when the Democratic Party was brought into the coalition, but just to accentuate the post-categorization politics at play here, this new coalition was, in turn, threatened when three Five Star Movement senators switched allegiance to the Northern League.

Bannon has also visited Germany, Poland, the Czech Republic, Austria, Hungary, Bosnia, Switzerland, Spain and France. Here, there is a certain reticence about very close associations with Bannon. The sensibilities of Marine Le Penn, the leader of National Rally, mean she is reluctant to have her party subsumed beneath the vulgarities of Trumpism, but there is undoubtedly a strong connection in terms of shared aims and strategies. Bannon has also worked closely with Boris Johnson and Jacob Rees-Mogg of the UK Conservative Party, which now has no political parties, other than the explicitly neo-Nazi British National and Britain First parties, further to the right. The Conservative Party's new brand of anti-European, science denying, nativist, English nationalism is very much in keeping with Bannon's vision. I would argue that it is in the combination of groups that are both populist and relatively new and the much older but radicalized parties like the UK Conservatives and US Republicans that are the real threat to the future of democracy. To reiterate, the problem is not Bannon and the Alt-Right, per se, but the way their vision and tactics have been adopted as the new political strategy by more traditional right-wing parties.

That the UK Conservative Party should choose to have close ties to Bannon rather than denounce him is a sign of the times. It cannot be stated just how far Bannon is even from the radicalism of Thatcher let alone the 'One-Nation' conservatism of the traditional party that Johnson likes to evoke. As Alexander notes,

> Bannon is engaged in a fierce struggle against the ideas and the spirit of democracy. When he references big thinkers [. . .] Bannon gestures admiringly to fascists, bigots, dictators, and reactionary theocrats. To Charles Maurras, for example: the rabidly anti-Semitic French Catholic political intellectual; fan of Mussolini and Franco; leader of the 'anti-Dreyfusards' who persecuted the Jewish Army Captain falsely accused of treason; decades-long agitator against the democratic and secular Third Republic; sentenced to life imprisonment after World War II for collaborating with the Nazi occupation. Or to Julius Evola: Italian professor at the weird but aptly named 'School of Fascist Mysticism'; ferociously anti-Semitic; intellectual and spiritual advisor to Mussolini; intimate of the Nazi SS; godfather of the Racial Laws that sent thousands of Italian Jews to their deaths in the late 1930s; key intellectual figure around whom the Italian neo-fascist movement reconstructed itself in the post-war period. (2019: 139)

He goes on to say how Bannon's ideology is rooted in a narrative that challenges 'the emancipatory humanism upon which democratic politics and a hopeful view of modernity are based' (146). Ultimately, 'Trump and

Bannon participate in a political process that democracy has constructed, but their aim is to destroy it' (147).

The greatest irony about Johnson, much like Trump, is that he has taken advantage of the mood that sees the 'elite' or the 'establishment', as much as the foreigner or migrant, as the enemy – this is the twin engine of populist incitement today – and yet Johnson is nothing but an establishment figure. Personally, I prefer not to refer to those with economic or political power as the elite as it suggests some kind of worth or merit when really it is more often simply the benefits of social and economic advantage, but Boris Johnson certainly is an establishment figure. He was schooled at Eton College and then studied Classics at Balliol College, Oxford, where he was a member of the exclusive and notorious Bullingdon Club, infamous for displays of opulence and bouts of vandalism. This is basic training for a role as post-war leader of the UK's Conservative Party. Despite his opportunism that made him the latest in a long line of politicians around the world to reap the rewards of climbing aboard the populist train, everything about the man, his attitudes and values remain profoundly aristocratic, believing that a significant segment of the population have little, if any, 'spiritual worth'.[12] Similar to the way in which the patrician elements of the Grand Old Party (GOP) have taken advantage of populism as they transition from the most traditional of US political parties to something emulating a Trump cult, Johnson can be added to 'the terrifying roster of distinguished men' (Arendt 1968: 326) that have flirted with the populist spirit that underpinned totalitarianism.

In this, we can see another of the factors that Mann (2004) highlighted as contributing to the rise of fascism. Speaking of the 1930s, he asks:

> Why did authoritarian nation-statism dominate one-half of Europe, liberal democracy the other half? It cannot have been some general crisis of modern society, such as the Great Depression or the defects of liberalism, for then it would have affected all of Europe, not just half of it. The difference is one that turns crucially on the behavior of political conservatives, 'old regimes', and the property-owning classes. For here class does matter, profoundly, if in a rather peculiar way. Right across one-half of Europe, the upper classes turned toward more repressive regimes, believing these could protect themselves against the twin threats of social disorder and the political left. But this does not seem to have been very 'rational' behavior. For they greatly exaggerated the threats and neglected safer means of avoiding them. (24–5)

Unfortunately, looking at the direction we are currently taking, it appears we are potentially set to repeat this irrationality, in part because aristocratic arrogance continues to believe itself impervious to the dangers of the populist forces it is happy to exploit.

In the conclusion to his book, Mann sets out five reasons that contributed to the 'upper classes' siding with right-wing authoritarianism. First, he cites the real threat of revolution (2004: 356). Although this may not be on the cards today, there is certainly the potential for a serious challenge from the 'left' due in part to the Financial Crisis and the collapse in the legitimacy of the dominant economic doctrine of neoliberalism. Indeed, we have already moved so far to the right economically that a politics based on substantial social democracy, such as that briefly offered by Corbyn in the United Kingdom or Sanders in the United States is presented as Bolshevism. We might then add to that the resurgence in environmental thinking in the wake of climate change and the level of state intervention required during the coronavirus pandemic that demanded anything but politics as usual. In addition, there was the incredible anti-racism and anti-colonialism protests driven by the Black Lives Matter movement. For the very wealthy, irrespective of the liberal platitudes they might repeat, the sense of a dangerous and imminent revolution is easily evoked.

The second related factor for Mann was the threat to property (356). This is not directly the case today, but something equivalent can also be seen in the challenge of climate change that threatens a range of economic interests built on fossil fuels. There is, then, some comparison with the way those with interests in the status quo have come out in support of hard-line, right-wing governments, and how much climate science denial is part of the rhetoric in the Alt-Right/Lite and neo-nationalist parties. The third element for Mann was the co-option of the military (356). This is perhaps the most veiled at the moment, but politics on the right has increasingly used mercenaries or what are euphemistically called 'private security forces' in sites of conflict. This has especially been the case since the second Iraq War (Scahill 2007). These forces act as something akin to a 'praetorian guard' for capitalist interests (Hirst 2001), and the Trump administration has been especially successful in appealing to the militias and armed patriots in the United States who are openly preaching civil war on social media while also refusing any challenge to fully militarized and largely unaccountable police forces.

The fourth and fifth reasons, according to Mann, included the support of the church (2004: 356). The connection between Nazism and German Catholicism is well known, and as I've already noted, Bannon is advocating against the liberal turn in the Catholic Church seen under Pope Francis. In the United States, the evangelicals have also moved squarely behind Trump and have effectively abandoned the Jesus of the Bible in favour of Trump as the God-Emperor (Denker 2019). There has been resistance, notably, from

Christianity Today that called for Trump's removal from office in December 2019, but across the board, far-right groups and politicians are claiming to be fighting a crusade to defend Judeo-Christian values, with Trump designated 'the chosen one'. Finally, for Mann, there was the geopolitical threat 'that made some ethnic, religious or political minorities seem especially threatening' (2004: 357). I deal with this in detail in Chapter 5, but it goes without saying how much the existential precarity of a supposed threat from Islam has contributed to the politics of hate today. For these reasons and all those outlined in the Introduction, I believe that far-right and right-wing authoritarians can continue to grow support, and we should not pretend otherwise.

2

Defining hate

It is neither difficult to define Richard Spencer's tirade following the 'Unite the Right' rally in Charlottesville as hateful nor is it controversial to similarly categorize the actions of Elliot Rodger, the Isla Vista shooter; but the politics of hate discussed so far includes a range of expression that covers outright threats or violent incitement to quotidian discrimination and insult. When thinking of how to understand hate today, we therefore need to be able to account for its crude brutality, its complex subtlety and its simplistic ignorance. Consequently, we have to account for Richard Spencer's claim that Martin Luther King Jr. was 'a degenerate in his life' or Andrew Anglin's promise that 'The day is coming when we're going to tear down the hoax [Holocaust] memorial in Berlin and replace it with a statue of Hitler 1,000 feet tall' while also comprehending the nature of Boris Johnson's naming of gay people as 'bum boys' and black people as 'piccaninnies with watermelon smiles'. In the current climate, where racist and discriminatory attitudes have been increasingly mainstreamed, it is the casual form of such language that significantly adds to the culture of hate and provides the fertile ground upon which the more volatile invective can take root and produce the toxic fruit of violent action. In addition to this, we need to think about what motivates hate, how it works and what it does for those seduced by a politics that promotes it. In other words, we need to think about hate as a complex set of relationships, contexts, investments, attitudes, images, objects and varying types of discourse. After Sara Ahmed, it is therefore important to understand that 'hate is economic' (2001: 347); it moves and is organized through a host of different cultural channels and social exchanges.

What is hate?

We often say we hate Mondays or our job. We regularly complain that we 'hate it when [insert your pet peeve here] happens', but on such occasions we are more likely expressing annoyance, irritation and dislike rather than a deep-seated abhorrence, but these examples do suggest a certain slippage in how we think about and use the term. Although Royzman, McCauley and Rozin (2005) argue that 'there currently exists no generally accepted definition of hate' (11) and, later, state that it is actually unhelpful to aim for one true, Platonic definition (30), some early effort ought to be made at defining the term. Emily and Arthur Reber (2002) have argued it is 'a deep, enduring, intense emotion expressing animosity, anger and hostility towards a person, group or object' (315). This works as an approximation of what most people would recognize as hate, I believe, but as Royzman McCauley and Rozin go on to point out, hate, even as just defined, can still bring about different types of action or behaviour ranging from withdrawal and avoidance to focused attack (2005: 4). It can also aim at diametrically opposed outcomes where in one instance hate might manifest as 'an intense desire for the annihilation of its object' (13), but this could also be a desire for their extended existence, only in suffering or pain.

The difficulty pinning down a definition of hate is therefore instantly revealed. This is only added to when we understand that as much as being a general disposition that might endure over time, hate can also be episodic (5). Here, the intensity we experience when we hate is periodically diminished or increased depending on a range of other contextual factors. Hateful feelings can therefore rise up or ebb away, and this offers us another very good reason why we need to think about hate as an economy: it goes through periods of investment and disinvestment dependent on the arrangement of social relations and political conditions, the dominance of certain narratives and the availability of material and emotional resources. Hate seems like it might be easy to define, but it is actually quite elusive, and a major part of our inability to guard against it is that we too readily believe we know what it is and what it is not.

Aside from these complications around hate as an emotion, hate also plays an important role in our identity formation, both individual and communal. Willard Gaylin (2003), for example, has argued that hate is a form of 'attachment to a self-created enemy' (240). In other words, the object of our animosity is not simply there but needs to be invented. In doing so, the constructed enemy is integral to how we see ourselves. Anti-Semitism is a classic example of this. From a religious perspective, as soon as Christians elected to take on the mantle of the chosen people, those who had held that honour earlier necessarily became the focus of their malice. Once we project ourselves as specially chosen by God, those who held the title previously need to be demeaned if not eradicated for our own claim to make any sense. Also, culturally, when Christians used to abide by the Christian ban on usury or money lending, Christian countries during the Middle Ages invited Jews to settle and act as bankers. The Jewish association with money was therefore created by the fact that Christians once adhered to a central aspect of Christian doctrine that they have now long abandoned. Among the Christian far-right, then, the myth of the conspiring, globalizing Jew is indeed a self-created enemy. Gaylin also regards this attachment to a self-created enemy as a psychopathology and calls it 'neurotic' (2003: 24), but it is important to not overlook how entirely normal and conventional the experience of creating an object of hate is. Where hate perhaps becomes pathological is when it cannot 'be extinguished either by countervailing experiences [...] or through new learning regimes' (Lerner et al. 2005: 107) or where 'the perpetrator is convinced that he must rid the world of evildoers, those outsiders who are destroying his racial heritage, his culture, and his rightful place in society' (Levin and Rabrenovic 2009: 42).

Ordinarily, hate is part of the human condition and the wide array of attitudes and emotions we hold and express, but in terms of its relation to self-identity, hate in particular is linked to the fragility of our world or way of life and the tentative place that world gives to our sense of self. Rather than a pathology, then, it is much more productive to follow Ahmed and think of hate as being about a fantasy in which both the hating subject and the hated object are brought into being in the very process of determining who we are (2001: 346). In so doing, the economy of hate shores up the world that provides and nurtures our identity. I will return to this in Chapters 4 and 5 because a challenge to our world can produce a deep sense of anxiety that is often remedied through hateful projection. Hate is therefore both an ontological and existential security blanket.

Developing the relationship between hate and self-identity a little further, Royzman, McCauley and Rozin (2005) argue hate is a compound of emotions including anger, fear and, perhaps – most importantly – for the purposes of this book, humiliation, all of which are directed towards a supposedly malicious threat that becomes the legitimate motivation for violence (9), be that physical, verbal or symbolic. In their view, 'humiliation (or something like it) appears to be the most commonly acknowledged antecedent within the hate script' (18). On this topic, Leonard Berkowitz (2005) argues that an inflated sense of self is often 'the key to aggression' (177) and that a 'grandiose but shaky self-image' (178) is one of the most regular precursors to hostility or violence. This is of particular interest in relation to our context. It clearly helps explain why *all* supremacist beliefs might be especially prone to hateful language and action. For those who have always assumed themselves to be cognitively, genetically or culturally superior, *any challenge to that inflated sense of worth is almost fatal.* This can also be seen at play in the language of Brexit where the constant repetition of claims about the days of empire speak to Britain's projection of itself as a superior nation as well as mourning the loss of that assumed greatness. This idea of humiliation would also apply to ideologies premised on strength and virility, as is the case in the Alt-Right's 'manosphere' and its 'incel' subculture. Again, any suggestion of weakness or vulnerability immediately becomes the focus of significant hostility. Thus, contradictory and conflicting feelings of power and powerlessness (Royzman, McCauley and Rozin 2005: 18) are crucial to the emergence of hate. In an increasingly precarious world, this is one reason why the politics of the far-right is especially dangerous.

This introduces a third way to think about the economy of hate. Here, C. Fred Alford (2005) argues that hate is regularly an amalgam of what is deemed bad or evil and what is believed to be good, just and worthy: 'hatred infiltrates these virtues, so that hatred of the enemy becomes so confused with love of country that it becomes almost impossible to sort them out' (249). The economy of hate therefore also includes various qualities we would not normally attribute to it. Returning to the abandonment of the Christian doctrine banning usury we still find some Christians are very happy to selectively deploy other aspects of Christian doctrine that support their prejudice against gay people, for example. Here, many will try to soften their hate by claiming they are doing it out of love and a desire to 'save' people they believe to be otherwise damned.

Furthermore, as Susan Opotow importantly recognizes, 'morals are likely to act as an accelerant, particularly moral justifications for harm doing, or moral exclusion' (2005: 122). In such situations, moral exclusion means the ability to separate out a group that are then excluded from the community's moral code that normally forbids persecution, violence or killing. In Ahmed's words, it is the fantasy of the hated object 'imagined as a threat to the object of love' – be that culture, nation or religion – that supposedly makes 'hate reasonable' and dangerously 'functions as a narrative of entitlement' (2001: 346). History has shown us how destructive this fantasy can be. For the purposes of discussing our current context and the following discussions of our variegated precarity, it will be necessary to return to this dual fantasy in the second half of the chapter, but – for now – it is worthwhile saying a little more about the declared morality of hate and its connection to supposedly reasonable action.

Ervin Staub (2005) argues, 'Hate is an intense negative view of, accompanied by intense feelings against, the objects of hate. A hater sees the object of his or her hate as profoundly bad, immoral, dangerous, or all of these. The intense devaluation and the associated feelings make it satisfying to have the hated other suffer, experience loss, and be harmed' (51). Importantly, for Staub, this attitude does not simply pre-exist but needs to be developed. In line with the analysis of Levin and Rabrenovic (2009), hate is 'an aspect of culture [and is] part of the totality of an individual's learned and accumulated experiences' mediated by the 'widely shared myths and stereotypes' (42) of the community to which a person belongs. Often, this process that can make hate appear reasonable is missed by simply equating hate with emotion or feeling. We tend to downplay the role of cognition and reasoning by accentuating the anger or rage in the expression of hate. For Berkowitz (2005), 'the distinction between affect and cognition is frequently highly artificial' (160). The two are readily drawn together through the telling of stories. Such stories arouse emotion and develop an understanding of the world by recounting specific versions of history that reproduce the community's identity and create the beliefs necessary for division between in-group and out-group.

As Aaron T. Beck and James Pretzer (2005) point out, these stories produce 'cognitive distortions' (68) about the frequency, nature and severity of events the said community regards as offensive, hostile or duplicitous (or whatever vice is preferred at the time). Such stories will also regularly recount how particular injustices have been disproportionately aimed at the same community or group. In this regard hate might be said to have a virtual aspect where the threat it is directed at always has the potential to be actualized. Beck and Pretzer go on to note how such 'beliefs and assumptions lie dormant until a relevant situation arises and then automatically become active and shape the individual responses when a relevant situation is encountered' (68) or, as is perhaps more pertinent to our context, when a relevant situation is manufactured. In relation to Trump's America, while the diversity index in relevant US states has certainly increased, and neoliberalism has taken its toll on working communities, Trump has purposefully activated cognitive distortions about the nature of America and its 'enemies'. He easily tapped into very old stories about white America, Christian mission and national greatness in order to trigger the primed responses he desired. In much of the rhetoric, it was Muslims who were singled out as either non-American, anti-American or un-American (Braunstein 2019). This worked because in communities that make up much of his base there is a strong sense of in-group and out-group, rooted as it is in the identity politics of white, Christian America. In such a situation, each member of the group is inculcated with what Robert J. Sternberg calls story-based, hate propaganda (2005: 41) where the out-group is presented as backward, primitive, barbaric, inhuman, animalistic, murderous, treacherous, untrustworthy, toxic, corrupting and a range of other characteristics that set them apart as evil-doers.

Very often, in order to reaffirm the superiority, morality and goodness of the in-group, the out-group or enemy will be rendered strange or alien by the exaggeration of small and relatively unremarkable differences. This is what Sigmund Freud, in four papers published between 1917 and 1939, called the 'narcissism of minor differences'. However, as Anton Blok (1998) points out, Freud never really knew what to do with this concept nor even fully understood what he had discovered, thinking of this narcissism more in terms of 'a harmless satisfaction of aggressive inclinations that could promote the solidarity of the members of a community' (35). He thus dismissed his theory of minor differences that helps explain the construction of distinctiveness among otherwise similar groups in favour of the obvious differences he thought were more 'fundamental'. Freud thereby failed to develop a significant heuristic device for understanding the minutiae of human behaviour and reinforced the seeming naturalness of established prejudices around supposed differences such as 'race'.

Blok goes on to note how this concept, while overlooked in the end by Freud, was important to sociologists such as Emile Durkheim and Marcel Maus, and later Claude Lévi-Strauss who used it to explain totemic classifications that set neighbouring tribes apart. It was also of central importance to Norbert Elias's work on the civilizing process where minor differences in manners signify supposedly major differences in social stratification. As a member of the petite bourgeoisie, I remember being told as a child all the things that we don't do that members of the working class – from where the social mobility of the post-war boom had jettisoned us – still do. This theory was in turn influential on Pierre Bourdieu's (1984) groundbreaking study of social distinctions and the cultural capital that gives someone access to social circles their lack of economic capital might normally disallow. Bourdieu's great insight was to explain that being middle class was not simply about how much money a person had but more about the ability to display the requisite taste. Of course, such minor differences are also crucial for articulating national identity. Just watch the reaction of a British person abroad when they are not let into a line of traffic or aren't acknowledged when they let others in. Where many other things are shared, such a lack of consideration is seized upon as something warranting a declaration of war, or at least a little bit of repressed road rage. On returning home, the traveller will recount such instances of discourteousness, and his friends will all confirm what a privilege it is to be British.

Rephrasing the conclusions of Pierre Bourdieu, Blok writes, 'social identity lies in difference, and difference is established, reinforced, and defended against what is closest – and what is closest (in several senses of the word) represents the greatest threat' (Blok 1998: 49). Perhaps this is one reason Jews, Christians and Muslims have trouble getting along. Sharing the same God and the same book means they have to work extra hard to enforce their absolute, undeniable differences. Blok also works through a series of historical examples that confirm how violence is linked to a perceived loss of difference. These examples include the genocidal violence in the Balkans and in Rwanda, but using a historical moment close to the concerns of this book, Blok also cites the work of John Dollard in the post-bellum American South. Noting how the Ku Klux Klan was founded in the same year slavery was abolished in the United States, Blok writes: '[white people] feared being put on a par with former slaves, and derived their identity and self-esteem from their social distance from the black population' (40). According to Dollard, the Klan was primarily concerned with 'the reestablishment of the social difference that formerly existed' (41). As a consequence, Blok goes on to conclude that 'the theory of minor differences finds confirmation in figurations characterized by greater ones' (41). Returning to the issue of humiliation as a source of hate and how the far-right today continually makes claims about their sense of displacement, Sternberg argues that 'when people's self-esteem is threatened, their tendency to seek to restore it by exaggerating minor differences may be increased' (2005: 42).

This is also central to Paul Gilroy's analysis of race. For him, 'the entities we know as races derived from the very racial discourse that appeared to be their scientific product' (2005: 8). In other words, 'race' as a concept emerged out of the way we speak about difference, and then that socially constructed difference was represented as the natural element that made the language of difference necessary. As a consequence, 'the "race" idea is powerful precisely because it supplies a foundational understanding of natural hierarchy on which a host of other supplementary social and political conflicts have come to rely' (8). In this analysis, it is the stipulation of minor differences that are at the root of in-group and out-group, friend and enemy distinctions that – in turn – found our politics. For Gilroy, this also means that racial divisions are therefore not 'anterior to politics' (33). They don't come first. 'Race' is neither a natural category nor can 'race' be seen as 'an eternal cause of racism' (14). Rather, 'race' is racism's 'complex, unstable product' (14). 'Race' therefore emerges out of the prejudicial desire to establish minor differences. It is not a given, natural or biological fact (Rutherford 2020).

The expansion of hate

Through the narcissism of minor differences, we can also see how hate can be directed at a variety of objects including a person, a group, an event, a practice, a cultural ritual or even an inanimate thing. However, while hate is often specific and localizable in its focus, it also has a tendency to expand. Here, Royzman, McCauley and Rozin turn to the work of Mick Power and Tim Dalgleish (2016) who talk about hate as 'generalized anger. It is a strong negative emotion which has ceased to be about one event or one thwarted goal and has broadened to embrace parts of, or indeed all aspects of the person or object, and continues across time' (293). Hate is therefore extendable and escalates, moving via displacement from part to whole (because the whole becomes reduced to or stands in for the part) or via association from instance to instance (because each instance is assumed to be the same). The multiplication of hate is further enhanced because an important part of its economy includes, as already noted, its transmission through stories, which for a very long time have stopped being tethered to a specific place, and through our globalized mediascapes can now spread around the world. These stories can then be modified and adapted for any fresh context, producing new forms of displacement and association.

This is why Ahmed argues 'hate cannot be found in one figure, but works to create the very outline of different figures or objects of hate, a creation that crucially aligns the figures together, and constitutes them as a "common" threat' (2001: 347). This conception is also central to Barbara Perry's (2001) analysis of 'hate crimes' where the assault is based on a stigmatization that all members of a community are deemed to share via these processes of displacement and association. This 'dynamic process' (1) where hate is in a 'constant state of movement and change' (8) is what potentially makes hate all-encompassing and difficult to contain. Again, accentuating the economy of hate, Perry argues,

> hate crime is a crime like no other. Its dynamics both constitute and are constitutive of actors beyond the immediate victims and offenders. It is implicated not merely in the relationship between the direct 'participants', but also in the relationship between the different communities to which they belong. The damage involved goes far beyond physical or financial damages. It reaches into the community to create fear, hostility, and suspicion. (10)

The different objects of hate that Ahmed speaks about, therefore, include both intentional targets as well as accidental or incidental ones that are caught up in hate's economy.

Hate can therefore be said to be expansive because it moves from the perception of minor differences to the creation of major differences and from socially cohesive prejudice to socially catastrophic genocide. In this process, a community's hate preachers like Tommy Robinson and Katie Hopkins in the UK take on the function of 'malignant group therapists' (Post 1999: 337). They cherish and cultivate enemies 'because if people lose them, they also risk losing their self-definition' (Sternberg 2005: 42). For Roy F. Baumeister and David A. Butz (2005), this is compounded through 'instrumentally aggressive victimization' (89) in which 'aggression against an out-group can be motivated by a desire to obtain rewards from the in-group' (91). Here, hate is not just given 'societal permission' (Berkowitz 2005: 172) but is actively encouraged if someone is to belong to a specific community. This is another reason why hate is contagious within a group. Such animosity can often be performed through jokes and forms of ridicule that express and reproduce the minor differences. Hence, given this is a primary route for hate's expansion, it is hardly surprising there is a call to limit certain types of speech. This issue is underscored by what I would call *the entropic tendency of hate*. On this issue, Susan Opotow (2005) makes the crucial observation that 'because milder, more subtle, and narrower forms of moral exclusion more readily give way to blatant, active, and wider forms of moral exclusion than the reverse, it is quicker and easier to bring about an increasingly intolerant social climate that excludes more widely and severely than to bring about a social climate that is more tolerant, inclusionary, and peaceful' (129). It cannot be stressed how important this is. In our current climate where opportunistic politicians believe they can make immediate gains from stoking xenophobia and racism, they could quickly learn their assumption about being able to control what they have encouraged is an illusion.

This issue of 'milder, more subtle, and narrower forms of moral exclusion' requires that we say a little more about how we might define hate in emotional terms. Arguing, after Ahmed, that 'hate is economic' has meant needing to show how it is structured socially through beliefs, values and modes of understanding that are all created and sustained through rituals and circulated through stories and the media that carry them. These stories set the boundaries for in-group and out-group, friend and enemy and self and other, resulting in periods of hostility and animosity that might steadily endure over time or peak in episodes of intensity activated quite often in relation to environmental factors pertaining to the abundance or scarcity of resources or even challenges to a community's sense of identity. Together with Kathleen Blee, we therefore need to understand that hate is also 'an outcome of social action' (2004: 96). Of course, it is the basic premise of this book that there are a range of social actions currently contributing to the rise of and even legitimation of hate. One of these actions is the increased tolerance of 'hate speech'. This is such a complex issue that I will return to it in Chapter 3. However, it is possible to say that simply based on the issues raised here – especially in relation to stories, discourses, cognitions, identities and social actions – the expansive and entropic nature of hate suggests that we do need to pay particular attention to the forms of social action and types of speech that helps it grow. For the rest of this chapter, however, we still need to understand more about the individual experience and expression of hate and what it is that drives an individual towards a particular type of social action.

The fantasy of hate

Another way to think about the economy of hate, and one that is especially important for a consideration of precarity, is how it might be 'mobilising or motivational for human action' (Brown, A. 2017: 463). Here, Brown is thinking specifically about motivating action towards an *object* of hate, but I am more interested in the motivation for the *subject* doing the hating, especially in someone experiencing a range of precarities. What I will focus on for the remainder of this chapter, then, is how we might understand the *expression of hate as especially empowering*, which will help explain why the politics of hate is so seductive in times of heightened precarity. Given that all theories of hate share the idea that hateful speech or action is in some way designed to devalue an object either by demeaning, degrading, diminishing or reducing to nought (insulting, killing, disappearing, negating, annihilating), it might be assumed this has the opposite effect for the subject doing the hating. Hating, both in the value it affords and the sensation it arouses in the person doing the hating, is advancing, promoting, elevating, entitling, heightening and aggrandizing.

In this area, important work has been done by Alford (2005) who proposes: 'hatred is a relationship with others, and it is a relationship with oneself, which is another way of saying that in structuring their relationships with others, people are at the same time structuring [. . .] themselves' (236). Hatred, he goes on to say 'is self-structure on the cheap' (239). Rather than the hard work that is required to improve oneself, the devaluation and demeaning of someone else provides a quick route to feeling better. In keeping with the analysis of hatred as an economy, he argues: 'The structure created by hatred is history, the history of people's hatreds, narratives of their malevolent attachments that help hold self and world together' (239). Consequently, he argues that hate has myriad functions that, in Brown's words, motivate or mobilize the subject. Among these, Alford lists the prevention of 'psychic fragmentation' or the maintenance of self; the provision of a source of 'attachment' that can substitute for love; the production of a sense of intimacy with others who share the object of hate; the insurance of a meaningful world and a place within it (a matter discussed at length in Chapter 4); the provision of pleasure, comfort and satisfaction and the certainty of knowledge (haters always seem to know the hated better than the hated know themselves). In this, and echoing Gilroy's argument that racism precedes 'race', Alford argues, 'hatred is a primordial science' (252). Ultimately, though, hatred 'energizes the self, keeping feelings of helplessness at bay, while imprisoning the self in its hatred in a way that is experienced as preferable to the terror of freedom' (240).

This final motivation is very much in line with Jean-Paul Sartre's thesis about hate as the opposite of freedom in his famous work, *Anti-Semite and Jew*. Here, the empowerment of hate is understood in similarly negative terms, that is, as a form of denial that keeps a lid on the feeling of helplessness and insecurity. For Sartre, what the anti-Semite denies, and this can be applied to any expression of hate, is the fallibility of the position from which they speak. He proposes that 'hate is a faith' (1976: 13) that is further strengthened by being 'uttered in a chorus' (15). As with Alford and others, this is the important communal and cohering function of hate, where the hated object (person or group) helps establish and reproduce collective identity. Comparing someone who seeks truth against someone who prefers their own prejudice Sartre writes:

> The rational man groans as he gropes for the truth; he knows that his reasoning is no more than tentative, that other considerations may supervene to cast doubt on it. He never sees very clearly where he is going; he is 'open'; he may even appear to be hesitant. But there are people who are attracted by the durability of a stone. They wish to be massive and impenetrable; they wish not to change. Where, indeed, would change take them? We have here a basic fear of oneself and of truth. What frightens them is not the content of truth, of which they have no conception, but the form itself of truth, that thing of indefinite approximation. It is as if their own existence were in continual suspension. But they wish to exist all at once and right away. [It is] the kind of life [. . .] wherein one seeks only what he has already found, wherein one becomes only what he already was. This is nothing but passion. Only a strong emotional bias can give a lightning-like certainty; it alone can hold reason in leash; it alone can remain impervious to experience and last for a whole lifetime. (12–13)

This is also in line with the long tradition that links humanity to the uncertainty of freedom. If animal behaviour is largely determined by nature or instinct, what defines humanity is our spontaneity; but that spontaneity also includes the choice to evade the fallibility that freedom opens up. 'If', Sartre continues, 'the anti-Semite is impervious to reason and to experience, it is not because his conviction is strong. Rather his conviction is strong because he has chosen first of all to be impervious' (14). Using imagery that perfectly captures hate speech today, Sartre goes on to note: 'The anti-Semite is a man who wishes to be pitiless stone, a furious torrent, a devastating thunderbolt – anything except a man' (38). This is the attitude, expressed by radical right pundits, that fills column inches and saturates the airwaves of shock jock radio.

This denial has one other very important implication and one that expands on Alford's brilliant designation of hate as 'primordial science'. Having locked themself inside an impervious castle of hate, Sartre points out that the only focus for those who hate is the eradication of evil, and if all they have to do is remove evil, 'that means that the Good is already given' (31). The hater 'has no need to seek [the Good] in anguish, to invent it, to scrutinize it patiently when he has found it, to prove it in action, to verify it by its consequences or, finally, to shoulder the responsibilities of the moral choice he has made' (31). In other words, 'the more one is absorbed in fighting Evil, the less one is tempted to place the Good in question' (31).

This desire, or even claim to be impervious, has only one outcome for Sartre, and that is for the anti-Semite to characterize Jewish people as being 'completely bad' (23). In keeping with their wish, as already noted, 'to exist all at once and right away', the hater characterizes the Jew as the epitome of absolute or limitless evil: as wholly determined by but also the agent of a total malevolence. Commenting on the anti-Semite's construction (fabulation, even) of the Jew, Sartre comments: 'There is only one creature, to my knowledge, who is thus totally free and yet chained to evil; that is the Spirit of Evil himself, Satan. Thus the Jew is assimilable to the spirit of evil. His will [. . .] is one which wills itself purely, gratuitously, and universally to be evil. It is the will to evil' (28). In the contemporary politics of hate, other targets have also been associated with this world-destroying malevolence including feminists, gay people, Muslims and migrants. This becomes a Manichaean struggle in which the anti-Semite as the 'Knight-errant of the Good [. . .] is a holy man. The Jew also is holy in his manner – holy like the untouchables, like savages under the interdict of a taboo' (30). This gets to the heart of what is so devastating about hate and the economy it circulates within. It is no surprise that anti-Semitism and white supremacy have been so destructive and that so many resources might be committed to their cause.

One of the most brilliant studies of this Manichaean relationship with evil and one that also explains our desire 'to exist all at once' can be found in François Flahault's book, *Malice* (2003). His theory of our relationship with evil, which is really a projection of evil onto another, is based on Freudian psychoanalysis and the sociology of Georges Bataille, both of which posit a desire to experience or attain limitlessness that Flahault places at the heart of the phenomenon of hate. From Freud, Flahault takes the concept of primary narcissism, a stage prior to the development of the ego when an infant has no sense of self and is indistinct from the world and others around it. Here, the infant exists in a state that Flahault calls 'non-bounded, non-differentiated, proto-subjectivity' (41). To become who we are we must 'give up [. . .] this infinite *self* (41; emphasis in original), but the desire to be infinite remains present as a potential psychopathology in later stages of development and is connected to forms of aggression, a desire for control and the narcissism of self-expansion.

In the work of Bataille, limitlessness has a more metaphysical source that for him explains the sacred character of social life. Here, it is the idea that each individuated being emerged out of cosmic continuity, a sense for which remains a part of each individual. For Bataille (1992), it is the desire to reconnect with continuity that is the foundation of religion and our desire to commune with God or the gods. Theology and forms of religion are therefore responsible for connecting us with this continuity, while social rituals such as music and dance are about finding other forms of access. Such rituals are well known to produce some sense of limitlessness as we lose our sense of self in both the rhythm and the crowd. The use of drugs and hallucinogens are also closely linked to such rituals. For Bataille, artistic practice, eroticism and sacrifice were all ways in which we might achieve a loss of self (through experience of the sublime, orgasm and proximity to death).

Fundamentally, this means Flahault's understanding of hate rests on a tension – that we can understand ontologically or psychologically – between 'the desire to be *undivided*' (2003: 84; emphasis in original) or complete in oneself, and the experience of our particular, limited and bounded existence. Linguistically, we like to exaggerate or even fantasize about being undivided. We even refer to ourselves as individuals, meaning undivided or indivisible, when in fact we are *dividuals*; divided by the language we received from others, the history bequeathed to us by others, the social place maintained by others and a life sustained by myriad other non-human (biological and chemical) elements. In Flahault's words: 'our fundamental propensity to exist as a complete whole clashes with the fact that in order to exist, we must exist in the mind of at least a few other people; we need to occupy a defined place in a shared world. [. . .] So, doomed to incompleteness and the hazards of dependency, we strive by every possible means to escape the walls of our prison' (70). In a line that resonates so strongly with the contemporary politics of hate, Flahault writes the following: 'being nice means internalizing the split between oneself and the other; it means limiting oneself in order to make room for the other, and is therefore a kind of renunciation of being whole' (87). The absolute refusal of such a limit, especially when it is presented in terms of empathy is crucial to the Alt-Right/Lite and the range of neo- and ethno-nationalisms currently ascendant. It is epitomized in their opposition to 'PC culture', which is simply the recognition of everyone's human right to dignity and respect. However, it is more than simply not being nice or empathetic. According to Flahault, we actively take pleasure in the suffering of others because through it we a get a sense of our own self-expansion. The plight of refugees is a very good example of this. In her study of totalitarianism, Arendt also noted how crucial this antisocial behaviour was in the formation of a link between different strata of society. 'The temporary alliance between the elite and the mob rested largely on [the] genuine delight with which the former watched the latter destroy respectability' (1968: 333).

In his work on the Alt-Right, Neiwert discusses a study by Erin E. Buckels of antisocial and aggressive trolling on the internet. According to Neiwert (2017), Buckels's study 'found that trolls share what psychologists call the "dark tetrad" of psychological traits: Machiavellianism (willingly deceptive and manipulative), narcissism (self-obsessed and egoistic), psychopathy (an absence of empathy or remorse), and sadism (enjoys the suffering of others)' (219). All four suggest the sort of indifference towards, and control of, other people that is perfectly in line with Flahault's analysis of the unlimited expansion of the self. In fact, online communities such as boards on Reddit or 4-Chan can increase the sense of expansion because troll attacks can function very much like mobs, and 'in mobs, there can be a speedy loss of the boundaries of the self' (Staub 2005: 60), or in Berkowitz's words, the 'anonymity arising from immersion in a group' (2005: 172) can lead to precisely the kind of 'deindividuation' (174) our desire seeks.

Such antisocial behaviour also requires the discussion of another feature of Bataille's (1993) work that is crucial here, namely, the idea of transgression. One way a society or community might manage the desire for limitlessness is to permit moments of law breaking and hence overcome the proscriptions that limit us. It is not uncommon for cultures to have various occasions when the usual social norms, rules of etiquette or structures of dominance are overturned. This is often referred to as the time of carnival. However, permission is not transgression. Genuine transgression needs to cross a line that is still in place, and Flahault suggests this can happen through what we might call the practice of perverse justice. He writes: *'another need not have injured us for us to desire reparation from him'* (2003: 121). Consequently, 'taking revenge on those who have done nothing to us affords a kind of supreme compensation' (127). In this sense, the migrant or refugee would seem to be the exemplary target. Not only have they not done anything to us, we might have already wronged them. Their displacement and need for refuge might be the direct result of our military actions overseas in the numerous foreign interventions we declare necessary but execute with so little thought.

Punishing the refugee provides precisely the sort of compensation of perverse justice that Flahault describes.

In contrast, many have considered love as a path to the consummation we desire. Since Socrates told the story of the gods splitting in two the humans they believed could threaten their power, we have continued to look for our 'other half' and the supposed completion they will bring. Flahault also considers love as an expression of 'the desire for self-totalization', acknowledging 'the person who loves expects the beloved to actualize and complete his or her own existence' (71). However, not only is love a risk and a gamble because it repeats and even intensifies the dependency we have on others, but it is also another way to limit our self. Any loving relationship requires compromise and reciprocity and demands 'we present an aspect of ourselves that finds favour, that we take up positions which suit the other' (71). By contrast, in hating someone it doesn't matter what they do because I can still hate them all the same. In other words, 'by hating, I can enjoy the power of affirming myself absolutely and unconditionally' (71). What is more, because there is no need for reciprocity in hate, I can project an absolute malevolence onto the other, which simply increases and intensifies the sense of self-expansion. Ultimately, then, for Flahault, 'only hatred can provide the dream of love with its complete fulfilment' (71).[1]

For all of the above-mentioned reasons, especially the capacity hate has to expand itself, and the way it is structured or organized through stories circulating across globalized media that aid its expansion, I am particularly troubled by the rise of hate today. However, because of the explanation offered by Flahault, I am especially concerned by *hate in precarious times*. What precarity accentuates is our sense of dependency and vulnerability that activates a profound anxiety for which hate is almost an immediate fix. This is why the politics of hate is such a challenge today. Also, once people whose lives are increasingly precarious have had a taste of what malice can do for them, it becomes quite addictive because, in Flahault's words, 'hating produces an immediate extra-being which is hard to give up' (126–7). Hate, as spontaneous and unconditional self-expansion, is therefore very powerful.

3

Slow hate and free speech

While the politics of hate is certainly ascendant, the rise of neo-Nazism, fascism and the array of reactionary groups gathered under the names Alt-Right or Generation Identity has not gone unchallenged. As the racism and xenophobia of these groups are seemingly legitimized by a white nationalist White House and a Brexit campaign that spoke in private about 'Empire 2.0', other groups have successfully sought to resist the white supremacy, misogyny and homophobia endemic in far-right thought by removing their platform. This has been most noticeable in universities that cancel invitations to speak – even if the number of these cancellations is regularly overplayed (Eaton 2019). However, this issue also raises a number of concerns about liberalism's ability to resist the rising tide of hate and so-called hate speech. This term is open to numerous definitions and is not 'bound by the assumption of univocality' (Brown, A. 2017: 467), but it might be described as public speech that incites discrimination and/or violence against historically marginalized groups based, for example, on race, religion, gender or sexuality.

Both the 'hate' and the 'harm' in hate speech are regularly contested, so I would like to briefly return to the definitions of hate in Chapter 2 to add another that I believe is crucial for our current context. Addressing the complexity of the economy of hate, Sternberg (2005) described seven types. These are *cool hate* or disgust, resulting in aversion or the negation of intimacy; *hot hate* manifesting in a mix of anger and fear; *cold hate* resulting in a judgement that diminishes or devalues a person or object; *boiling hate* described as revulsion plus anger and fear; *simmering hate*, which is a deep loathing accompanied by devaluation; *seething hate*, characterized by a sense of revilement premised on the object being perceived as a threat and the precursor to mob violence, and *burning hate*, which is the felt need for annihilation (39–40). These seven indicate that hate is not simply a crude, individual emotion but has subtle variations that manifest at different points in its economy. However, to these seven types, I would like to add an eighth. This is something I will call *slow hate*.

Slow hate

Slow hate is named after Rob Nixon's (2011) analysis of 'slow violence', which he defines as 'a violence that occurs gradually and out of sight, a violence of delayed destruction that is dispersed across time and space, an attritional violence that is typically not viewed as violence at all' (2). In this sense, slow hate would be something akin to the low-level malice and generalized spite of shock jocks, sofa-sitting media pundits, populist politicians complaining about 'PC culture', and right-wing journalists who sell newspapers and grab viewers through the manufacture of outrage. I will return to this in Chapter 8, but for now it is important to include this ubiquitous malice in our thinking around both the politics and the conceptualization of contemporary hate precisely because it is 'attritional' on democratic principles of equality and in terms of the harm it does to those targeted.

Nixon's specific aim in his discussion of slow violence is the damage done to the environment: the almost imperceptible degradation and pollution bringing about climate change and species depletion around the globe. Coupled with the violence, though, is a second challenge that he calls 'representational' (3). In a world of 'flickering attention spans' and 'spectacle-driven corporate media' (6), how can we 'devise arresting stories, images, and symbols adequate to the pervasive but elusive violence of delayed effects'? (3). In a world where events such as the 'Unite the Right' rally and the murder of UK member of parliament, Jo Cox, rightly get instant media attention, how do we develop awareness of, for example, the spike in acts of aggression towards Muslim women after Boris Johnson epitomized today's pervasive spite with his casual comments about them looking like bank robbers and letterboxes? For Nixon, it is not only the fact the media live off the spectacular but also the structural privilege of *'who counts as a witness'* (16; emphasis in original). He continues by making the very important point that 'contests over what counts as violence are intimately entangled with conflicts over who bears the social authority of witness, which entails much more than simply seeing and not seeing' (16). It has traditionally been white men who take this authority upon themselves.

Over that last five decades significant counters have been made against this structural privilege, as I will discuss in Chapter 7, but it has still been insufficient and requires more work. In fact, the attack on so-called PC culture by the right is precisely an attempt to curtail and even roll back these advances. Ensuring the effects of slow hate remain invisible is, then, an attempt to reinforce or bolster the structural privilege that remains. The invisibility of slow hate is therefore partly because of the difficulty in defining the harm done by such small acts. As if he were responding directly to Nixon,

Jeremy Waldron offers us an 'ecological analogy' (2012: 96) for thinking the problem.

> Suppose we said that unless someone can show that *my automobile* causes lead poisoning with direct detriment and imminent harm to the health of assignable individuals, I shouldn't be required to fit an emission-control device to my car's exhaust pipe. It would be irresponsible to reason in that way with regard to environmental regulation; instead we figure that the tiny impacts of millions of actions – each apparently inconsiderable in itself – can produce a large-scale toxic effect. (97; emphasis in original)

He concludes that a lot of progress has been made in our moral philosophy by 'taking causation of this kind, on this scale and at this pace, properly into account' (97), and yet we seem unable to do it in relation to speech.

Returning to Nixon, the problem is in part because of who is called or, more often, who isn't called to witness the action as harm. Given that we outsource so much of our pollution and environmental depletion to poorer often post-colonial nations, their voice is less important. In relation to speech, though, there was a brief period in 2019 when milkshakes were used as a variation on efforts to deplatform racist speech. The tactic was simply to cover said speakers in milkshake as a protest against the discriminatory politics they advocated. Quite often, this was presented in the media as an anti-democratic practice that curtailed free speech, but I would prefer to think of it as the sort of opportunity Nixon calls for to visualize the invisible effects of slow hate and help make victims of it more visible. A milkshake doesn't physically injure a person, but it does stop or at least interrupt them expressing their opinions, while also producing a moment of social shaming. As such, is this not exactly what racist and discriminatory speech does? And isn't the accumulative effect of such slow hate precisely a form of intimidation and social shaming that undercuts a person's capacity and willingness to openly express themselves? If so, how can a commitment to free speech or a critique of 'prohibitionism' (Heinze 2016) ever truly enhance democracy? Until we, as a society, address the structural privilege that prevents the necessary people being given the chance to bear witness, is it possible that the stain of the milkshake might offer us a way to see what all too often remains unseen? If the throwing of a milkshake, which causes no physical injury, can be seen as harmful because such action inhibits or stigmatizes, can we not by analogy see the harm done by slow hate?

Understanding slow hate is also a call to develop what we might include in the term hate itself. In the preceding chapter I attempted to show, in line with Ahmed's work, that hate is a complex economy of relations, exchanges, values, judgements, resources and contexts. It is also rooted in cognitions, modes of understanding and stories. A conception of slow hate also supports Sternberg's efforts to specify different types of hate but also move beyond basing it purely in feelings of anger or rage, disgust or revulsion, revilement or the desire to annihilate. Slow hate is, thus, closest to Sternberg's 'cold hate' as a judgement that diminishes or devalues, but I use slow hate to speak of the gradual, accumulated effect of such diminishment and devaluing, as well as its invisibility. In doing this I would also call in support from Alexander Brown (2017) who argued that in attempting to define hate speech we must not 'fall into the trap of blindly accepting the myth of hate' (441), by which he means hate understood in terms of the violent expression of rage and revulsion.

In attempting to think through the varied types of speech that people regularly collect under the term hate speech, he suggests we treat 'hate speech' as a 'partially transparent idiom whose meaning is not directly deducible from the literal meanings of the words "hate" and "speech"' (462). He likens this to other idioms such as 'zebra crossing' and 'pillow talk'. In 'zebra crossing' the term 'zebra' is not used literally but assumes the crossing is like a zebra in one sense (it has black and white stripes). Applying this to hate speech, Brown proposes 'the word "hate" in "hate speech" means *like hate in a least one of its attributes or qualities*' (462). As for 'pillow talk', he notes that in this idiom 'pillow' doesn't relate to a quality but to a relation. Pillows are found on beds, a context of intimacy, and the talk that takes place there is at least potentially as unguarded as the other activity it is understood to follow. Applying this to hate speech, 'the word "hate" in "hate speech" means *analogous to hate in at least one of its relational structures*' (463; emphasis in original). Using these two examples, slow hate, or low-level malice, is like hate because it has the *quality* of seeking to devalue and demean in *relation* to a person or group of people understood to be non-dominant and historically marginalized, oppressed or persecuted. In this way, I believe it is possible to encompass a broader range of speech and action including the more pervasive forms of slow hate that seem to be moving from the margins back into the mainstream of political discourse. If we are unable to do this, we will fail to comprehend the extent of the politics of hate and its gradual normalization.

Unfortunately, this is precisely what we are doing. All too often, in response to attempts to de-platform racist or misogynist speakers, the radical right have countered with appeals to 'free speech'. The phrase has also been taken up by the mainstream media and presented as evidence that it is those who actively oppose the rise of the far-right that are the real threat to democracy. For the rest of this chapter, then, I want to raise some concerns about 'free speech' both in terms of those who advocate for it and its robustness as our main defence against fascism. Given that the United States considers itself the world's leading democracy and adopts an almost absolutist defence of free speech, it will be my primary focus here. I believe it also provides a very good test of our Biedermann syndrome.

Free speech

When I began to write this book, Boris Johnson's racist remarks about Muslim women published in *The Telegraph* on 5 August 2018 encapsulated the problems with free speech absolutism. In an article about banning the Niqab, a proposal he rejected, he still couldn't help offering the sort of cultural insensitivity that this empire-loving Etonian is well known for. He wrote 'it is absolutely ridiculous that people should choose to go around looking like letter boxes' and that if 'a female student turned up at school or at a university lecture looking like a bank robber' he'd ask her to remove her veil before having any discussion with her. Although the article was supposed to be a more general critique of what he sees as an oppressive religion, an issue we should always be allowed to discuss and critique, these comments target specific individuals by dehumanizing them (likening them to inanimate objects) and criminalizing them (likening them to bank robbers) thereby servicing a host of prejudices that demean Muslims and Muslim women in particular. His words also display a range of ignorant assumptions about Muslim women and blithely repeat the idea they are unable or not allowed to make their own decisions about how they dress when this is not the case. Deciding to wear the Niqab can be a religious decision based on the interpretation of the Koran, but it is often a cultural one linked to a sense for the rituals that bind a community. In a number of instances the decision will be political one, often as an act of resistance and a direct response to the rise of Islamophobia. Rather than a simplistic sign of oppression, then, the Niqab represents a complex set of religious, cultural and political issues of which Boris Johnson is willingly oblivious.

While there was an outcry in response to Johnson's remarks, not least because of the then ongoing investigation into Islamophobia in the Conservative Party (an investigation, incidentally that has gone nowhere despite the revelation in 2020 of 300 allegations), plenty of people came to his defence, again citing the 'democratic' principle of free speech. Social media users also took to re-sharing comedian Rowan Atkinson's speech in favour of freedom of expression from 2012. Atkinson has long been committed to the right to make jokes about and ridicule religion and, indeed, the right to offend. In a passionate speech in response to *Charlie Hebdo* publishing cartoons of the Prophet Mohammed, Atkinson glossed over an issue that takes us to the heart of what is at stake in this debate. Echoing Barak Obama, who in response to calls to suppress certain types of speech famously said we need more speech not less, Atkinson made an argument that we need more speech in the way a body needs to ingest germs to build up its defences. What we need, he proposed is to 'build our immunity to taking offence'. At one level this sounds sensible, but on another it smacks of our love for lazy analogies that make social processes appear to be as necessary and inevitable as natural ones. Most importantly, though, for people to use this speech as a defence for insulting Muslim women is deeply problematic because the speech contains no understanding of power dynamics. In other words, it assumes an equality that exists only abstractly in our legislation but is absent from our histories and our socio-economic realities.

Viewed in relation to the Johnson scandal, it implicitly assumes that when a powerful, wealthy white man insults Muslim women – who are more likely to be economically, socially and politically disadvantaged – it is the same as her insulting him. This is completely blind to the realities of social inequality and is a highly privileged position to hold. Rowan Atkinson is a wealthy, middle class, middle-aged, straight, white man. He is the least likely to be subject to the consequences of racist, classist, sexist, homophobic 'hate speech' and is therefore a poor example when discussing the realities of everyday, casual, yet systemic discrimination and the violence that often accompanies it. Yes, he might receive hostile criticism, even death threats in his role as a comedian. We are all potentially at risk from the actions of extremists whether we draw cartoons in Paris, have a drink in the Admiral Duncan in Soho, attend college in Isla Vista, go to an Arianna Grande concert in Manchester or a black church in Charleston, but Atkinson will never face the everyday prejudice, discrimination and abuse that a Muslim woman is regularly exposed to, so, again, it is a misleading choice of defence.

A little over a year after Johnson's column was published, it became clear the sort of effect the speech of the most powerful man in the country could have. According to Lizzie Dearden (2019) in the *Independent*, 'Islamophobic incidents rose by 375 per cent in the week after Boris Johnson compared veiled Muslim women to "letterboxes" [. . . and] was followed by the biggest spike in anti-Muslim hatred in 2018, as his words were repeated by racists abusing Muslims on the street and online' (np). Returning to Atkinson's speech, what its recirculation actually did was show how advocates of free speech regularly belong to socially dominant positions that have been undermined to some extent by both the democratic move towards greater representation and the technological developments that have opened the public sphere to a much greater diversity of voices. Former gatekeepers are troubled by what they perceive to be their waning influence and thus the diminishment of their world view. These developments have been largely responsible for curbing speech that might be deemed racist, sexist or homophobic. As a society, we had fortunately become increasingly sensitive to the harm such speech can do and had developed what might be called a voluntary social code that deemed certain language unacceptable. These limitations are relatively minor, and, yet, the defenders of free speech act as if they are completely silenced on all manner of issues when in reality we still seem to be constantly talking about all the things free speech absolutists are claiming we are not allowed to talk about. Simply put, for those who still hold socially dominant positions, these limits seem quite alien. Previously, the mark of social privilege has been the ability to say whatever you want wherever you want to say it. The privileged have never experienced limits and don't see why they should now.

If you have experienced the limitations and, indeed, the various forms of violence that accompany racism, sexism and homophobia or are a member of an ethnic group or a culture that has been enslaved, transported, dispossessed, tortured, raped or bought and sold, limitations being placed on you are part of your living history. You may come from people who had their language stripped from them, weren't allowed to use their own name, practice their cultural rites or who had their children taken away. You may have been excluded, denied entry, confined, overlooked or demeaned based on your gender. You may have been banned or physically attacked because of your sexuality. While many of these debasements and restrictions are part of the history and lived experience of people or groups often referred to as minorities, for white people and white men in particular any suggestion of limits is unacceptable. This is what is so interesting and effective about the current social proscription around white people using the n-word. As Ta-Nehisi Coates once cogently explained, being unable to utter this word is probably the only way a white person can have any sense of the limitations and exclusions placed on people of colour living in both colonial and post-colonial societies. Each time we are required to *not* say the word is potentially an educational moment. Ultimately, while free speech has no doubt contributed to the advancement of the previously marginalized, *the concept itself still needs to be radically de-colonized* if it is to genuinely continue that advancement and not find a natural 'limit' in the level of progress that white (straight, Christian) men, in particular, are prepared to tolerate.

Critics of free speech absolutism regularly point out the contradiction whereby Alt-Right hate preachers are happy to be liberal allegiant when trying to justify their right to speak but will denounce the very liberalism they have used to secure a platform once they are given the opportunity. These critics also turn to Karl Popper's paradox of tolerance presented in

The Open Society and its Enemies where he argues: 'Unlimited tolerance must lead to the disappearance of tolerance. If we extend unlimited tolerance even to those who are intolerant, if we are not prepared to defend a tolerant society against the onslaught of the intolerant, then the tolerant will be destroyed, and tolerance with them' (2002: 581).

In his speech in favour of building our immunity to offence, Atkinson indirectly referred to Popper's argument about tolerance and made a claim that such an argument simply replaces one form of intolerance for another. This is certainly a potential problem, but otherwise tolerant people being intolerant of intolerance is hardly equivalent to intolerant people being intolerant of tolerance. In other words, people who are happy to let others live and practice their culture being intolerant of those who aren't is qualitatively different from people who advocate a monoculture and are intolerant of difference. At the extremes of these two views is, on the one hand, a celebration of diversity, admittedly with all the problems around cultural relativism that this may include, and on the other a celebration of a socially dominant identity with all the problems of exclusionary violence and oppression that may include. The two are fundamentally and diametrically opposed political positions. Any conflation is disingenuous. However, the issue surrounding what to do about 'hate speech' does raise a number of very important legal and political questions, and in the most laissez-faire of Western democracy's approaches to the topic – the First Amendment to the Constitution of the United States – there is both a vigilant defence of freedom and a deeply troubling, Biedermann-esque complacency that all will be well if that right is simply protected. As this attitude is central to the politics of the radical right in other Western countries, it is important we work through it in detail.

The First Amendment to the US Constitution reads: 'Congress shall make no law respecting an establishment of religion, or prohibiting the free exercise thereof; or abridging the freedom of speech, or of the press; or the right of the people peaceably to assemble, and to petition the Government for a redress of grievances.' In recent years, opponents of 'hate speech' have argued that some speech should indeed be abridged because of its capacity to inflict harm and therefore contravene other aspects of the Constitution pertaining to the protection of life, liberty and equality. For a summary of the complex problems involved in the limitation of free speech, the most informed and thorough – yet also concise – account is Nadine Strossen's *Hate: Why We Should Resist It with Free Speech, Not Censorship*. In a series of seven meditations that consider equality, the type of speech that is already punishable, the difficulty in defining both 'hate' and 'harm', overreach, counter-productivity and non-censorial methods, Strossen offers a brilliant defence of free speech that benefits from her considerable expertise and is strengthened by both her family history that includes the loss of family members in the Holocaust and her recognition that 'entrenched structural discrimination' (2018: 8) is a reality.

In short, Strossen, like Obama and Atkinson, is an advocate of more speech not less and provides a detailed and often very convincing justification for her position. The main thrust of her argument rests on the importance of ensuring 'viewpoint neutrality' as a cornerstone of American democracy and political life and a recognition that 'emergency principles' already guard against speech if 'it causes specific imminent serious harm' (38). Given the fundamental nature of the emergency principle to the preservation of US democracy, I will return to it specifically in the next section. More generally, though, while I have immediate concerns with the legal-centric conception of neutrality that has a very limited sense for wider issues of social power and political hierarchy – as noted in her ludicrously uncritical defence of 'ideological neutrality' in US classrooms (175) – the most sobering aspect of her argument for advocates of limiting 'hate speech' is the fact that this often turns out to be counterproductive and is turned against minorities or dissenting positions.

On the topic of overreach, she argues that given society's 'entrenched racism and other types of discrimination [. . .] it is predictable that the institutions and individuals enforcing "hate speech" laws will not do so in a way that is helpful to minorities' (15); going on later to note that 'just as free speech always has been the strongest weapon to advance reform movements, including equal rights causes, censorship always has been the strongest weapon to thwart them' (81). Importantly, she cites numerous examples from across Canada and the EU where 'hate speech' laws have been used against the very groups arguing for those laws. On this topic, she notes that the US Supreme Court enforced the '"bad tendency" standard' (40) until the middle of the twentieth century. This was a standard whereby the government could suppress speech they judged 'might cause harm at some future point', using it to limit speech critical of US entry into the First World War and engage in 'rampant viewpoint discrimination' (40). Reading this book is, therefore, essential for anyone like myself who believes some limits must be placed on our right to speak freely. It is a timely reminder that such a decision is a genuine risk and could, in fact, further entrench already existing discriminatory forces.

Strossen's argument for free speech is also indicative of the many assumptions that underpin the position. First, there is the claim that 'Encountering "unwelcome" ideas, including those that are hateful and discriminatory is essential for honing our abilities to analyze, criticize and refute them' (2). While this is a wonderful liberal ideal, the truth is that a significant number of people do not proceed to their opinions through the mode of reasonable, evidence-based deduction that Strossen advocates – a point, incidentally, that Popper includes as a reason for not tolerating intolerance. If people were rational, it is unlikely they would believe in the Rapture, the conspiracy of the moon landing, race science, 'Pizzagate' or any other similar story popular with the radical right. Too often, it is believed that the reasonable exchange between positions will lead to the delegitimation of the 'unwelcome' ones, but this is clearly not the case. In fact, it would be unreasonable to assume so. In many respects this is the fantasy known as 'the marketplace of ideas', an idea akin to the great neoliberal fantasy of the 'free market' but this time applied to political discourse. As with the 'free market', it is assumed to be free from influence, emotion, bias, manipulation and power, which it certainly is not. It is a concept as fabulous as a unicorn.

In keeping with this is another liberal fable that 'free speech [. . .] facilitates the search for truth' (21), and yet no consideration is given to the widely discussed move towards post-truth, accelerated by Trump's preference for disinformation and 'alternative facts'. This is a problem accentuated by his undermining of journalism as 'fake news' and the framing of journalists as 'the enemy of the people', along with broad and sustained attacks of any expert that counters the veracity of his own proclamations, all of which is distributed via the new propaganda vehicle of unregulated social media. Omitting any reference to the current context is therefore a significant oversight, and an example of the complacency that is so troubling. Yes, free speech has indeed been a major contributing factor in discovering and establishing the truth, but when the message from the White House is profoundly illiberal, deliberately deceitful, dismissive of scientific evidence and what is proven to be true – and the '"government speech" doctrine' states 'the government has the prerogative to choose which messages it will convey' (59) – this deep-seated assumption about the relationship between free speech and truth needs serious attention and cannot be taken for granted.

This idea of what is reasonable also surfaces in Strossen's discussion regarding adjudicating true threats, incitement and what is called '"hostile environment" harassment' (65). She notes how the Supreme Court held that 'threatening language in a public debate was mere hyperbolic rhetoric that would not instil reasonable fear of an actual attack' (61), but what is this position from where the reasonableness of speech and action is being judged? Despite some element of racial and gender diversity creeping into the Supreme Court, this supposedly neutral, 'unmarked' position of adjudication is another myth. This problem was epitomized when B-list white supremacists, Lauren Southern and Stephan Molyneux, visited New Zealand. Discussing their visit in relation to an earlier judgement around a racist cartoon that was deemed not to be, Moana Jackson (2018) eloquently summed up the problem:

> Cartoons published a few years ago depicting fat and lazy Māori taking advantage of free school lunches were found by the court to be objectively offensive but protected by free speech and the fact that they weren't offensive enough to incite a 'reasonable person' to hatred or violence against our people.
>
> The reasonable person in the common law was for a long time described as the 'man on the Clapham omnibus', and while that fictional being is now genderless, it is still presumed to be some amorphous Pākehā [the Māori word for white person].
>
> Rather, as the term 'a trial by a jury of one's peers' has a default meaning, where Māori can never be tried by a jury of Māori peers, so the reasonableness of a cartoon or speech is judged by the standards of an invisible and unnamed Pākehā.

Here, Jackson simply dismantles the idea of neutrality by showing how such a position is revealed to be partial from an indigenous perspective. The United States is in no way immune from such bias, and this is very clearly another idea in need of decolonization.

Quoting British scholars, Dennis J. Baker and Lucy Zhao, Strossen also talks about the importance of the dominant social message being one of equality and how "'strong majority attitudes" should "prevent denigrating expression from making those denigrated feel as less than full members of society'" (131), and yet this completely fails to recognize how quickly the dominant message can change and how quickly it has changed under Donald Trump, or indeed how the dominant message, like much of the formal legal theory Strossen relies on does not translate into actual social, political and economic equality. The argument also fails to recognize that 'free speech' is not simply a legal issue but is also a cultural one, and it gets applied differently depending on the culture concerned.

As Christina Carron (2018) reported in *The New York Times*, Baraboo School District would not punish a class of white students who collectively posed for a photograph while making a Nazi salute, and yet just over a year earlier, Jacey Fortin (2017), also in *The New York Times*, reported that two black students at the Victory and Praise Christian Academy in Texas were kicked off a school football team for kneeling during the national anthem in protest against police violence and killings. If the latter case went to court, a First Amendment defence could no doubt be made in favour of the students, but the 'free speech' doctrine is not just a constitutional amendment linked to set of legal rulings it is also a cultural norm that regulates everyday behaviour, and because those norms are often riddled with the structural discrimination that Strossen acknowledges, but quickly seems to forget, they are applied differently in the minutiae of everyday life. As such, 'hate speech' has much greater and more immediate social efficacy than a legal defence of free speech in a federal court. It is for this reason that unregulated 'free speech' can easily contribute to a shift in political culture that, in turn, renders the laws protecting freedom more precarious. Speaking purely of the United States, given the deeply politicized nature of its Supreme Court, this ought to be more of a concern.[1]

The problem of *emergency bias*

While Strossen does an exemplary job unpacking the problems and dangers of limiting free speech, her failure to interrogate some of the widely held assumptions integral to a free speech position raises a number of concerns that leaves me still believing in the need for some form of limitation. However, nothing convinces me more than her failure to consider the 'emergency principle' in the context of the Trump presidency. This is by far the most pressing issue that leads me to speak of the liberal complacency that takes us back to the tragic Biedermann reading the newspapers and thinking it could never happen in his house. Although she argued that the 'bad tendency principle' was overturned by the middle of the twentieth century, it wasn't actually replaced by the 'emergency principle' until the Supreme Court ruling in *Brandenburg v. Ohio* in 1969. This ruling is important because it rejected a statute used to charge Clarence Brandenburg with inciting violence. As a Ku Klux Klan leader, Brandenburg had organized a rally calling for violent action to be taken against 'N*****s' and 'Jews', but the Supreme Court ruled he was protected under the First Amendment because his speech didn't constitute 'imminent lawless action'. However, for the purpose of our situation, it is worth noting that this means the current interpretation of the 'emergency principle' came into existence specifically in relation to quashing charges against members of a white supremacist, far-right group.

Although there were earlier rulings relating to the idea of a 'clear and present danger', the most famous is probably the Smith Act of 1940 that is regarded as a precedent for the hysteria of post-war McCarthyism. Amid rising tensions in Europe, the Smith Act 'forbade any attempts to "advocate, abet, advise, or teach" the violent destruction of the U.S. government' (Thompson nd). This was followed ten years later by the Internal Security Act of 1950 that viewed the Communist Party of the United States of America (CPUSA) to be an agent of a foreign power and hence a national security threat. Aside from the viewpoint denial and hostile environment harassment that defined McCarthyism, there were some notable Supreme Court rulings, not least *Dennis v. United States* in 1951 that upheld the conviction of CPUSA members for advocating the overthrow of the US government. Interestingly, when *Brandenburg v. Ohio* overruled the conviction of Brandenburg in 1969, it upheld *Dennis v. United States*, and even cited it as exemplary of the newly confirmed 'emergency principle'. It is as if white supremacism is less of a challenge to the instituted order of the United States than communism, which is deeply revealing of the complete lack of neutrality within the world view inherent to the US judiciary. This also makes me mindful of signs often held at Black Lives Matter protests saying that America is so racist that protesting against it is seen as a protest against America.

Anyway, with an almost absolutist approach to free speech, it is this thoroughly biased emergency principle that is supposed to ensure American democracy is protected. But, given the current situation, how might the Trump administration and the politics around it be understood as an emergency? Why should we be concerned? Why hasn't the emergency principle been evoked, especially after he blatantly abused the First Amendment by proclaiming he will 'dominate the streets' during BLM protests in June 2020? But there were numerous calls for concern prior to this. Aside from the appointments Trump makes being evidence to support the claim that his administration is a white nationalist one with autocratic if not authoritarian tendencies, there is also the alleged statement from Steve Bannon describing himself as a Leninist out to destroy the state. *Daily Beast* reporter, Ronald Radosh, presented this boast in August 2016. 'I'm a Leninist', Bannon is supposed to have said, 'Lenin wanted to destroy the state. I want to bring everything down, and destroy all of today's establishment.' This may have simply been bravado, or another example of disinformation. He may never have said it at all. Radosh could never get him to reconfirm what he claims Bannon said to him. However, given Bannon's influence over Trump, and Trump's direct attempts to scupper the EU with blasé support for Brexit and far-right nationalist movements across the continent; his desire to undermine NATO; his failure to appoint staff to countless government positions (while also dismantling the pandemic response team); declaring the press 'the enemy of the people'; undermining White House and congressional protocol; brazenly contravening the emoluments clause of the Constitution; enacting gross nepotism; ignoring advice on National Security clearance; surrounding himself with criminals (Gates, Flynn, Manafort, Papodopulous and Cohen); threatening a state of emergency to build a racist monument on the southern border; enacting the longest government shutdown in US history; purging voters from registers under false claims of voter fraud; coming out in support of a foreign enemy rather than his own intelligence services; destabilizing long-established diplomatic alliances and friendships; pulling trillions of dollars out of the US economy for tax breaks to billionaires in a move that every expert not invested in the tax cut said would radically destabilize the US budget; firing a slew of inspectors general and withholding funding from a foreign power in a bid to get them to investigate a political opponent, it is not a wild exaggeration to say that Trump puts into practice what Bannon allegedly said.

In fact, we know that Bannon had been a close adviser to Trump well before the election, so when Trump told Fox News in February 2014: 'You know what solves [America's sorry state]? When the economy crashes, when the country goes to *total* hell and everything is a disaster. Then you'll have a [chuckles], you know, you'll have riots to go back to where we used to be when we were great,' you get the sense that Bannon might have already lit the fuse. Anyway, whatever the truth is regarding Bannon's Leninist leanings, the litany of Trump's attacks on normal governance, established process, constitutional norms and diplomatic ties is indicative of a president willing to enact radical destabilization in pursuit of his goals. As Christopher R. Browning (2018) has argued, what is most disconcerting about the foreign policy arm of this agenda is

> the ideological preference of Steve Bannon and the so-called alt-right for the unfettered self-assertion of autonomous, xenophobic nation-states – in short, the pre-1914 international system. That 'international anarchy' produced World War I, the Bolshevik Revolution, the Great Depression, the fascist dictatorships, World War II, and the Holocaust, precisely the sort of disasters that the post–World War II international system has for seven decades remarkably avoided.

Listed together like this, it sounds like an emergency.

On the domestic front there has, of course, been some judicial pushback against Trump's most egregiously discriminatory policies such as the Muslim ban, and yet the Trump administration is also remarkable for what Browning has also called 'the extreme politicization of the judiciary'. This began just prior to the election of Donald Trump with Senator Mitch McConnell blocking Obama's appointment of Merrick Garland to the Supreme Court, leaving a space to be filled by Trump with Neil Gorsuch. That appointment was relatively straightforward even if it was a stolen seat, but the extreme politicization returned with the controversial Senate confirmation of Brett

Kavanaugh based on the withholding of 100,000 pages of his rulings (Stolburg 2018) amid credible testimony of a history of sexual assault. Not only that, while the president was under investigation for collusion with a foreign enemy, this nomination was also notable because Kavanaugh had previously professed a legal interpretation arguing a sitting president cannot be indicted (Gerstein 2018). If we then add to this the fact that a president can personally choose the Attorney General, to whom the results of the investigation were given, and under whose authority decisions over public disclosure were made, I find it quite staggering that Strossen can have such confidence in the US judiciary and its sense of what constitutes an emergency.

This became even more pronounced with the appointment of William Barr to the post of Attorney General who immediately seemed to take on the role of Trump's personal defence lawyer. Barr undermined and obstructed every legal investigation of Trump's actions before the election and while in office. He interfered with the Federal Prosecutor's offices in DC and New York, appointed a criminal prosecutor to investigate members of the FBI and CIA involved with the investigation into Russian interference in the 2016 election, and another criminal prosecutor to investigate members of the previous administration, one of whom was Trump's opponent in the 2020 election. He was also integral to the impeachment acquittal and rather alarmingly showed that all a president needs to become seemingly unaccountable is a ruthlessly partisan Attorney General and a zealously partial Senate Majority Leader. Perhaps this was not out-and-out authoritarianism, but the Trump administration was certainly drafting the blue prints.

What makes Strossen's idealistic commitment to free speech more troubling, though, is the principle of viewpoint neutrality, a principle that has never genuinely operated in a country that perceives one particular form of economic organization to be divinely ordained, and it patently does not apply to considerations of the 'emergency principle' today. The United States is very active against the imminent threat posed by viewpoints that oppose Christian-based capitalism but appears very lax when judging the danger of violent creeds that support that viewpoint. Despite the acts of white men with affiliations to a variety of far-right groups currently being responsible for the largest number of terrorist incidents in the United States – even when that number of incidents is greatly reduced by language that tries to picture them as lone wolves with mental health issues rather than representatives of a hateful ideology – it is still Muslims that are primarily portrayed as a 'clear and present danger'. In fact, an important, yet little discussed, policy of Trump was to remove the funding for the investigation of white supremacist and far-right extremism, while at the same time designating the left-wing group known as 'Antifa' – a diminutive of Anti-

Fascist – as domestic terrorists (Zanona 2017; Tracy 2018). This reared its ugly head again during the protests in 2020 following the killing of George Floyd, where an almost mythical construction of 'Antifa' became the focus of the Trump administration's ire rather than police departments that were clearly out of control and riven with racist attitudes and populated with officers clearly holding white supremacist views. At a time when the UN is reporting a 320 per cent increase in white supremacist terror globally,[2] this reveals a profound blind spot in the emergency principle that Strossen argues is sufficient to protect people against harm. In fact, it implies a distinct *emergency bias* when it comes to the assessment of a 'clear and present danger'. Ultimately, the neutrality that governs US law is nothing of the sort. Like Biedermann who can't quite believe Schmitz and Eisenring are arsonists, the United States can't quite bring itself to accept that far-right white men are a true threat to democracy. Therefore, if the only real limit to free speech in the United States is an emergency that the implicit bias of the law cannot see, I would contend we are in serious trouble. To consider how we ended up in this situation where the United States was just one of the numerous democratic countries that succumbed to the illiberalism of the radical right, we need to examine the range of precarities that have fuelled the disaffection.

Part 2

Precarity

World or ontological precarity

In *Postcolonial Melancholia* Paul Gilroy offers a brilliant and prescient commentary on the state of our politics. He argues a radical shift in consciousness took place over the second half of the twentieth century and then dramatically sharpened in the early years of the twenty-first. Immediately after the Second World War and its genocidal horrors, racism was understood to be a problem for civilization (Gilroy 2005: 15) – a disease of the political sphere that threatened to destroy Western culture. However, just under fifty years later, with the publication in 1993 of Samuel Huntington's *Clash of Civilizations*, it seemed that racism had been transformed into Western culture's best chance to save itself. Huntington's article, later expanded into a book, was both celebrated for anticipating the hostility that underpinned the War on Terror, while also being heavily criticized for having a completely unworkable model of distinct civilizations and for its repetition and reframing of colonial prejudices and imperial hierarchies. For Gilroy, it was as if we had moved from a conception of open and variegated human civilization to a point where civilizations were 'now closed or finished cultures that need to be preserved' (58).

Sadly, this has become even more pronounced today with the re-emergence of racism, generalized xenophobia and white supremacy. Even after the Holocaust and the supposed end of empire, which precipitated the gradual turn towards multiculturalism, these forces have always implicitly – and often explicitly, depending on your ethnicity and geographic location – organized our politics; but there was a time when they were seen to be corrosive of political life and the dominant discourse at least made some effort to disavow them. This is not so today when a sense of embattled racial and/or ethnic culture is central to the stories we tell about ourselves. Inspired by Guillaume Faye's *The Colonization of Europe* and Renaud Camus's more recent *The Great Replacement*, the resurgence of racism has also precipitated the fantastical claim of 'white genocide' that unites ethno-nationalists across the Western world. It is also a fantasy that many mainstream politicians have ruthlessly exploited.

In the UK and the EU, while Islamist terror attacks have been used to stoke Islamophobia and anti-immigrant rhetoric, there is no single event that can be said to have triggered the upsurge in end-of-the-world rhetoric. In the United States, the opposite is the case. According to David Neiwert, 'The gradual coalescence of the alternative-universe worldviews of conspiracists, Patriots, white supremacists, Tea Partiers, and nativists occurred after the election of the first black president, in 2008' (2017: 231). Neiwert offers an even more precise summation when quoting the words of a central Alt-Right figure, Don Black. When interviewed by the *Washington Post*, Black lamented that 'White people, for a long time, have thought of our government as being for us, and Obama is the best possible evidence that we've lost that' (90). This attitude was also presented plainly by Bill O'Reilly in December 2016 on Fox News when he declared 'the Left wants power taken away from the white establishment. They want a profound change in the way America is run.'

Although various groups have made inroads into the dominance of the white man, society remains largely patriarchal and Caucasian in terms of its distribution of advantage, and yet this group still feels its world is under threat. Over previous decades, despite the spike in the scapegoating of foreigners, immigrants and Muslims, there has largely been a progressive but glacial shift in cultural outlook around the issues of race, gender and sexuality. The myths that previously supported patriarchy, white supremacy, heteronormativity and the privileging of Christianity were no longer repeated with the same certainty as they had been. As a result, the rise of Islamist terrorism was taken as an opportunity to reassert them in the face of a supposedly decadent and weak liberalism. This sense that a world or way of life is under attack is, of course, not new, and is an echo of the feelings expressed in the earlier white power movement where liberal and left-wing politics 'were seen as threats to the white supremacist racial order' (Belew 2018: 62). However, the idea that our worlds are contestable, fragile and not quite as robust as we would like is the first form of precarity that needs to be addressed because it is a universal condition that affects how we react to the others.

World as meaning and reference

We are all familiar with the fact that *life* is precarious. Our vulnerability to illness or accident teaches us this from an early age, while our global media testify to the magnification of that vulnerability for others. However, to understand the precarity of the *world*, which we ordinarily understand as being robust enough to continue after our deaths, we need to take our lead from the work of Martin Heidegger. This is for a couple of reasons. The first is because in place of an objective definition he talks about the world as a 'referential totality' (1962: 99), that is, a set of meanings and purposes that organize, maintain and legitimize our beliefs and actions. Everything I do in my everyday activities while at work or at leisure *refers* to a collection of aims, goals, reasons and rationales that warrant that behaviour and ensure it makes sense. At the same time, a set of concepts pertaining to nation, gender, race, sexuality and class, to name only a few, help create and maintain my sense of self. Any interruption of or breakdown in these references, he argues, can be catastrophic for my sense of self. In this way, Heidegger challenges our understanding of the world as a collection or arrangement of things that simply exist around us. This is not to refuse the world can also comprise facts about those things or events that happen, it is rather to acknowledge that much of what makes up our world, namely, definitions of the good, notions of justice, conceptions of God, interpretations of our purpose, remain stubbornly resistant to proof by scientific method. So, Heidegger's analysis is helpful in the first instance because he understands the world as a creative or an interpretive project through which we make sense of our self and the life we live.

The world is thus a collection of values and beliefs, reasons and purposes that all refer to each other in a coherent way, and this world is maintained through the stories and myths, both ancient and modern, we circulate and repeat. However, as a creative project in need of constant reinforcement, our world is always susceptible to being challenged and on such occasions can feel like it is slipping away. My point is that an awareness of this fragility can help understand why far-right politics that seeks to root itself in the guarantees of nature is so seductive today. While politics on the left has come to terms with democratic challenges to entrenched power and is increasingly open to the idea that our understanding of nation, class, race, gender and sexuality are socially constructed or are produced and maintained through established yet contestable ways of speaking and doing, politics on the right, especially the far-right, has consistently defended these categories as God-given, innate or inherent. Hence, as I noted earlier, the far-right's obsession with what they call 'race realism' (Hawley 2019: 101) and 'sex realism' (103) where race is reified in terms of essential, inborn traits – both genetic and cognitive – that supposedly justify separation and claims to supremacy. Similarly, biological differences based on reproductive organs supposedly legitimize differentiated and clearly demarcated social roles. Most importantly, these support the assumed naturalness and inevitability of the world and justify existing forms of malice, discrimination, subjection and exclusion. As Alford has argued, our worlds are structured through stories that form history and the 'history of one's hatreds constitutes the single most important, most comprehensible, and most stable sense of identity for many people' (2005: 240).

The second reason for using Heidegger's analysis is because he himself fell prey to the far-right politics I am seeking to counter by talking about the danger of hate in precarious times, so it is important to consider why this might have happened. In 1933, as documented in his infamous Rectoral Address, he threw his intellectual weight behind the National Socialist Party when he became the Rector of Freiberg University. After the war, when his Nazi affiliations became known, attempts were made to excuse this as simply an expedient attempt to protect the university, but since the very late translation and publication of the *Black Notebooks* his anti-Semitism became irrefutable. In these 'ponderings' from the late 1930s and early 1940s, this deeply conservative philosopher targeted 'world Judaism' as a central driver of the instrumental and calculating Western modernity he believed was so dangerous.

For Heidegger, this instrumentality was epitomized by the two global industrial machines of American capitalism and Soviet communism. This precursor to the 'globalism' that remains the *bête noir* of the Alt-Right is what led Heidegger to search out a place from which such nihilism might be challenged. For him, this was Europe's task, but, more importantly, it was Germany's. His philosophy is therefore replete with calls for securing the place from out of which a more essential and authentic understanding of being might be brought forth. As a result, his anxiety about the nihilism of the modern West, coupled with his anti-Semitism and his privileging of authenticity as a practice that clears a (national) space for truth, all contributed to his fatal error. Today, at a time of heightened anxiety, the promise of security and power through membership of a supposedly superior or more important race, nation or culture is the main reason far-right politics is so seductive. The task, then, is to consider how we might begin to address our own anxieties about our precarious world such that we don't fall foul of the chauvinism Heidegger did. If we don't begin to address this, the dark forces that Heidegger thought he could rein in and steer will rise again and consume us, too.

To do this, it will be helpful to offer a more philosophical discussion of what constitutes the world and our relation to it in order to understand the fundamental anxiety that other more specific forms of precarity exacerbate. This precarity was introduced in Heidegger's lecture series from 1921–2, published under the title *Phenomenological Interpretations of Aristotle*, where Heidegger describes the world as 'the content aimed at in living, that which life holds to' (2001: 65). This holding to is important because its ambiguity suggests that life and world are to some extent stuck together in an unbreakable bond, held like glue, but this might also be a clinging to, like a capsized sailor desperately trying to hold on to an overturned boat. Either way, life and world are distinct, even while being intimately connected. Here, life signifies the animated existence that all beings share, while world is the content – meanings, purposes, values and myths – that makes sense of our life and gives it a direction. This making sense of or making meaningful is the world that Heidegger argues life holds to and aims at. Hence, life always refers to a meaningful world, and this meaningful world is always realized in a life; but there's the rub. It isn't always realized or isn't realized in the way we had hoped or even expected: there is a tendency for the meaning we ascribe to life to ebb away, recede or even collapse.

Life, then, always aims at something, and what it aims at is based on what we inherit, be that the values and beliefs of our family, our generation or wider society. The importance of such an inheritance can be seen in the violent practices of colonialism where colonized people are removed from their history, tradition, ancestors and language. For the colonizers to succeed, they must cut off the colonized from their way of life. Breaking bodies is not enough as long as their world is sustained. Once the colonized are left derelict, unable to find their way, forcing them to accept the 'life' imposed by the colonizers becomes so much easier. This idea is also crucial to Elaine Scarry's (1985) brilliant conception of war in *The Body in Pain* where the 'unmaking' of your enemy's world – and therewith the 'substantiation' of your own – is crucial to any conclusive victory.

Returning for a moment to the idea of the physical world, life is always lived among things that are already presented to us as meaningful. This means the objects in our world cannot be said to 'run around naked' (Heidegger 1962: 69). Just as there is no mere life, there are no bare objects; they are part of our world because they are already meaningful in some way, and this is what life 'holds to' – although it should again be pointed out that this is what life is *directed* to hold to. This also means that without naked objects, there is no naked subject. Despite what our egos might try to claim, there is no pure interiority that isn't already directed in some way. The history of Western philosophy is littered with failed attempts to secure this thing that is supposed to exist independent of language, history and world, but these are often nothing more than vain attempts to run from the world and its contingencies in search of a secure place of everlasting security. As such they are completely at odds with any attempt to understand our ontological precarity.

In the lecture series from the summer of 1923, Heidegger discusses this precarity in relation to hermeneutics, traditionally understood as the scholarly interpretation of religious texts. For Heidegger, however, hermeneutics refer to our lived experience which is something 'in need of interpretation and that to be in some state of having-been-interpreted belongs' to that experience

(1999: 11). Hence, there is neither naked object nor naked subject, for both are mutually implicated in this interpretive process. This being-interpretive, for want of a better phrase, is how we are in the world. We always already exist in a meaningful world, but we reflect on and interrogate the world into which we are born. In other words, we further contribute to the world by asking why we are here, who we are and what we should do, but we will also receive an answer and an explanation that we are expected to adopt and abide by. The world is, then, always given to us *as* this or *as* that, but we can in turn engage with it under the knowledge that it might possibly be understood *as* something else or conceived in another way. This is the underlying condition of our politics.

However, the interpretation we are born into is so familiar that it withdraws or fades into the background. Here, we are not consciously aware of it and more often than not go about our lives unreflectively. Heidegger asks us to think of this like the pen we write with. As long as the pen is full of ink, the nib is in good working order and the paper is dry, I will not be especially conscious of the act of writing or of holding the pen. If I am working at a computer, reaching for and manipulating the mouse becomes second nature. I only become aware of it if it breaks or stops functioning, or if I read about myself using the mouse as I edit these words. Ultimately, this means that the world directs us, but it is largely inconspicuous. As long as 'life' is *working* for me, the world that directs it remains withdrawn despite continuing to direct my every move.

In this withdrawal, it takes on a sense of naturalness, with all the inevitability and certainty we attribute to that term. However, should any part of my world malfunction by being challenged as illegitimate, immoral or even out of date, what normally and unproblematically directs my thought and behaviour suddenly becomes an issue for me. The world itself becomes a problem. This may only cause a minor, temporary disturbance, but it can be a profoundly unsettling experience. So while the world is so familiar as to be unnoticeable, it remains a 'disturbable familiarity' (Heidegger 1999: 74); this is absolutely crucial for understanding our ontological precarity. Ordinarily, the 'naturalness' of the world functions to hold off any self-questioning that the gap between life and world always makes possible, but should any of this be challenged, the world can be thrust before us like the pen that suddenly runs out of ink. Most often, such a challenge produces a pervasive and ill-defined sense of anxiety that might remain unarticulated, but it can also develop into fear and a strategy for eradicating the object identified as the source of the anxiety (Curtis 2007). As such, it can become the basis for the 'complex of cognitions and emotions' (Staub 2005: 52) out of which hate is built.

We are, then, genuinely concerned for the world that gives life a direction and shape, to the point of actually worrying about protecting and preserving its pattern. Here we are motivated to repeat a range of behaviours and stories that uphold and reinforce the cultural inheritance through which we understand who we are. This is the fabric of our culture, the fine texture of our mundane relations with each other. This is also central to Mary Douglas's (2001) analysis of the regulation of social systems in *Purity and Danger*. In this study of how dirt and defilement function in relation to the creation and maintenance of a meaningful social order, she offers a wonderful account of how a world is structured and how patterns of thought and behaviour are maintained and made 'holy' by the expulsion of anything that doesn't fit. In the central methodological chapter entitled 'The Abominations of Leviticus', Douglas counters various traditional interpretations of why certain things are taboo based on, among other things, allegorical readings of appearance or behaviour suggestive of vice or uncleanliness. What she offers instead is a structural analysis that shows how the 'unholy' is simply that which doesn't conform to an already established category.

This is summed up in relation to the rules regarding what animals are deemed 'holy' and hence edible. In *Deuteronomy XIV*, the holy animals are described as those with a cloven hoof who chew the cud. Effectively, it is the combination of this type of hoof and diet that is regarded as normal. Hence, any animal with a cloven hoof that doesn't chew the cud (swine) or animals that chew the cud but don't have a cloven hoof (camel, hare and rock badger) are exceptions and, by logical extension, unclean and taboo. There is nothing inherently wrong with these animals apart from the fact that they challenge and confuse the meaningful order (world) and therefore must be separated off or cast out in order to maintain the *way* of life. Consequently, Douglas concludes that 'Defilement is never an isolated event. It cannot occur except in view of a systematic ordering of ideas. [. . .] For the only way in which pollution ideas make sense is in reference to a total structure of thought whose key-stone, boundaries, margins and internal lines are held in relation by rituals of separation' (2001: 42).

In this analysis, dirt is not derived from an entity's inherent quality or lack of it, it is simply 'matter out of place': it is 'that which must not be included if a pattern is to be maintained' (41). This goes a long way to explain cultural judgements of behaviour, language or persons that are regarded 'dirty' or 'evil' and is a perfect anthropological illustration of the ontological structure through which we maintain the world our life holds to. For me to retain a place in a culture, a place that gives my identity a sense of substance through categories that might include reference to nation, tribe, religion, ethnicity, civility or rank, it is necessary for me to observe the separation between sacred and profane, holy and taboo, good and evil, clean and dirty that maintains them. As I noted earlier, we do this all the time. It is neither exceptional nor especially remarkable; and while it is an integral part of everyday life, it is also the lifeblood of politics. In essence, the world is a struggle to maintain and reinforce the inclusions and exclusions that reproduce it and make it appear natural. In our current moment, though, there is a very powerful move to counter the world of liberal multiculturalism and social equality and reassert the world that was dominant until very recently. This world privileges social, racial and gender hierarchies and supports myths of national superiority. We have entered a time when, from this perspective, multiculturalism, tolerance and equality are seen as defilements in need of removal: diversity as dirt.

Returning to Heidegger, this means that in holding to a world I am always already outside of myself, sustained by the cultural rites, norms, codes, values, beliefs, meanings, goals and references that I in turn commit to reproducing. This is another crucial component in understanding our ontological precarity and the profound anxiety that accompanies it. In stark contrast to the way we commonly think about our relationship to the 'outside world' – as if we view things from within the safe confines of our cranium in the same way a security guard might survey a territory from his tower – we are always already on the other side of any perceived bodily limit, caught up with everything that is meaningful or of value and which affords us a place to stand. We are always already in the world and our understanding is rooted in the social pattern that we must necessarily maintain. Through this, 'I' see myself in all things and all things confirm the naturalness, normality or holiness of 'me'. This distributed self is another way we might think of Ahmed's economy of hate where '"the subject" is simply one nodal point in the economy, rather than its origin and destination' (Ahmed 2001: 348). From this perspective, we can also think of our being in the world as a form of ontological rather than psychological narcissism. The experience whereby the world reflects and reinforces my sense of self is akin to the limitlessness Freud evoked in his discussion of 'primary narcissism'. Any interruption of that relation necessarily introduces limits that block the perceived naturalness of my beliefs and behaviour. For a supremacist, be that supremacism based on race, religion or gender, the world of equality is precisely such a limit or block.

The idea that 'I' am the 'world' and the 'world' is 'me' also means there is no closed interiority to which we might retreat at times of crisis. There is no immunity or safe haven from the fate of the world. Although the world feels robust, we effectively reside on top of an abyss. This abyss is invisible as long as the world holds, but if it is challenged and starts to crack, the gap between life and world can yawn open and the experience can be profoundly unsettling. To be explicit about this, *our sense of self is wholly dependent upon the chain of references that combine to organize, arrange and give meaning to our life.* If those references are broken in any way and the world we depend on becomes unstable, the instability in turn threatens to capsize us, which is why we will fight so hard to re-establish those references. It is hardly surprising, then, that these references need to be regularly repeated and their boundaries constantly policed. It is the continual repetition of them as part of the communal liturgy that seems to *substantiate* or *realize* our worlds. As long as we continue to tell the stories, circulate the myths and practice the rituals that define us, they take on a sense of reality and incontrovertible naturalness. Consequently, our own sense of self seems so much more expansive and secure. Those who refuse the liturgy or try to rewrite it threaten to *de-realize* our world and are treated as hostile. This is what is happening today.

The world under threat

As I have already mentioned, religion, with its definitions of sacred and taboo, good and evil is the foundation of our world making, but other keystones for the architecture of a world invariably hinge on conceptions of gender, race and nation, all of which are crucial to the world of the radical right. I will discuss examples of race and nation shortly – especially as they relate to the resurgence of white supremacy in the United States and the xenophobic neo-nationalism that underpins Brexit. However, I will begin with gender because it is especially useful for thinking about how the world works and the anxiety that manifests when an alternative interpretation contests it. As noted earlier, in response to feminist challenges to the world of patriarchy, the Alt-Right in particular has reaffirmed what they call 'sex realism' (Hawley 2019: 15). This argues that biology and gender are coterminous and that biology determines prescribed social roles. A less rigid version of this 'realism' is also part of the common sense about sex and gender. There is a popular assumption that gender is inextricably linked to sex, and sex is designated according to the empirical presence of specific sexual and reproductive organs.

However, sexing children male or female according to their genitalia already erases the reality of intersex people whose genitalia don't clearly match this either/or option. In one study (Blackness et al. 2000), instances of intersex in all their variety are reported to be as high as 2 per cent of the population, making intersex people as common as those with red hair. Unfortunately, however, our conception of sexed bodies doesn't allow for both/and. In fact, our desire for a binary world is such a powerful frame for our thinking that we will put intersex children through all manner of invasive, dangerous and psychologically damaging treatments to force them to comply with the way we have decided to abstractly divide up the world. This is, then, made 'legitimate' by presenting intersex people as unnatural or monstrous.

Although I will concede that the behaviour expected of someone sexed male might have some basis in genetic elements and chemical triggers that have contributed to the connection between masculinity, strength and aggression, the fact that many men are not aggressive or are smaller and weaker than some women is evidence that these physical attributes are already unreliable witnesses in the debate around the naturalness of gender. In contrast, gender is a set of cultural expectations that defines the behaviour of someone sexed either male or female. From a very early age we learn this behaviour through cultural osmosis, but it will often need reinforcing through explicit schooling or social shaming. From a very young age we are aware that girls and boys perform their ascribed gender in multiple ways, but we are also taught names to apply to those children that don't behave in a manner that reproduces the preferred pattern of our world.

Why we can't accept that gender is a continuum and that people *naturally* place themselves in all sorts of positions and in all kinds of combinations along it baffles me. We have numerous examples of culturally recognized third genders available to us that ought to help us think this through. The Khanith in Oman and the Muxe in Mexico, for example, or the Fa'fafine of Samoan culture who are sexed male yet raised as female members of the family offer us identities beyond the confines of binaries. That gender is a performance and is not naturally determined by sex is also evident from the variety of ways men and women behave in different countries and have been expected to behave in different historical periods or even across different social strata. The most obvious example of this to me was as a child learning about the Tudors and Stuarts. Looking at images of Stuart aristocracy and courtesans, it was immediately obvious that my short hair, lack of make-up and rather dreary attire had little to do with some essential masculinity as had been suggested. Not that long ago, if I were wealthy enough, I would have failed to perform my masculinity appropriately if I hadn't worn very large wigs, lipstick, foundation, artificial moles, ribbons, garters, sequins, tights and high-heeled shoes with big, shiny buckles.

From this historical and cultural diversity, it is hard to argue that gender performance is predetermined by nature. However, if the world your life holds to is centred around rigid definitions of gender – as is the case for many on the political right or who self-identify as conservative – you will be especially disturbed by any failure to see them repeated. This is most evident in the regular outbursts from a Trump supporter like Piers Morgan, who is predictably outraged and vociferously vocal about any representation that doesn't support his interpretation of what men should do and how they should present themselves. Although there are numerous examples of his pronounced sensitivity is this area, his tweet directed at actor Daniel Craig lambasting him for carrying his baby in a papouse, with the accompanying #EmasculatedBond, says everything about Mr Morgan's anxiety.

However, the social requirement to comply with gender expectations is intense and encourages a whole range of compensatory behaviours designed to ward off the anxiety that arises when the world of predetermined, supposedly natural gender relations is challenged. This is most apparent when women challenge men, and it becomes even more pronounced when black women challenge racist men. Donald Trump's treatment of Loretta Lynch, Donna Brazile, Jemele Hill and Myeshia Johnson are very good examples of this. In most cases, a challenge from a black woman is met with the demand from Trump that she is fired, or in the case of Myeshia Johnson, he'd rather attack the bereaved wife of a recently killed US soldier than accept the slightest criticism. Any push back from a woman, especially one declaring her feminism, is often met with a barrage of insults and threats. For a significant number of conservative men, especially those identifying as Alt-Right/Lite, this compensatory behaviour makes it necessary to attack any woman who challenges a man's sense of ownership, access or entitlement.

Shortly before I began thinking about this book, a few events brought home to me just how strong this sense of ownership, access or entitlement was. When the remake of *Ghost Busters* was released in July 2016, a rather fragile group of men imploded. We were led to believe they simply didn't want a favourite childhood film ruined, but it was the sense of replacement that they really couldn't handle. Women assuming the roles of their heroes and wielding the potent symbols of ghostbusting power – the strangely phallic proton guns hanging from their hips – came to stand for the 'feminazis' who were threatening to castrate men on Twitter, Reddit and 4Chan. Leslie Jones, the one woman of colour in the team, was singled out for some especially vile online abuse, and while remakes and reboots always run the risk of raising the ire of fans, this was a sustained campaign aimed at a perceived incursion into the world of men.

Almost a year later, in June 2017, another group of men had a similar collective tantrum when the Alamo Drafthouse in Austin, Texas, announced a women-only screening of the *Wonder Woman* film, directed by Patty Jenkins. Even though the film carried only the mildest of feminist messages, the making of it was nevertheless hailed as a significant advancement in the gender politics of Hollywood blockbusters, which were still dominated by male leads and directors. These men couched their challenge to the Alamo Drafthouse's political hen party in the language of the law, declaring it discriminatory, but it couldn't hide the fact this was a deliberate attempt to prevent women enjoying this film in the exclusive company of other women. Despite women historically having been denied access to so much, this exclusion was too much for these men to bear. As a consequence, the screenings were cancelled, with the owner forced to issue a letter of apology promising to pay a settlement as 'deterrence' to the sum of $8,892.

Not long after, the internet blew up with allegations about Harvey Weinstein as a serial sexual predator. This was also when #MeToo, a phrase first used by Tarana Burke on MySpace way back in 2006, went viral after Alyssa Milano encouraged its use to promote the regular forms of assault that women experienced not just in Hollywood but in all walks of life. When all the Weinstein stories were breaking in the United States, a woman journalist in the United Kingdom made an allegation about Defence Secretary Sir Michael Fallon, who later resigned. As further allegations about rape, assault, bullying and sexual misconduct in parliament surfaced, there was a vigorous backlash in the conservative parts of the media that were not prepared to let the challenge stand. Two notable, and frankly embarrassing, examples came predictably from Charles Moore and Peter Hitchens. On 3 November, Moore wrote in *The Telegraph*: 'The scandal shows that women are now on top. I pray they share power with men, not crush us.' While on 5 November, Hitchens wrote in *The Mail on Sunday*: 'What will women gain from all this squawking about sex pests? A niqab.' The fragility of these responses and their sense of entitlement are staggering, but they also indicate how a challenge to a particular interpretation of the world can immediately precipitate a perceived threat of annihilation. Rather than reflect, which may only intensify the sense of anxiety, these men chose to attack.

As far as race is concerned, it goes without saying how central the story of white supremacy has been to the United Kingdom's sense of its greatness, sustaining it throughout the age of empire, and to the United States' sense of 'manifest destiny' in the colonization of the New World. With regard to the United States, the current resurgence of white supremacy is part of a long historical pattern marked by moments when the world of white domination and entitlement was threatened by the political advancement of people of colour. This is documented in Carol Anderson's (2017) book, *White Rage*. Unlike the hatred we saw in Charlottesville, white rage for Anderson 'doesn't have to wear sheets, burn crosses, or take to the streets' (3). Instead, it 'works its way through the courts, the legislatures and a range of government bureaucracies. It wreaks havoc subtlety, almost imperceptibly' (3). Echoing Neiwert and Belew, Anderson argues white rage is triggered by any sense of black advancement, and the election of Obama was 'the ultimate advancement, and thus the ultimate affront' (5). It is also worth noting how well this idea of supremacy works with narcissistic theories of hate discussed in Chapter 3. Here, 'aggression and violence may arise in people who have positive self-views but receive negative appraisals from others' (Beck and Pretzer 2005: 93). When supremacy is rooted in nothing but its own myth, it is a powerful source of hatred once challenged.

According to Anderson, however, to understand the contemporary expression of hate, we need to view it historically and see the current politics of race in the United States as one moment in a series of attempts to prevent the derealization of a world premised on white advantage and superiority. This is a history dating back to the passing of the Thirteenth Amendment of the US Constitution in 1865 that ended slavery, and it is sobering to read just how much pushback the Amendment generated.[1] It is also important to remember how catastrophic this would have been to a world built on white supremacy. The keystone to such a world is the inherent superiority of white people, which in turn refers to the superiority of white bodies, white minds, white culture, white history, white religion and white civilization. The suggestion that black people were equal, even in a formal or abstract sense, threatened this world with collapse. In fact, equality – in the formal sense – was perhaps more devastating because it meant no matter how much white people might continue to enforce inequality in practice, the truth was always the opposite.

While Abraham Lincoln is widely celebrated as the great abolitionist and advocate of freedom, in reality he cared little for the welfare of the new Americans. Anderson notes how in 1862, Lincoln had a plan to resettle millions of former slaves in Chiriquí, Panama, and actually blamed them for the civil war that was ravaging the country. In trying to persuade black leaders to accept relocation he told them: 'But for your race among us there could not be war' (9).[2] He was in fact far more interested in securing the union than the welfare of freed slaves. His plan to unite the country was merely to ask Confederate states to adopt the Thirteenth Amendment and for 10 per cent of eligible voters, namely, white property owners to swear loyalty. He had explicitly stated he had no interest in promoting equality among the races (14), and as a consequence, the franchise was not extended to the four million newly freed black Americans.

This was an attitude continued by the new president, Andrew Johnson. In March 1865, Congress created the Bureau of Refugees, Freedmen and Abandoned Lands, which was charged with leasing 40 acre plots of abandoned plantations to former slaves to enable a modicum of self-sufficiency. Johnson immediately overturned this 'commanding the army to throw tens of thousands of freed people off the land and reinstall the plantation owners' (16). Aside from the persistent white supremacy, Andrew Johnson also called on the principles of capitalist competition, arguing 'the government "never deemed itself authorized to expend public money for the rent or purchase of homes for the thousands, not to say millions, of the white race who are honestly toiling from day to day for their subsistence"' (24). However, as Anderson notes, Johnson had done exactly this with his support of the Homestead Act that took land for white settlers from Native Americans (26).

In addition, Johnson was quick to pardon a significant number of Confederate leaders such that the political institutions of the defeated Confederacy quickly resembled the ante-bellum South. This resulted in a new regime of violence against black people as Southerners felt 'they now had a friend in the White House' (17) – a sentiment eerily repeated by the Alt-Right today.[3] The reassertion of the 1856 Dred Scott decision ruling 'that black people have "no rights which the white man is bound to protect"' (18) was another piece of legislation aimed at preserving the supremacy of the white man's world. Furthermore, despite his argument against using the state to assist the black Americans that slavery had left derelict, Johnson was happy to employ the state 'to derail the very market forces he touted as the cure for the post-slavery blues' (26). The Black Codes required African Americans to 'sign annual labor contracts with plantation, mill, or mine owners' (19), and labourers could be charged with vagrancy or auctioned off if they refused. The contracts also meant 'African Americans were forbidden to seek better wages and working conditions with another employer' (19).

There were also a series of decisions that started with *Hall v. DeCuir* (1877), which ruled 'a state could not prohibit racial segregation', and continued with US Supreme Court decisions '*Strauder v. West Virginia* (1880), *Ex parte Virginia* (1880), and *Virginia v. Rives* (1880) [that] provided clear guidelines to the states on how to systematically and constitutionally exclude African Americans from juries in favour of white jurors' (35). Anderson then draws the chapter to a close with a quote from the Democrat Senator for Georgia, Walter George, who proudly declared: 'We have been very careful to obey the letter of the Federal Constitution – but we have been very diligent in violating the spirit of such amendments and such statutes as would have a Negro to believe himself the equal of a white man' (37). In other words, the time known as Reconstruction did far more than rebuild the Union. As the Thirteenth Amendment threatened to overturn the world of white supremacy, everything was done to ensure the freedom of black people made no incursions upon the meanings, values and practices that placed whiteness at the top of the tree.

Throughout the years that followed, these attempts to block the advancement of black people were compounded by the anti-enticement statutes (47) introduced in the early twentieth century. These sought to stop the movement of African Americans northwards in search of a better life. 'Black flight', Anderson writes, 'threatened much more than the economic foundation of a feudal society; African Americans' determination to achieve their full potential endangered the legalistic, biological and philosophical tenets of a racially oppressive system' (54). In other words, it further threatened the world of white supremacy. She then documents efforts to undermine *Brown vs Board of Education* in 1954 that outlawed segregation in schools. Here, a range of legal challenges to what states saw as federal violation of their constitutional rights delayed implementation, while any interruption to the schooling of white children was blamed on the 'black aggressors' (87) who supported integration. The Voting Rights Act of 1965, 100 years after the creation of the Freedman's Bureau, was then met with similar tactics that continue up to the present day. As recently as 2013, the Voting Rights Act was gutted under *Shelby County v. Holder* where 'justices treated the rationale for the Voting Rights Act as now obsolete' (149), thereby making legal Shelby County's 2008 redrawing of district boundaries that lost the only black councilman his seat. In sum, in the words of Tressie McMillan Cottom: 'Whiteness defends itself. Against changes, against progress, against hope, against black dignity, against black lives, against reason, against truth, against facts, against native claims, and against its own laws and customs' (in Anderson 2017: 172).

These successive attempts to secure the meaning, values and references of a white world also help us think about the anxiety surrounding the conception of Britishness that contributed to the decision in 2016 to leave the EU. While we might concede that 'Britain' does in part refer to an empirical reality designated by the physical territory that collects England, Scotland, Wales and Northern Ireland (the latter making Britain the UK), this is insufficient to get at the *idea* of Britain that significantly surpasses any geographic area or verifiable object. Britain cannot be thought, at least by British nationalists, without some sense of greatness, both in terms of imperial expansion and the supposed natural superiority that justified that expansion. Here, the idea of Britain or Britishness is mixed with a fantasy of global supremacy and authority, the ghosts of which nationalists still conjure when imagining the country's global influence. Furthermore, this is an idea based on the supposedly positive legacy of development, improvement and the advancement of civilization. This is a narrative that is only possible by excluding the violence of Britain's colonial rule, the evidence of which is discounted like the dirt excised from the diet of the ancient Hebrews. Again, in terms of what motivates hate, it is also worth noting how such a 'grandiose self-concept' is prone to 'aggressive reaction' when threatened (Berkowitz 2005: 168).

This loss of the established interpretation of the world can be seen in an analysis of the far-right English Defence League (EDL) by Simon Wilson, Steve Hall and James Treadwell (2017), this version of Britain is also evoked on the part of the white working class as a response to their desire for belonging while experiencing a sense of 'out-of-place-ness' (173). It includes the reimagining of a romanticized traditional community that provided them 'a sense of place, a sense of belief and a structure of feeling that enabled forms of psychic security to be established and reproduced across generations' (173). According to interviews conducted, this was a 'perfect world [. . .] in which their skills were valued and their jobs paid enough money for them to live a good life free from perennial anxiety and competition. In this perfect world men like them were listened to' (174). In keeping with Gilroy's analysis, this exhibits a melancholy for a world that was meaningful and placed them at its centre. That world now exists as a lost object mobilizing both anxiety and hostility. In the first place, those interviewed could not 'bear the humiliating prospect that it will be their generation that allows the lost object [. . .] to disappear forever' (Wilson, Hall and Treadwell 2017: 177). They also carried with them 'the unconscious belief that Muslim communities possessed the spirit of solidarity and brotherhood precisely because white working-class communities did not' (170).

Another key aspect of this world that British nationalists are determined to preserve is a specific interpretation of the Second World War, something that has become a cultural industry over the last couple of decades. As Paul Gilroy explains, 'Revisiting the feeling of victory in war supplies the best evidence that Britain's endangered civilization is in progressive motion toward its historic completion' (2005: 88). He goes on to argue the war has 'totemic power' and carries 'the status of an ethnic myth'. It makes 'it a privileged point of entry into national identity and self-understanding [and] reveals a desire to find a way back to the point where national culture [was] both comprehensible and habitable' (89). In this dominant interpretation of Britain and Britishness, immigrants 'represent the involution of national culture [and] the perceived dangers of pluralism' (90). Encapsulating my main argument about ontological precarity, Gilroy claims that when 'the history of the empire became a source of discomfort, shame, and perplexity, its complexities and ambiguities were readily set aside. Rather than work through those feelings, that unsettling history was diminished, denied, and then, if possible, actively forgotten' (90).

Again, supporting the idea that a challenge to our world induces hostility born of anxiety, he continues by saying the 'invitation to revise and reassess often triggers a chain of defensive argumentation that seeks firstly to minimize the extent of the empire, then to deny or justify its brutal character, and finally, to present the British themselves as the ultimate tragic victims of their extraordinary imperial successes' (94). The logic is that Britain brought civilization to other countries only for the inhabitants of those countries to return to Britain and destroy the very civilization the British had gifted them. In keeping with the structure of hate I set out in Chapter 3, Gilroy uses the work of Alexander and Margarete Misterlich who he says warned us 'that melancholic reactions are prompted by "the loss of a fantasy of omnipotence" and suggest that the racial and national fantasies that imperial and colonial power required were, like those of the Aryan master race, predominantly narcissistic' (99). Triggering this narcissism, British citizens from former colonies and more recent migrants 'carry all the ambivalence of empire with them. They project it into the unhappy consciousness of their fearful and anxious hosts' (100). Ultimately, Gilroy explains, this 'melancholic pattern has become the mechanism that sustains the unstable edifice of increasingly brittle and empty national identity' (106). However, once migrants and even naturalized citizens are seen as the villains and hostility towards them is deemed legitimate, what appears brittle feels so much more robust.

Nicholas Boyle (2017) has eloquently argued it was the loss of this sense of British exceptionalism – both as an imperial nation and a victor in the Second World War – that led to the decision to leave the EU. Being just one member of a club, no matter how important we liked to project our role, was at odds with a country that to this day still tells the story of how 'the sun never set on the British Empire' and how 'we stood alone against the might of Hitler'. This was also a major contributor to the election of Boris Johnson, a man who works so hard to channel the spirit of Churchill as both author of *The History of the English Speaking Peoples* and 'We shall fight them on the beaches'. All of this increasingly articulates the long-held belief that Britishness (and Englishness especially) refers back to a mythical time of uniformity, which is always equated with whiteness, and that this whiteness, despite all the contrary evidence of genetics and demographic movements, is autochthonous and 'indigenous'.[4]

Consequently, in the words of Gilroy:

> racial difference and racial hierarchy can be made to appear with seeming spontaneity as a stabilizing force. They can supply vivid natural means to lock an increasingly inhospitable and lonely social world in place and to secure one's own position in turbulent environments. Acceptance that race, nationality, and ethnicity are invariant, relieves the anxieties that arise with a loss of certainty as to who one is and where one fits. The messy complexity of social life is thereby recast as a Manichean fantasy in which bodies are only ordered and predictable units that obey the rules

of deep cultural biology scripted nowadays in the inaccessible interiority
of the genome. The logics of nature and culture have converged, and
it is above all the power of race that ensures they speak in the same
deterministic tongue. (2005: 6)

If our sense of identity is dependent on the ideas and values to which it refers,
it is not surprising we need to regularly repeat the stories that carry those
values in order to make them appear real. However, such ideas are prone to
a high rate of attrition if they are not continually reinforced in our everyday
utterances or go undefended against a counter-interpretation. As has already
been noted at length, the human condition is an interpretive one, so if stories
are not told, new ones will come along in their stead. Looking forward from
where we are now, then, the challenges are only going to be more pronounced
as the resource depletion threatened by rampant consumerism and climate
change puts even greater pressure on land, food and water and precipitates
even larger demographic shifts. If we cannot come to terms with the fact that
our world is in a fundamental way an interpretation, the ontological precarity
set out here is likely to become more pronounced. This is because it is further
exacerbated by other forms of precarity to which I will now turn – these are
the existential threat of terrorism, the material threat of unregulated capital,
the social threat of challenges to privilege and the epistemological threat of
post-truth.

Terror or existential precarity

The attacks of 11 September 2001 were designed with our ontological precarity in mind. They were intended to cause maximum disturbance to the way Americans and their allies saw themselves. They were orchestrated to radically undermine the world understood as a collection of values, meanings, references and signs and thereby destabilize America's sense of itself. The attacks were an act of mass murder that killed 2,996 people; yet, despite the massive destruction and horrific loss of life, it was a symbolic attack as much as a physical one. It was quickly determined Al-Qaeda was responsible, and that this group, well known for their iconoclasm, had explicitly chosen to destroy symbols of American economic, military and political power – and had piggybacked on the media technology of America's 'soft power' – to generate and distribute the most spectacular counter-image of its vulnerability. The planning and audacity needed to pull off the attacks suggested the perpetrators could have killed many more and, no doubt, would have chosen a different strategy if they were only looking to maximize the death toll, but, as the public relations and marketing strategies of our image-saturated society tell us, it's all about the 'optics'. '9/11', as it was dubbed, was a message; it was an attack on what America thought it was.

In terms of the precarity this event generated, the naming of Al-Qaeda as the enemy was only the beginning. The rhetoric quickly established they were representative of an even more disturbing foe, one that is formless, globally networked, zealous and able to hide in plain sight. This enemy was, of course, militant or radical Islam. Their tactics of using leaderless, quasi-autonomous cells was pawed over by security analysts, academics and media pundits and presented as some entirely new threat, which was odd given this had been the method of 'leaderless resistance' in America's white power movement since the 'revolutionary turn' in 1983 (Belew 2018: 105). Nevertheless, the newly elected US president, George W. Bush, ensured that the powerful symbolism of the attacks was not overlooked, declaring in his address to the joint session of Congress and the nation on 20 September 2001: 'These terrorists kill not merely to end lives, but to disrupt and end a way of life.' The United States was now at war with faceless yet fanatical adherents of an ideology that wanted to destroy the very idea of America.

This was then picked up and amplified by right-wing academics such as Eliot Cohen (2001) who was quick to point out that the War on Terror – which Bush also announced in that September address – was in fact World War IV. Here, he was invoking the sense that this war had global implications, but just like the Cold War (which he now called World War III) it also had 'ideological roots' and was a confrontation over the very status of the world itself. Following Cohen's lead, Norman Podhoretz (2002) published an article setting out the scale of the task he believed President Bush had legitimately set for the country. Having already toppled the Taliban in Afghanistan, he wrote 'we may willy-nilly find ourselves forced by the same political and military logic to topple five, six or even seven more tyrannies in the Islamic World' (29), creating a 'new species of an imperial mission for America' (29). The article was also a classic example of the Islamophobia that neoconservatism cultivated so effectively and which is a cornerstone of far-right and broader ethno-nationalist rhetoric today. Implicitly exempting Christians from the historical litany of Christian violence, Podhoretz wrote: 'there is something in the religion itself' (27) that obliges Muslims to kill. This attempt to claim authoritative control of the meaning of '9/11' was crucial for the full fruition of the existential threat. The War on Terror was nothing less than absolute good facing down absolute evil.

When Bush announced the first phase of Podhoretz's 'imperial mission' with the completely illogical (Saddam Hussein was a sworn enemy of Al-Qaeda) and unnecessary (he had no weapons of mass destruction) invasion of Iraq, there had already been strong resistance to the policy within the United States, much of which came from the US far-right, soon to become the Alt-Right. As (white) nationalists, they had no interest in foreign wars 'justified by abstractions like the spreading of democracy' (Hawley 2019: 90). Their anti-Semitism also led them to believe that US foreign policy was done in the service of Israel, a belief fuelled by conspiracy theories pertaining to a Jewish-led world government. As noted in Chapter 1, the predecessors of the Alt-Right therefore had stronger ideological connections to paleoconservatism, which was sceptical of military adventures abroad, especially ones extending global 'free trade' (Wendling 2018: 18). However, despite their 'antipathy to neoconservatives' (Hawley: 90), I believe neoconservatism, through its policy and rhetoric, became a significant ally for the emerging Alt-Right and the wider xenophobic nationalisms that weaponized the Islamophobia neoconservatism stoked.

Despite the resistance to the rhetoric from many areas of society, an important aspect of American culture made it especially amenable to a story of an absolute existential threat. Since its founding, the country has mobilized a deep-seated apocalyptic tendency where it sees itself as either the manifestation of heaven on earth or the entity that is single-handedly holding back Armageddon. In many respects, George W. Bush, a recovering alcoholic and born-again Christian, was the perfect man to carry the baton in 2001. As Ira Chernus noted, his own brand of 'compassionate conservatism', which sought to reverse immorality and secure 'a safe and pure homeland' (2006: 147) easily dovetailed with the eradication of evil abroad. This, in turn, chimed with America's long-standing belief in its own role in the wider execution of God's will. After '9/11', Bush's faith story became a perpetual struggle against personal and public, domestic and foreign monsters. Chernus writes:

> If sin is a metaphysical reality, then it can never be eradicated. A true patriot will have to fight and sacrifice endlessly just to keep the national dwelling safe, just as true Christians must work hard every day to stave off the temptations of sin. The war will have to be waged on two fronts simultaneously: keeping foreign enemies beyond the nation's borders and purifying moral life inside the borders. [. . .] As long as Americans fight and show conservative compassion [. . .] the nation and the world will be pure, stable and safe from the ravages of sin. [. . .] To be sure we are doing God's will, we need monsters to fend off and destroy. But we cannot destroy them all. Some monsters must remain, so that we can continue to fight them and thus show the strength of our faith. (147)

For Donald Trump and his supporters, there are still monsters abroad, but it is the presence of monsters at home, most notably Muslim and Mexican migrants that are eroding the very fabric of God's white, Christian kingdom. They have consequently become the primary targets of Trump supporters who remain in a perceptual state of emergency driven by apocalyptic visions of decay. While erstwhile neoconservatives such as Bill Kristol and David Frum are vocal critics of Trump, it was their own amplification of apocalyptic rhetoric and the demonizing of Muslims that chimed with already existing white supremacist beliefs about the death of the white nation and fed more recent Alt-Right fantasies of 'the Great Replacement' and 'white genocide'. This chapter, then, is an assessment of how the rhetoric around the War on Terror greatly intensified the existential precarity that has been a major contributor to the mainstreaming of far-right sentiment in the United States and seamlessly merged with Trump's own invocation of the apocalypse coming from an 'open' southern border.

Premillennialism and postmillennialism

In the early years of the War on Terror, books from neoconservatives touting the end of the world became a publishing industry in its own right, with each author looking to tap into Americans' existential dread in ever more visceral ways. David Frum's own apocalyptic fervour was clearly in evidence in the book he co-authored with Richard Perle dramatically entitled *An End to Evil*. Although Frum and Perle seem to have missed the memo about the need to keep some monsters alive against which true believers might test their faith, they made it very clear to those who might still be ambivalent about the threat of militant Islam: 'There is no middle way for Americans: It is victory or holocaust' (2003: 9). In these early years, Islamist extremists were a composite of nihilistic cultists, ruthless dictators and fantasy figures drawn from comic books: they were destroyers of worlds. However, Frum and Perle's rhetoric is interesting for another reason. In keeping with the Christian evangelism that had increasingly taken hold of the Republican Party, the Holocaust was used to evoke the idea that the chosen people were once again under attack; only this time God's people are a specifically anointed section of the American population now braced for a final confrontation with Satan.

It is also worth noting how this is a perfect illustration of Flahault's analysis of our desire to touch limitlessness with which I closed Chapter 2 and which Flahault used to explain our propensity to hate. Specifically, he argues that because we have split the concept of infinity between a good infinite (God) and a bad infinite (Satan) it is only through an encounter with Satan that we can truly touch limitlessness (Flahault 2003: 142). God, as the creator of all things and the giver of laws, is the source and protector of the ordered world and all the limited beings it contains. Only Satan remains truly chaotic, exceeding every boundary and limit. For Flahault, then, our narcissism or the desire to be all-powerful means we must pit ourselves against an entity that threatens total destruction. Indeed, we must actively conjure such a monster, which remains our only access to limitlessness and the means to satisfy our repressed megalomania. The hyperbole and extremity of the rhetoric – 'victory or holocaust' – that surrounded the Islamist threat encapsulates this desire to test what Flahault calls our 'abyssal narcissism' (7).

In keeping with this, neoconservative rhetoric drew on centuries old stories of all-devouring beasts, which meant the message fell on already fertile ground. As a consequence, it was quickly established and had such efficacy that it remains firmly planted in the imagination of white Westerners today, who even after the massacre of fifty-one Muslims in Christchurch, New Zealand, could still wheel out the argument that they deserved it for being members of a murderous religion.[1] As for Frum and Perle, they went on to say that militant Islam is 'the great evil of our time, and the war against this evil, our generation's great cause' (2003: 9). I have no doubt this was a genuinely held belief, but it is both fed by and feeds into the widespread apocalyptic foreboding that I have already noted is endemic in US popular culture and which, according to Lee Quinby, has an 'unusual elasticity' (1994: xii) in the scope of its application.[2]

Most importantly, though, as the United States was embarking on its new imperial mission, the threat of total annihilation seemingly legitimized an unlimited response where the supposed immanence and magnitude of evil permitted us to throw off all previously established ethical and juridical limitations. The extra-legal, exceptional logic that became known as the Bush Doctrine will need to be returned to below, but the argument was clear; the threat to democracy was so great that the norms it enshrined (namely, international law and rights around privacy, a trial, imprisonment, torture, oversight and accountability) all needed to be cast off if we were not to descend into the yawning abyss opened up by militant Islam. As a consequence, and in contrast to its stated intention, the legacy of neoconservatism has been the continued weakening of democracy in favour of strong, charismatic leaders, hostility towards foreigners and minorities, suspicion of the rule of law (especially where it is seen to be liberal) and an undermining of the separation between church and state; all of which have been seized upon by Donald Trump.

Before taking a closer look at the philosophical underpinnings of the Bush Doctrine and the apocalyptic culture it spoke to, it is helpful to introduce the work of Leo Strauss as an important tributary of neoconservative thought. Strauss was a deeply conservative thinker. He was opposed to modernity and argued for the importance of virtue to any political community. According to Mark Gerson (1997), Strauss only advocated for freedom as a means to serve such virtue. In this, Anne Norton (2004) ironically likens Strauss's thought to that of Sayyid Qutb, a leading member of the Muslim Brotherhood and a major influence on the ideology of radical Islam that neoconservatism was supposed to be pitting itself against. Their respective sets of disciples, she writes, see 'the modern world as corrosive of public and private virtue. Each has condemned modernity for nihilism. Both longed for a single standard of conduct for all. Each has displayed distaste for mass culture and distrust of mass politics' (114); and while the Muslim Brotherhood cultivated 'a romantic view of the time of the Prophet, the Straussians cultivated the romance of the Ancients' (115). Without this commitment to virtue, society was under threat from what another important figure, Reinhold Niebuhr, called the 'children of darkness, who prey on the naiveté of their often soft-headed opponents' (Gerson 1997: 17).

Ultimately, then, the neoconservative persuasion was rooted in a classical sensibility based on a principle of aristocratic virtue that believed itself to be on the brink of a chiliastic struggle (Norton 2004: 197) against the children of darkness for the redemption of America. As another disciple noted, it was 'fundamentally an ethical and religious movement. [One that believed] in the importance of liturgy, community, ethnicity, and roots' (Novak in Gerson 1997: 272). There was a sufficient sense of a sacred mission to neoconservatism, and enough parallels with the ideology it was opposing, for Norton to call it 'an American jihad' (2004: 191); but what is it about American culture, in particular, that made it such a fertile ground for this theological language of a total and final war against evil?

In *An Angel Directs the Storm*, Michael Northcott analysed the widespread belief in the United States that the world is approaching God's final judgement. Known as millennialism, he shows how a significant segment of the US population believe they are literally living in the end times and that the increase in war, violence, natural disasters and social decay are all signs that Armageddon is nigh, and that within this narrative the United States is the divine instrument charged with securing this most providential path. The belief that the world is approaching the end times is a specific strain of millennialism known as premillennialism. This is the most widespread version of millennial belief, popularized in the bestselling book series, *Left Behind*, by Tim LaHaye and Jerry B. Jenkins. Unlike postmillennialists, who believe they are building a godly commonwealth and ushering in the 1,000-year rule of the saints – an idea in keeping with the American Civil Religion that Robert Bellah famously defined as a 'living faith' (1967: 19) – premillennialists believe the Judgement and the Second Coming will be preceded by the final decisive battle against Satan.

The genealogy of this apocalyptic thought is expressed in the title of Northcott's study and is another element that appears in Bush's speech to the joint session of Congress and the nation on 20 September 2001. In the same speech that he announced the War on Terror in defence of the American way of life, he also declared that America's destiny to shape the world according to its interests would take courage and perseverance but would ultimately succeed 'because it is "the angel of God that directs the storm"' (2004: 6). This phrase originated in a letter written by John Page to Thomas Jefferson shortly after the Declaration of Independence where Page declares: 'We know the race is not to the swift nor the battle to the strong. Do you not think an angel rides in the whirlwind and directs this storm?' (6). This is the reassertion of Page's postmillennial, revolutionary faith that from its founding America was and always will be the instrument of God's will on earth.

In contrast to postmillennialism, premillennialism believes we are moving towards the 'Great Tribulation' that precedes the millennium of peace. The Great Tribulation, Northcott explains, is defined by an increase in wickedness, war and disaster as well as a weakening of faith. This is also indicative of the continuity between the apocalyptic vision of neoconservatism and Trump's own use of the Christian Right (as well as the fractious coalition of Evangelical Christianity and anti-Semitic Alt-Right that he seeks to hold together) where Israel plays an especially important role. Part of premillennialist doctrine is the belief that one of the major signs for the immanence of the Judgement and Second Coming is the building of the Third Temple in Jerusalem on the site of the al Aqsa mosque (Revelation 21: 2 describes Jerusalem 'prepared as a bride adorned for her husband'). Hence, Trump's recognition of Jerusalem as the capital of Israel on 16 December 2017 was of major importance for those with a premillennial disposition.

However, what is especially disturbing in relation to this creed is that each new war and every new disaster, natural, social or political, is just one more sign permitting Reuben Torrey, for example, to declare on the outbreak of the First World War: 'the darker the night gets, the lighter my heart becomes' (Northcott 2004: 61). According to James Robison, who prayed with George W. Bush during the presidential campaign in 1999 and was a religious mentor to Ronald Reagan, all peace activists are heretics because the teaching of peace prior to the return of Christ is against the Word of God (67). In much of the premillennialist literature, the United Nations is taken to be a sign of an 'insidious one-worldism', and the pacific ideals of liberalism are seen as one of the Antichrist's 'great "counterfeit" missions' (Melling 1999: 78). This belief is, of course, closely aligned with the Alt-Right's vision of the evils of global government.

After the Berlin Wall fell in 1989, the suggestion of global peace encapsulated the satanic balm of one-worldism. Pat Robertson's book, *New World Order*, also epitomized the premillennialist foreboding regarding the Soviet Union then preaching perestroika and glasnost. Americans should remain on guard because one-worldism signals the coming of the Antichrist's dominion. This also became a particular focus of the apocalyptic vision of the white power movement in the United States. The specifically theological version of apocalypse had long been part of the white supremacist group, Christian Identity, but up to this point the white power movement more broadly had always named communism as the annihilating threat. For Belew, the end of the Cold War was the 'historical shift that rendered obsolete much of the anticommunist rhetoric [. . .] but also worked as a bridge issue with the evangelical right' (2018: 188) as both groups sought a new enemy.

As Belew goes on to note, the New World Order came to reflect a globalized version of white supremacists' anti-government stance. It replaced the older national vision of the supposedly Jewish-controlled ZOG that threatened 'racial extinction' (188). It also motivated members of the white power movement to migrate to the Northwest of the United States in search of a white homeland. In the words of Robert Miles, leader of the white power congregation, Mountain Church, they were seeking 'a sanctuary for our Folk . . . since we are an endangered species in America' (Belew 2018: 162). Taking this sentiment even further, Order leader Bob Mathews wrote in the epigraph of James Coates's book *Armed and Dangerous: The Rise of the Survivalist Right*: 'We are the legions of the damned. [. . .] The army of the already dead' (Belew 2018: 224). Today, the threat posed by the New World Order is referenced in the far-right's use of 'globalism', which at one level wants to address problems caused by economic globalization but on another is a very clear invocation of white supremacists' long-standing, anti-Semitic and apocalyptic fears of annihilation.[3]

Friend and enemy

It is unsurprising, therefore, that neoconservatism's heady mix of permanent vigilance in the face of a hostile entity preparing to annihilate America in a conflagration of apocalyptic proportions would find its doctrine crystallized in the political theory of a Catholic academic whose thought was premised on the need for a perpetual struggle against chaos, disorder and the work of Satan. Neoconservatives would have been introduced to Carl Schmitt by reading Leo Strauss whose own encounter with Schmitt did much to reveal the Nazi jurist's apocalyptic bent; and it is in Schmitt's definitions of the political and the nature of sovereignty that we can see the essence of the neoconservative world view and how its legacy continues in Trump's approach to the southern border of the United States.

Carl Schmitt's *The Concept of the Political* was published in 1927, followed by revised editions in 1932 and 1933. This final version is important because it appeared the same year Schmitt became a member of the National Socialist Party and because the 1933 version was a response to Leo Strauss's review of the 1932 edition. This exchange also explains how, given Strauss's profound influence on neoconservative thought, Schmitt's concept of the political will have had an influence on the ideology of the Bush administration and is now central to the world view of Trump's Attorney General, William Barr.[4] As a conservative, Schmitt was obsessed with the maintenance of order and believed that liberalism – premised as it is on a fundamental understanding of diversity – was a permanent threat to it. Here, there is a direct spiritual link between Schmitt, paleoconservatism, neoconservatism and the Alt-Right. With typical precision, Strauss summed up Schmitt's philosophical 'chain of thought' and the existential danger threatened by liberal pluralism. In an essay from 1940, he writes:

> There is not one ideal, but a variety of conflicting ideals; therefore, ideals cannot have an obligatory character; more precisely, any value judgment is a free decision, which concerns exclusively the freely deciding individual himself; it is essentially a private affair; therefore, no one can expect of any other man that that man sacrifice anything for the first man's ideal; but no political community can exist without asserting that there are *obligations* which can overrule any private decision; whatever may be the ultimate source of these obligations, they cannot be derived from free decisions of the individual, or else they could be no more than *conditional* obligations, not *absolute* obligations, the obligation to sacrifice life itself. (in Meier 2006: 127–8; emphasis in original)

What Strauss highlights in Schmitt's thought is the centrality of existential survival premised on upholding the distinction between friend and enemy. Maintaining this distinction is essential to the authority of the sovereign whose primary power is the capacity to decide when a hostile situation has arisen.[5]

Currently, the hostile situation takes the form of a threat to 'Western European culture'. This is central to the rhetoric of Trump supporters and conservative commentators such as Ben Shapiro and Jordan Peterson, but it is also important to recognize how this civilizational conflict had been an essential mark of the neoconservative persuasion for at least two decades prior to the War on Terror. Writing in 1980 in the wake of the Soviet invasion of Afghanistan and the Iranian hostage crisis and deeply critical of the 'anti-American upsurge' (Gerson 1997: 88) that had created a culture of appeasement, Podhoretz was adamant that what he called the 'neonationalist' or 'neoconservative' intellectuals were in a 'fateful struggle' (Gerson 1997: 89) for the future of civilization. It is this vision of potential death, decay, invasion and loss that binds paleoconservatives, neoconservatives and the Alt-Right, despite their protestations, and has laid the foundation for the weakening of democracy and the emboldening of racism and illiberalism today.

To understand the extra-legal and anti-democratic nature of the Bush Doctrine (and in turn, I believe, Donald Trump's hostility to any legal or 'liberal' limitation being placed on his desire to 'secure' the American way of life), it is necessary to understand the basic premise of Schmitt's

1922 publication entitled *Political Theology*. This book is one of the most important and influential books on the subject of sovereignty, which he defines as the capacity to decide on the exception (2005: 5). In other words, the sovereign is the entity or person that can decide when the normal, legal situation no longer applies and the law can be suspended through the announcement of a state of emergency. For Schmitt, this means sovereignty 'is the highest, legally independent, underived power' (17). It is a 'superlative' (17) and 'inexplicable identity' likened to the 'indivisible person [. . .] derived from theology' (38).

According to Schmitt, no matter how much liberalism believes sovereignty is a matter of democratic discussion, technical deliberation and legal procedure, in this moment of decision, it remains deeply theological in its reliance on the idea of an authority not subject to any other authority. As the United States enacted their sovereign right in the face of a supposedly existential threat, this conception of authority came to define the Bush Doctrine. From the logic of 'pre-emptive defense', to mass surveillance at home and abroad, to its pro-torture stance, to its 'black sites' and imprisonment without trial, the War on Terror operated according to this extra-legal sovereign principle whereby the emergency legitimized suspending both the law and the democratic norms that underpinned it. Although the principle was veiled under the Obama administration, despite a huge increase in summary executions via the US drone apparatus (Curtis 2016), I believe it was this extra-legal approach to domestic and foreign security prosecuted by the 'neonationalist' Bush administration that laid the foundations for Trump's signature extra-legal practices at the southern border of the United States.

As we have seen, as far as neoconservatism was concerned, the existential threat took the form of a 'holy war'. As anti-communist rhetoric slowly morphed into the open-ended fight against Islamist terror, America continually presented itself as 'holding back' the advance of evil (Podhoretz 1980: 100). Here, the United States can be seen to take on the role of the 'restrainer' (or *katechon* in the original Greek). This is a curious and little understood figure, obliquely referred to by Paul in 2 Thess. but which also appears in the later work of Carl Schmitt. In *The Nomos of the Earth*, Schmitt directly makes the argument for the katechon in terms of a Christian empire in which its role as prosecutor and persecutor is of central importance (Schmitt 2003: 59–62). According to Meier, while this was primarily the role of the Catholic Church, other entities can take on the role of holding back Satan. Schmitt therefore believed in the possibility of a plurality of katechons and 'the uninterrupted succession of the historical bearers of this force' (1998: 160–1). This is what neoconservatives assumed themselves to be. It is also something Bannon has evoked. As Alexander (2019) notes, this imagery is not alien to the Alt-Right: 'In his 2004 documentary about Ronald Reagan, *In the Face of Evil*, Bannon condenses his long list of dangerous others into a meta-antagonist that, drawing from the Old Testament's Book of Daniel, he metaphorically identifies as "the Beast"' (143), and with that identifies Reagan as the restrainer of the 'red menace'. During the War on Terror, this would morph into the 'green menace' of radical Islam. However, the ideological force of such a menace was only created through apocalyptic rhetoric being aimed *indiscriminately* at a *generic* Muslim enemy that brought with it a significant rise in the Islamophobia that has been a rallying call for the radical right today.

Islamophobia, Mexicans and migrant caravans

As Leonie B. Jackson has argued, over the course of the last two decades, a simplistic narrative about the dangers of Muslims and 'the Muslim world' has come to have an extraordinary 'explanatory power' (2018: 2), informing a 'common sense' (19) that underpins our ontological and existential precarity today. While we must acknowledge there are a range of Islamophobias because it 'is always expressed in a local context' (13), the term first came into popular parlance in the 1990s on the back of events like the fatwa issued against Salman Rushdie as well as spurious yet popular academic theories such as Samuel Huntington's 'Clash of Civilizations'. In the UK, for example, the Runnymede Trust's report from 1997, entitled *Islamophobia: A Challenge for Us All*, understood Islamophobia as a set of 'closed' rather than 'open' positions (Zempi and Awan 2016; Jackson, L. 2018). In other words, and paraphrasing Jackson, Islamophobia sees Islam as monolithic ('*the* Muslim world', for example) rather than diverse, separate rather than interacting and inferior rather than different. It rejects rather than considers Muslim criticism of the West, defends rather than criticizes discrimination against Muslims and sees Islamophobia as natural rather than problematic. It also sees Muslims as enemies rather than partners and manipulative rather than sincere (3). Although Jackson is suspicious of this procedural approach (4), the idea of 'closed' interpretations goes some way to articulating Islamophobia as a generalizing discourse where negative attributes of Islam are seen to reflect innate characteristics of a specific group of people. This, in turn, results in the 'essentialisation of a culture' (178), and most importantly for the argument in this book, the hate directed at members of this group 'restores fantasised power' (181) to those who believe their identity and culture are under threat.

According to Khaled A. Beydoun, the Islamophobia of the War on Terror meant that Muslims were effectively "'raced" as "terrorists'" (2018: 120). To some extent, though, this did require careful semantic gymnastics given the United States' earlier support for political Islam. As Todd H. Green notes, during the Cold War 'secular Arab nationalism, socialism and communism were making inroads in the Middle East [. . .], all to the benefit of the Soviet Union' (2015: 106). As a response, the United States often supported Islamist groups and governments in the region. Islamism, as Green goes on to explain 'was therefore not anathema to US foreign policy in the Middle East but rather an integral part of its Cold War strategy' (107), with Reagan, for example, famously calling the Mujahideen in Afghanistan 'the moral equivalents of America's founding fathers' (110).

The Islamophobia cultivated during the War on Terror, however, was profound and multifaceted. It took the form of *political Islamophobia* where, for example, the report by 9/11 Commission chose to ignore any political or economic grievances resulting from earlier US foreign policy in the region that might have contributed to the attacks. It preferred instead to blame the violence solely on Islam as a pathological religion (117) that rendered Muslims 'guilty until proven innocent' (Beydoun 2018: 98). This is, of course, rooted in long-standing *cultural Islamophobia* that goes all the way back to the Crusades of the Middle Ages but was developed in the Orientalist discourses (Said 1978) that presented Muslims as lazy, devious, irrational, sensual, backward and effeminate, and which both accompanied and enabled Western imperial expansion across the region. It also manifested as *structural Islamophobia* (Beydoun 2018) in the form of legislation like the Bush administration's National Security Entry and Exit Registration System (NSEERS) where 'twenty-four of the twenty-five countries of interest listed in the NSEERS legislation were Muslim-majority nations' (101).

Such structural Islamophobia remained during the Obama administration via the introduction of Countering Violent Extremism (CVE) policing, but it was also evident in a metastasizing anti-Sharia movement that reached its zenith in 2011 with forty-seven anti-Sharia law bills in twenty-one states (Beydoun 2018: 108). The frenzied unreason of this was more like a symbolic, ritualistic attempt to erase or purge Muslim presence from the United States. It was a curious case of sacrificial magic where a crude and demonic image was conjured and legal incantations used to cast it out. As such, it brings to mind eliminationist discourses that David Neiwert (2009) has argued especially plague the American Right.[6] As Neiwert explains, eliminationism is 'a politics and a culture that shuns dialogue and the democratic exchange of ideas in favour of the pursuit of outright elimination of the opposing side, either through suppression, exile, and ejection, or extermination' (12).

In hindsight, this should have clearly signalled that something like the Trump phenomenon was brewing.[7]

Trump clearly benefitted from the apocalyptic rhetoric of neoconservatism that had so meticulously crafted a sense of existential threat. Without feeling the need to dampen down the language of the coming Armageddon, as Obama had at least attempted to in his own rhetoric, Trump was all too happy to reignite it and unapologetically co-opt Islamophobia for his own ends. His call for and attempt to instigate a ban of Muslims entering the country – Executive Orders 13769 and 13780 and Presidential Proclamation 9645 – was one of the primary ways he appealed to his base. The brazen nature of the 'Muslim ban' is testimony to just how heightened the fear of Muslims and Islam had become over the preceding fifteen years. It also speaks volumes about the irrationality of this fear given it came at a time, as I noted in Chapter 3, when the greatest threat to security and the highest incidence of terrorism on US soil was coming from white supremacists.

Interestingly, however, while readily deploying Islamophobia, the specific enemy in the Trumpian apocalypse was Mexicans, and more generally Central American migrants crossing the southern border. On a number of occasions, he has presented migrant 'caravans' as an existential threat to America, and while it is difficult to see a few thousand largely impoverished people as the enemy set to end the American way of life, the appetite for images of an impending annihilation remained very high. This was no doubt in part due to anti-migrant rhetoric regularly spouted by the likes of Sean Hannity, Tucker Carlson and Laura Ingraham on Fox News, but it should also be noted that some version of this threat has been an important part of conservative and white supremacist concerns throughout the twentieth century (Belew 2018: 97). This goes back to 1977 and David Duke's Klan Border Watch but also includes Glenn Spencer's American Patrol founded in 1995 and the Tombstone Border Militia started by Chris Simcox in 2003 (Neiwert 2017: 81). So, Trump did not need to generate a sense for this specific threat himself. He simply needed to reactivate long-standing white supremacist concerns about invasion from the south.

With reference to Mexicans in particular, Trump uses a very specific rhetoric to conjure up his own vision of impending dissolution. He has repeatedly referred to them as drug dealers, criminals, rapists and animals, with the latter being an especially disturbing form of dehumanization. He has also offered rather lurid improvisations on the subject, such as this account from 11 January 2019 on the topic of border security: 'Human trafficking – grabbing women, in particular – and children, but women – taping them up, wrapping tape around their mouths so they can't shout or scream, tying up their hands behind their back and even their legs and putting them in a back seat of a car or a van – three, four, five, six, seven at a time.' This attitude towards Mexicans and illegal immigrants (known as 'Dreamers') has also seen an especially draconian use of US Immigration and Custom Enforcement (ICE) by the Trump administration and significant increase in detention camps. At the same time, his fabled wall across the southern border – that many see as just a giant monument to racism – is said to be the only way to stop the invasion. In the meantime, the numbers being detained has dramatically risen and a policy that separated migrant children from their parents was introduced (as well as roundly condemned). After the separation, the children were detained in camps such as the Tornillo tent city on the border between Texas and Mexico. In these camps run by ICE, there has been widespread concern about human rights abuses as well as the number of deaths.[8]

To understand the legal status of these camps and the intellectual continuity from the Bush Doctrine to Trumpism, it is useful to return to the work of Carl Schmitt and the particular interpretation offered by Giorgio Agamben. In his important study of sovereignty entitled *Homo Sacer*, Agamben highlights how the camp – with all the horrors we have associated with camps over the course of the twentieth century – is the logical conclusion of the type of politics based on the sovereign exception. In the final chapter, he asks what is the nature of the 'juridico-political structure' (1998: 166) of the camp such that the crimes with which we are all so familiar can take place there. In the early part of the book, Agamben points out that Schmitt's distinction between friend and enemy is really a secondary phenomenon and what is really at stake here is a decision about whose life deserves the protection of the law and whose doesn't. He notes the ancient Greeks had two words for life, *zoē*, or the 'bare life', as he calls it, that all living things share, and *bios*, the life of a political community. The decision to name the enemy is thus a decision about who belongs and who doesn't, those who are protected by the laws of a political community and those who aren't. When an enemy is named and the law is suspended, protection is effectively withdrawn from those who are designated as not belonging to the political community.

Defined in this way, they are reduced to 'bare life' and are potentially exposed to the full force of violence without any mediation. This was done most effectively during the War on Terror with the creation of Guantanamo, a prison under US control but not on US soil – meaning it is not subject to US law – housing 'enemy combatants', a completely invented nomenclature that meant detainees weren't protected by international law pertaining to the treatment of prisoners. Consequently, Agamben says we should not ask how it is possible to commit crimes against humanity, but analyse 'the juridical procedures and deployments of power by which human beings could be so completely deprived of their rights and prerogatives that no act against them could appear any longer as a crime' (171). It is not, then, that humans are capable of inhumanity, but that we have a juridico-political structure that enables it.

As for the migrant camps, Tanvi Misra (2019) writing for *City Lab* evoked the children's reduction to bare life when she noted how 'soccer balls that the incarcerated kids had kicked over the fence […] had been signed with their names, almost as if they were saying, "We were here"'. The children are there in the first place because under the *Flores vs Reno* ruling, or the Flores Agreement, children cannot be kept in detention beyond a specified time. They have to be released to the 'least restrictive' setting suitable, in this instance to shelters run by the Office of Refugee Resettlement (ORR). They are also required to receive a certain amount of education, welfare and medical assistance, rights that in June 2019 were reportedly being revoked (Sacchetti 2019).[9] They were also supposed to be released from these places as soon as a relative or guardian can sponsor them.

What was happening in practice, though, is that these children entered a legally indeterminate state due to a stipulation set up by the Trump White House. As Victoria López reported for the American Civil Liberties Union (ACLU): 'A recent agreement between ICE and ORR now requires background checks and fingerprints – not just for potential sponsors of immigrant youth but for any person living in the same household as sponsors – that can then be shared with ICE. The effect is to instil fear of arrest and deportation in those who come forward to sponsor a child' (np). In a separate ACLU article, Madhuri Grewal adds this has resulted in 'a record-setting number of children being held by ORR. The number of children – as young as babies and toddlers – detained by our government has skyrocketed, from 2,400 in May 2017 to more than 14,000 in November 2018. Children are also being detained for longer periods of time, dramatically increasing the chances they will suffer severe and irreparable harm, according to the American Academy of Pediatrics' (np).

Although it might be argued that in viewing Trump's migrant camps through the lens that Agamben used for understanding Nazi concentration camps I am suffering from my own apocalyptic fears of dissolution, while also perhaps diminishing the full horror of the Shoa, I think it is important to be very clear that Trump's camps are rooted in the same juridico-political structure as the Nazi extermination camps. This means we also have to take note of the historical amnesia that Jonathan Katz (2018) has spoken about in relation to his own attempts to draw a likeness. He writes: 'in dismissing any such historical comparisons out of hand, people are making the common mistake of reading history backward' (np). In other words, we think only of what the Nazi camps were like at the end not what they were like when they started – an origin that emerged out of the Prussian law of 1851 pertaining to *Schutzhaft*, or 'protective custody' (Agamben 1998: 167).

Although these camps were used by the Obama administration and the removal of immigrants was high under his watch, they never featured as propaganda in the development of a presidential persona that appealed to belligerent forms of ethno-nationalism. My point, however, is that Trump was able to tap into the sense of ontological and existential precarity that had become especially intense over the course of the War on Terror and remains especially high today to use these reserves of anxiety for his own purposes. Ultimately, neoconservatism re-energized apocalyptic narratives of a nation and a civilization under existential threat from rampant evil, both at home and abroad, and in that it bequeathed an undermining of the rule of law and democratic principles, especially where *liberal* advocacy for that law and the human rights it protects is represented as weakness and a threat to national security. Cast in this light, the liberal underpinnings of democratic life have become very fragile and are highly susceptible to strong leaders ready to name the enemy. Such a strategy also has the added benefit of working very well as a form of distraction. At a time of global economic crisis, it is easy for the architects and major beneficiaries of the system that created that crisis to mobilize fear of foreigners and misdirect any attention that might otherwise come their way. It is to this economic precarity that we turn next.

Crash or economic precarity

In June 2019 the UK's Institute for Public Policy Research published a study claiming that, since 2012, 130,000 preventable deaths in the UK could be put down to the effects of austerity (Hochlaf, Quilter-Pinner and Kibasi 2019). Like all numbers, these are of course contested, but it was supported by an earlier study published in *BMJ Open* (Watkins et al. 2017) showing a marked increase in mortality rates since the Conservative-led coalition implemented dramatic public spending cuts as a response to bailing out the banking sector in the wake of the 2008 Financial Crisis. These reports have been supplemented by a steady tide of media stories about deaths and suicides linked to Universal Credit, a supposedly streamlined version of the UK social security system. It has become synonymous with severe delays in payments that have left families destitute, while seriously ill people or people with profound disabilities have been found fit for work by the Department of Work and Pensions, thereby stripping them of any claim to support and leaving them with no income. However, this is just the latest in the four-decade assault on the post-war consensus and the welfare state that has been central to the economic doctrine known as neoliberalism. This doctrine has been marked by sustained and targeted attacks on labour protections and welfare rights; coupled with the off-shoring of jobs linked to globalization; structural adjustments (selling off public services, assets and resources) in exchange for loans; de-industrialization through the shift to a service economy and the socialization of losses in times of crisis. The resulting economic precarity has compounded many communities' fragile sense of identity and security, with several commentators noting blue-collar anxieties as a key issue when explaining both the Trump and Brexit phenomena. An understanding of the Financial Crisis of 2008 is therefore crucial if we are to escape the cycle of ever-deepening economic inequality and the social and political scapegoating that has helped feed the resurgence of the far-right.

It is quite common to hear the pejorative 'sharks' being used for lenders, but in this situation the term is perfectly accurate for two reasons. Especially egregious, predatory lending was certainly a major contributor to the Financial Crisis, as will be shown below, but also like sharks, if money doesn't continually move around the system creating new loans and new assets, it dies. Liquidity, or the movement of money, which is based on the confidence that you'll get it (plus a profit) back, is the oxygen our economic system depends on. If it stops, which is what happened, the results are catastrophic. Ultimately, the entire system was only revived – although it has been in a close to critical condition ever since – by being bailed out with massive amounts of public money. It was effectively a giant transfer of wealth from the bottom to the top. However, according to Mariana Mazzucato (2020), this injection of liquidity 'only ended up back in a financial sector that was (and remains) unfit for purpose' (np). The flood of public money enabled banks to quickly return to the culture of paying out obscene bonuses and ensured the top 1 per cent continued to vacuum up the greatest share of the wealth (Brown, R. 2017), but it did little to strengthen the economy as a whole. While the crisis had immediate causes, it also had a long history, and it is important to address this at some length in order to understand how we developed an economic system that fuels so much social division and resentment.

A history of a crisis as the emergence of groupthink

When the post-war boom became the bust of the 1970s, we were told that the Keynesian economics of state intervention that helped the world recover from the 1929 crash and great recession was no longer adequate to deal with capitalism's inherent fluctuations. Instead, it was argued, state intervention was part of the problem and the time was right to embark on a form of free-market capitalism that rolled back 'state interference', privatized resources and services and allowed capital to do its magical work unimpeded. So, by the end of the 1970s, Ronald Reagan in the United States and Margaret Thatcher in the United Kingdom were ready to roll out the new doctrine – developed by the likes of Friedrich Hayek and Milton Friedman – and for the next three decades, neoliberal economics became an unquestionable dogma underpinning a new common sense. The high priests of the new creed were so confident that just prior to the Great Financial Crisis of 2008 significant figures such as Ben Bernanke, then chairman of the US Federal Reserve, spoke in hallowed tones about the 'Great Moderation' where more efficient markets, deregulation and financial wizardry were celebrated as the cure for the perennial problem of the boom and bust business cycle, and that we had entered a brave new world of continual growth and stability.

Throughout this time, what remained hidden was the fact that, while the top percentiles of society were doing extremely well out of the new creed, there had been a stagnation in growth and a decline in the share of wages as a percentage of GDP for everyone else (Foster and Magdoff 2009: 129–30).

In the United States, for example, 'while average pre-tax national income per adult [had] increased by 60% since 1980, it [had] stagnated for the bottom half at about $16,000 a year' (Brown, R. 2017: 14), showing the extent to which the exponential growth of wealth at the top skews the median figure. In addition, neoliberal ideologues were also unconcerned by arguments that the financialization of the economy was little more than a sticking plaster covering the innate tendency of capitalism to stagnate and crash. In other words, increasing the size and profitability of the financial sector compared to other aspects of the economy led to the well documented process of deindustrialization as money sought short-term financial gains rather than long-term profits from investment in the real economy (Lapavitsas 2011: 615); post-crisis, it was no doubt a major contributor to the 'jobless recovery'.

In fact, on this front, neoliberalism and the attendant financialization is better understood as a form of politics rather than economics. It enables a small class of people to be the primary beneficiaries of growth and capture vast amounts of wealth at the expense of other sections of society. It is, therefore, unsurprising that those who benefit so much from it refuse to let it die. In fact, we remain so in hock to the banking sector both as economies and as individuals – through what is called 'the financialization of personal income' in the form of credit cards, car loans, student debt, re-mortgaging and pensions (Lapavitsas 2011: 623)[1] – that this 'zombie economics' (Quiggin 2010) has continued to stagger around for the last decade. With every alternative quashed via widespread propaganda decrying any form of left-wing economics, neoliberalism finds its only challenger to be the reanimation of an older form of naked (anti-welfare) and belligerently nationalistic capitalism.

After the 1979 election of Margaret Thatcher, financialization and the attendant principle of privatization came to define both her economics and politics. With regard to the latter, the UK embarked on a radical project to sell off publicly owned companies, services and resources, including energy, transport, communications and other assets such as social housing and even school playing fields. However, while this brings in immediate revenue for the government, it is often a net loss to the public purse in the long run because the public enterprise can be used to service higher levels of lending than its sale can pay off (Quiggin 2010: 191). Ultimately, then, while privatization is of very dubious benefit to the public, it is very advantageous for capital.

Aside from the sale of public assets to private companies at knock down prices, though, privatization has a second element, namely, the cutting of state regulation, which was absolutely crucial to the second principle of financialization. Almost immediately on taking office, Thatcher abolished the exchange controls that regulate trade in currencies, which put the UK at the forefront of the free flow of global capital (Helleiner 1994). This shift towards expanding the financial side of the UK economy was then completed in 1986 in a series of legislative changes known as the 'Big Bang' that repositioned London as the world's leading financial centre, which also intensified the gentrification (or 'social cleansing') of numerous London boroughs. This also enabled the development of a consumer culture fuelled by cheap credit and a massive increase in personal or household debt, all of which was sold to the public on the back of a new common sense that spoke of the democracy of share options and the association of political freedom with a consumer-based notion of 'freedom of choice' amid a cornucopia of branded 'lifestyles'. Thatcherism's solution to capitalism's over-accumulation problem (Lee 1993; Harvey 2010) therefore combined a bargain basement clearance sale that offered up new resources for capital to exploit coupled with a massive increase in the capacity of individuals to purchase the products of capitalism's expansion, not through increased wages but through the accrual of debt.[2]

Deregulation therefore comes to underpin both privatization and financialization, becoming *the* economic and political driver of the neoliberal revolution inaugurated by Thatcher and Reagan. However, while it encapsulates the doctrine's antipathy to the role of the state on a number of levels, such antipathy is nothing new. It stems from capitalism's historical and deep-seated paranoia about the dangers of government. As Mark Blyth (2013) has argued, if we return to the earliest philosophers – John Locke and David Hume – of the emerging capitalist class, we find a redefinition of the legitimate functioning of the state in terms of the defence of private property (105). Writing not long after the Glorious Revolution of 1688 that saw parliamentarians establish what is now known as the system of limited government with the passing of the Bill of Rights in 1689, Locke was determined to resist any repetition of the right to confiscation that had existed under the previous (pre-1640) model of absolute monarchy. Hume, on the other hand, was the first exponent of the now widespread myth of the corporate class as wealth creators. For Hume, merchants are 'at the center of everything [and are] "one of the most useful races of men"' (Blyth 2013: 107). Their work, he argued, is threatened by the state's issuance of debt serviced by the raising of taxes. Hence, the state should let the merchants do what they do best. Deregulation worked on many fronts, then. It sought to open up new resources through privatization but was also a process that degraded all forms of legislation that placed a limit on the free decisions of the owners of capital.

In relation to the Financial Crisis, deregulation was an assault on the laws stipulating how financial organizations, in particular banks could trade and lend. A cornerstone of the financialization of the economy was therefore the deregulation of the banking system to the point where regulatory oversight was practically non-existent. In the United States, the apex, although not the end of this legislative cull was the abolition of the Glass–Steagall Act in Bill Clinton's Financial Services Modernization Act of 1999. Glass–Steagall had originally been passed in 1933 to create a firewall between retail and investment banking in the wake of the 1929 crash. The idea was to end catastrophic bank runs by ensuring that any crisis in the investment side could not spread to the commercial sector, but arguments were made that this piece of legislation diminished the capacity of banks to grow sufficiently in size to compete on a global scale. Its repeal is the primary reason that banks became 'too big to fail', that is, not too big to be failures but too big for us to allow them to fail. Of course, with the banks now being so powerful that economies are completely beholden to them, any effort to reinstate Glass–Steagall, or something like it, has failed. The closest to it is the Volcker Rule contained in the Dodd–Frank Wall Street Reform and Consumer Protection Act that came into effect in the United States in July 2015. This rule, described as 'Glass–Steagall Lite', is an attempt to limit the liabilities a bank can hold, but it remains relatively light touch compared to earlier regulations.

The repeal of Glass–Steagall was preceded by the repeal of the Garn–St. Germain Depository Act of 1982 permitting savings and loans companies to expand into new businesses. Reagan hailed this as the 'first step' to 'comprehensive deregulation' (Johnson and Kwak 2010: 72). The Secondary Mortgage Market Enhancement Act of 1984 then allowed investment banks to buy up mortgages, pool them together, slice them up and resell the repackaged slices in a process known as securitization. If there was one innovation that is key to the successful financialization of the economy and then that economy's catastrophic collapse, it is securitization. This practice of slicing and dicing mortgages and re-selling the bundles on to other investors allowed banks to mix elements of high-risk loans with medium- and low-risk loans, thereby spreading and supposedly lessening the volatility of investment because the instability of high risk was now believed to be off set and therefore 'secured' against the low-risk investments in the new bundle.

The point is that securitization enabled banks and other financial institutions to expose themselves to higher risks and therefore higher yields because they believed securitization meant risk had been diluted to such an extent it had effectively been removed.[3] These securitized bundles were then sold on to other investors in what was known as a collateralized debt obligation (CDO), meaning that risk was passed from banks to countless other financial institutions, funds and vehicles. Given this movement of risk from the initial lenders to the investors who had purchased bundles of these sliced and diced loans, lenders 'now had no need to be particularly bothered about whether or not the borrower could repay' (Lanchester 2010: 99). This opened up the now infamous and predatory sub-prime lending that would eventually bring the system to its knees. Selling mortgages to people on low incomes became attractive because lenders could still benefit from a high yield while believing they were no longer exposed to the risk that normally came with lending to people in precarious financial situations. However, the sheer quantity of this high risk lending and its distribution across the sector meant that the entire system became contaminated. In Lanchester's words, securitization was like people using 'the invention of seatbelts as an opportunity to take up drunk-driving' (65).

As Blyth notes, because this created a situation where everyone believed there was little chance of default, no one believed there was a need 'to keep very much capital at all in reserve to cover anticipated losses because no losses [were] anticipated' (29). In effect, lenders were given the green light to lend money to anyone irrespective of the ability to pay, all under the misguided premise that, with house prices continuing to rise, everyone would continue to benefit. On top of this, was the hubris that an industry 'making so much money had to be good, and people who were making so much money had to know what they were talking about' (Johnson and Kwak 2010:6). Hence, once the poor people who never stood a realistic chance of repaying the mortgages they were sold defaulted and because so much – up to $1.4 trillion (Morgensen and Rosner 2011) – had been distributed through the system via CDOs alone, the contamination brought down the entire financial system.

In fact, it is even possible to say that the reason such confidence could arise within the financial sector was not simply because of this misguided faith in their own technical innovations but because they also knew if the whole thing fell apart they would be given a parachute and a soft landing. The Keynesian compact that arose from the Great Depression gave an increasingly important role to central banks as lenders of last resort. In this role the function of central banks was to add stability to a system that had been shown to be very fragile. The relatively minor Financial Crisis in 1987 saw Alan Greenspan, then chairman of the Fed, inject liquidity into the system, an action that became known as the 'Greenspan put', named after a put option that guarantees the price of an asset, and by the time the Fed again bailed out LTCM in 1998 (Krugman 2009: 134–8), the financial sector came to believe that the Fed could and would bail them out of any crisis. So, by the end of Greenspan's tenure, the role of the central bank had shifted from prevention of crises to the guarantor of any wager a financial institution wished to make. While neoliberalism demands the rolling back of the state, in its role as the banker of last resort neoliberals are happy for the state to become the underwriter of casino capitalism.

Another reason CDOs looked like a safe way to make ridiculous amounts of money was because these financial tools had been given a AAA status by the big three rating agencies – Standard and Poor's, Moody's and Fitch – charged with assessing the likelihood of default. The AAA rating was equivalent to saying they were as safe as the very safest investment, which at the time was deemed to be US government bonds. What is interesting, though, is that the agencies take a fee from whoever is seeking the rating, thereby setting up a potentially catastrophic conflict of interest at the heart of a system totally dependent for all of its functioning on the ratings of these private, for-profit companies. After the crisis, the Dodd–Frank Act mentioned earlier tried to strengthen the regulation of them, as did the creation in 2011 of the European Securities and Markets Authority, but as Frank Partnoy has argued (2017), these reforms have had very little effect on curbing the dangers of this 'impenetrable oligopoly' (np).

Furthermore, because of the fact that these companies rate government debt, they have also become very powerful political players, not simply because a downgrade of a country's solvency can affect the policy of the government seeking the rating but because a government can use the threat of a downgrade to pursue specific political decisions. Here, neoliberal politicians can use the opprobrium of the rating agencies to confirm the validity of their political programme and set in place a new round of legislation favourable to the corporate and financial sectors. As such, back in 2005, Timothy J. Sinclair argued these agencies 'represent the shape of newly emerging authority' (175) whose power is 'camouflaged' (175). This power was epitomized in October 2009 when the new British prime minister, David Cameron, gave a speech declaring the UK's budget deficit to be a 'clear and present danger'. This was the leader of one of the world's largest economies using the dramatic language of the sovereign. As noted in Chapter 5, this is normally only used when declaring war or a state of emergency, but here it referred to the fact that Standard and Poor's had threatened to downgrade the UK's credit rating unless the government pursued a programme of deficit reduction, otherwise known as austerity.

So, not only had the financial system been brought to its knees by inept and deeply compromised rating agencies, these rating agencies were also still dictating political and economic policy in the wake of their failure. Effectively, they had been one of the major contributors to the Financial Crisis and the need for banks to be bailed out with taxpayers' money, and yet they remained in control of post-crisis politics by demanding and supposedly legitimizing a policy that meant taxpayers would continue to carry the burden for the foreseeable future. At the time of the crisis, the ideological sleight of hand that enabled this was quite remarkable. Within a week, certainly no more than a fortnight, the banking crisis had turned into a taxpayer-funded rescue package that resulted in 'the largest ever transfer of private losses from banks' books onto the public ledger' (Varoufakis 2018: 19).

In line with this financial switch came a discursive switch whereby a banking crisis suddenly became what was called a 'sovereign debt crisis' meaning that national governments no longer had the money to repay loans or pay for public services and welfare provisions. Very quickly, then, the focus was turned from the failures of the financial system to the *cost* of welfare provisions and public services, coupled with an upturn in discriminatory rhetoric targeting beneficiaries and migrants. A crisis in *private* debt had been discursively morphed into a crisis of *public* debt.[4] In other words, an economic doctrine that zealously pursued the deregulation that caused the Financial Crisis used that crisis to legitimize further deregulation of the public services that states could supposedly no longer afford, and victimize those most dependent on them. John Clarke and Janet Newman liken this to a form of mythical shape shifting, where political and financial 'wizards' found 'the alchemy that might turn disaster into triumph – the triumph being a new neo-liberal settlement' (2012: 300).

'Wealth creators' and austerity

While I've offered an explanation of the fragility introduced into the global economic system that persists today, it is important to understand an accompanying cultural shift that has contributed to the growing sense of economic precarity over the last few decades. Put simply, this is the shift from a stakeholder to a shareholder economy. Although I don't like the term 'stakeholder', it is suggestive of the varying entities, both human and non-human, that have a stake in how an economy is organized. We have a stake as workers, citizens, neighbours, consumers, patients, students and parents, and our children certainly have a stake because it is their future that we are shaping. Obviously, thinking more holistically, animals, both wild and domestic, have a stake, as do the forests, the oceans and the entire planet on which everybody's future depends. However, over the course of the last four decades, this diversity of interests has been made subservient to the interests of the shareholder or investor. In other words, every possible stake we can have in the way we economically organize ourselves has been reduced to the interests of people with money and their need to maximize profits from it – a shift that disproportionately transfers risk and the precarity resulting from it to the rest of us.

Just as the rating agencies have contributed to the macro-management of the economy in favour of shareholders (Sinclair 2005: 69), there has been a micro-level cultural adjustment in boardrooms. Writing in *Forbes* in July 2018, Steve Denning commented on what Jack Welch, former CEO of General Electric, had already described as 'the dumbest idea in the world' (Stout 20121: 6). According to Denning, from the 1980s, 'public companies began embracing a very different idea as to the purpose of a firm: the idea that the sole purpose of a corporation is to maximize shareholder value [. . .] at the expense of everything else'. According to Lynn Stout (2012), this is the philosophy of 'shareholder primacy theory' proposed by Milton Friedman in 1970. For Stout this meant 'that the only proper goal of business was to maximize profits for the company's owners, whom Friedman assumed [. . .] to be the company's shareholders'. This theory was then set out in Michael Jensen and William Meckling's seminal 1976 essay 'Theory of the Firm', which radically reconfigured the relationship between investors and the manager or executive, defining as 'aberrant' (308) any activity not in the best interests of the investor. This was an absolutely crucial component of the new common sense that enabled the rich to legitimize taking an ever-growing share of economic productivity and increasing the precarity of others.

Another essential component in this cultural shift was the widespread cultural propaganda that mythologized and fetishized the financial class as 'wealth creators' despite the fact that the financialization of the economy meant this made little sense. Aside from the obvious contribution to the production of wealth made by the workforce (made very clear during the coronavirus crisis) and by the state through the public funding of infrastructure, the financialization of the economy meant the vast majority of wealth being gathered by the rich was in reality, as Andrew Sayer notes, *unearned income*. This is income 'extracted by those who control an already existing asset, such as land or a building or equipment [or in this case, money] that others lack but need or want, and can therefore be charged for its use' (2016: 44). Where earned income is work based, unearned income stems from the control of an asset and is warranted solely by that power; people extracting wealth from such assets are better understood as rentiers rather than workers. For Mariana Mazzucato, those who live off the control of an asset are in fact better understood as 'wealth extractors' (2018: 4) who organize the economy for their own benefit.

So, when this house of cards came crashing down only to be rescued by taxpayers, there were two solutions to the artificially created sovereign debt crises. Governments could either raise taxes, especially on the wealthy who had caused the catastrophe, or austerity, meaning that the people who had paid once would be asked to pay again. As you would imagine, with higher taxes on the rich declared a threat to investors, it was austerity that won out. Austerity was not new, of course. It had been the go-to policy of neoliberalism for some time. Throughout the first few decades of the dogma's global expansion, the World Bank and the IMF used loans to demand structural adjustments to a country's economy that would make them more amenable to the free flow of capital. For David Harvey this constituted little more than 'mandated austerity' (2010: 19). The adjustments required cuts to public spending, the privatizing of public services and the opening up of national resources to international competition, thereby creating new forms of colonial dispossession (Venn 2018: 73).[5] Putting economies through austere economic reforms was the bread and butter of what was effectively the de facto, transnational neoliberal state.

The second reason austerity is favoured is that capitalism loves to eat itself, cannibalizing whatever doesn't survive a bust. Commenting on the work of Joseph Schumpeter, Blyth notes how for free-market zealots 'the process of liquidation, of failure, produces the raw material for the next round of innovation and investment' (2013: 120), and once again, it is imperative for the government to keep out of the way while capital renews itself via this necrotic feast. As a consequence, 'Liquidationism' argues:

> *for* an inevitability – *the slump must happen* – and also *for* intervention's unintended consequences – if you get in the way of that inevitability *you will end up making it worse*. The consequence of this line of thinking is *austerity* – purging the system and cutting spending – which becomes the essence of recovery. Austerity may be painful, but it is unavoidable since undergoing such emetic periods is the essence of capitalism's process of investment and discovery. (121; emphasis in original)

Again, we are supposed to believe that what is best for investors is best for everyone else.

The third reason is that this particular crisis was seized upon by the UK Conservative Party as a once-in-a-generation chance to fully degrade the welfare system and complete the project of privatization. This cynical use of deficits is also central to modern-day Conservatism in the United States. As Richard McGahey has argued, US Republicans have often advocated 'growth in the national debt in order to cripple the government's long-term ability to expand social programs' (2013: 719). When George W. Bush took office in 2000, Bill Clinton had returned the federal budget to a surplus, and Bush immediately ordered a programme of tax cuts equivalent to $1.6 trillion over ten years weighted heavily in favour of already wealthy Americans (720). The impact of the cuts was immense, still contributing to 40 per cent of the US deficit as late as 2013.

According to McGahey, the roots of this policy date back to the 1964 presidential campaign of Barry Goldwater – the candidate supported by Ronald Reagan. Goldwater

> was a strong advocate of limited government, states' rights, and lower taxes. He called for the federal government 'to withdraw from a whole series of programs that are outside its constitutional mandate – from social welfare programs, education, public power, agriculture, public housing, urban renewal'. He was anti-union and opposed mandatory Social Security participation, speculating about ending the program all together. (727)

Tax cuts became an effective way of controlling federal spending for Conservatives precisely because they grew the deficit. Economists like Friedman 'believed that cutting revenues would eventually force the government to slow spending because government bond markets would make additional borrowing too costly' (729).

Tax cuts for the rich are therefore doubly cynical. They further enrich the already wealthy while purposefully growing a deficit that can be used to justify further cuts to public programmes. Trump's Tax Cuts and Jobs Act of 2017 is the latest example of this political cynicism. The 2017 Act did little to significantly stimulate the US economy, while the projected Trump budget for 2020 (submitted in March 2019) included $1.9 trillion in 'savings' from programmes including Medicaid and Medicare, food stamps and housing support.[6] The proposed cuts to Medicare alone will total $846 billion over ten years, with $26 billion being cut from social security, which includes a $10 billion cut to Social Security Disability insurance. Like the Conservative government in the UK, Trump decided to make a particular target of disabled people.

For these political reasons austerity was the policy of choice for the wealthy and the corporate-aligned politicians and media barons who were more than happy to sell the story. However, because of a problem known as 'debt deflation', where 'debts increase as incomes shrink' (Blyth 2013: 150), austerity is nearly always bad economics. It is sold to the public using the false analogy of household debt where overspending can be corrected by some 'belt tightening'. Unfortunately, though, this seemingly simple and logical example fails to explain that households have a consistent (even if lower) amount of money coming in. For the economy as a whole, what actually happens during austerity is that, as spending is cut, both consumption and government income are reduced meaning the economy continues to shrink, and we end up chasing our tail in a dizzying slump; but, again, as Blyth notes, 'too many reputations and too much sunk political capital are at stake for mere facts to get in the way of this ideology' (216). Even when the IMF, one of the leading institutions of neoliberal governance, came out to say that neoliberalism had been 'oversold' (Ostry, Loungani and Furceri 2016) and that their assessment of austerity produced 'disquieting conclusions', there was no change in the approach of the ruling class because this was never about economics. Neoliberalism has always been a political project designed to remove accountability from a corporate-financial class in their pursuit of infinite wealth. Effectively, what Johnson and Kwak call 'the revolving door' (2010: 92) between Wall Street and Washington has completed the shift from democracy to fully fledged plutocracy.

The (ethno-)nationalist diversion

In short, what has taken place over the course of the last forty years is 'neoliberalism's intellectual capture of economic policymaking [. . .] resulting in the exclusion of most wage earners from the gains of economic growth' (Ghosh 2018). This has been exacerbated by the off-shoring of jobs – a policy that was a central part of globalization and capitalism's search for pools of cheap labour – coupled with the attack on unions that have further weakened the position of workers. Where there once were 'jobs for life', the experience for many soon became short-term employment followed by regular rounds of retraining and/or periods of welfare. It is this that has left many people feeling forgotten or ignored and therefore open to charismatic leaders who promised to help them.

The early years of this brave new world also involved government policies where programmes of 'work experience' amounted to unpaid labour, a phenomenon that has become even more pronounced in a contemporary culture of unpaid or even 'pay to play' internships where Sarah Kendzior notes 'volunteerism is par for the course' (2015: 121). While this further advantages those with some existing form of material support, because no one else can afford to work for nothing, at the other end of the social ladder are zero-hour contracts. Here, workers have to promise themselves to a company or business without that business having to reciprocate by promising a fixed numbers of hours, and therefore income, per week. During this time, the contracted worker cannot 'work' for anyone else and must be available at the drop of a hat (Southwood 2011). By 2017, the number of zero-hour contracts in the UK alone had reached 1.8 million, and for the new demographic of the working poor, privation had 'become part of the job description' (Kendzior 2015: 40).

All of this was accompanied by the diversionary tactics of anti-beneficiary rhetoric. Through 'relentless demonisation' (O'Hara 2014: 136), the public were convinced that the problem did not lie with the rich syphoning off all the wealth but with the poor who were dependent upon the dole and housing benefit. As late as 2011, the Conservatives in the UK were still pointing at the poor as the cause of what they called 'Broken Britain' (McKenzie 2015: 11). What is extraordinary in all of this, though, is that amid this anti-welfare propaganda there has been a significant growth in 'corporate welfare'. This comes in a range of forms from tax breaks for rich individuals to exemptions and subsidies for businesses; but it also comes in the form of social security paid to supplement people earning poverty wages. Again, in order for investors to maximize profits, the state steps in to pay the shortfall in the scandalously low wages they offer. In effect, we live in such a rigged economic system that the government is compelled to indirectly contribute to corporate profits by trying to lift people out of the poverty that their paid work keeps them in.

To illustrate this, I'd like to quote at length from a report published in 2014 by Americans for Tax Fairness that gives a particularly stark description of how corporate welfare works. They write:

Walmart is [...] number one on the Fortune 500 in 2013 and number two on the Global 500, had $16 billion in profits last year on revenues of $473 billion. [...] The six Walton heirs are the wealthiest family in America, with a net worth of $148.8 billion. Collectively, these six Waltons have more wealth than 49 million American families combined.

This report finds that [...] Walmart and the Walton family receive *tax breaks and taxpayer subsidies estimated at more than $7.8 billion a year* – that is enough money to hire 105,000 new public school teachers. [...]:

- *Walmart receives an estimated $6.2 billion annually in mostly federal taxpayer subsidies.* The reason: Walmart pays its employees so little that many of them rely on food stamps, health care and other taxpayer-funded programs.
- *Walmart avoids an estimated $1 billion in federal taxes each year.* The reason: Walmart uses tax breaks and loopholes, including a strategy known as accelerated depreciation that allows it to write off capital investments considerably faster than the assets actually wear out.

- *The Waltons avoid an estimated $607 million in federal taxes on their Walmart dividends.* The reason: income from investments is taxed at a much lower tax rate than income from salaries and wages.

In addition to the $7.8 billion in annual subsidies and tax breaks, *the Walton family is avoiding an estimated $3 billion in taxes* by using specialized trusts to dodge estate taxes – and this number could increase by tens of billions of dollars.

Walmart also benefits significantly from taxpayer-funded public assistance programs that pump up the retailer's sales. For example, *Walmart had an estimated $13.5 billion in food stamp sales last year.* (Emphasis in original)

In this climate, which for most people has at best been an experience of economic stagnation, but for many has seen an increased sense of economic precarity, people are looking for change. Unfortunately, throughout neoliberalism's reign, the scapegoating has been as severe as the wealth extraction, both of which have become more acute since the Financial Crisis. While the narrative of the 'scrounger' and the 'work shy' has always been present, this has taken on more ethnic and racial connotations in recent years as those in power seek to distract and deflect attention from the fact that what they euphemistically call 'trickle down economics' is really just a big bucket being dropped into the waters of the common wealth and hauled up to the top. The drips off the bucket are what trickle down.

In the United States, this has largely been done through Rupert Murdoch's Fox News, while in the United Kingdom, wall-to-wall right-wing press ably supported by the BBC has presented the British population with a regular diet of fear mongering about migrants and refugees. Rooted in long-standing racist rhetoric stemming from Britain's imperial past, this leaves people open to politicians offering a solution to the 'invasion' they are told is taking place. Genuine economic alternatives have also been derailed, even by pockets of the liberal press that remain wedded to the status quo. Over the course of the last four decades, then, the centre of politics has shifted so far to the right that even the moderation of Keynes is now cast as some radical leftist position.

Examining this shift, Mike Berry (2018) has done some very important work documenting attitudes to post-crisis austerity in the UK. He notes how there was a widely held conflation of government and household debt that cemented the idea we had been living beyond our means and therefore prepped the population for austerity: 'just under 70 per cent' he writes, 'saw the rise [in the deficit] as attributable to increased public spending' (178). When he completed his original research, the banking crisis was still fresh in people's minds and was the most often cited reason for the deficit, but importantly for our purposes here, the third most frequently cited reason for the increased spending was immigration and asylum seekers. Berry writes: 'what wasn't expected was that in 9 out of the 16 focus groups the view that immigration and asylum were to blame for the rise in public debt was firmly expressed. This perspective was particularly strong in groups of low income or older participants where it was often the first factor that was identified' (179). Berry also notes that much of this was linked to media reporting and the regular repetition of the myth that migrants come here just for welfare benefits and free housing. One group also argued that immigrants were taking money out of the country to support an international network of dependents and noted stories of benefit fraud they'd read in newspapers. Berry offers the following exchange as an example:

Respondent 1: You see the social security and all that there's millions and millions of people coming into Britain and they're claiming three or four times and that must be costing a fortune in money and they've got houses here and houses there.

Respondent 2: Look at that one a month ago in the paper she had ten passports for claiming for ten people. It was all illegal immigrants and she was claiming that they had kids and all the rest of it. (Low income group, Glasgow). (180)

Berry goes on to argue that three conclusions can be drawn from his data:

First, public understanding of the contours of public spending is extremely limited. Total benefit fraud in 2008–2009 was estimated by the DWP to £1.1 billion or 0.8 per cent of benefit spending. Family allowance claimed by EU migrants in 2012 was estimated to be £55 million or 0.035 per cent of total benefit spending. [. . .] Neither were significant factors in the rise in public debt post-2007 but loomed large in the minds of many of our participants. Second, people tended to see the economy as a container which some people were seen as contributing to and others were seen as draining. Responsible people were seen to be putting in at least as much as they took out. [. . .] This finding is supported in other research which noted that seeing the economy in this way had the effect of 'reinforcing the demonisation of groups who are portrayed as draining the pot, like immigrants and benefit claimants'. [. . .] Third, without an understanding of how public spending breaks down citizens will overestimate the contribution of issues that have high visibility in the media, especially if media accounts focus on emotive and atypical cases whose existence is then taken to be widespread. So the strong emphasis given in the press to highly charged accounts of benefit fraud by immigrants led our respondents to massively overestimate the impact that it had on the public finances. (181)

Berry also notes the regular repetition of the phrase 'benefits culture', an idea the right-wing press had carefully cultivated over preceding years. It matched a rhetoric dominated by a Manichaean division between givers and takers, between 'paying' and 'drawing', 'strivers' and 'shirkers', that was hugely important to the early phase of neoliberalism's assault on welfarism. This attitude had also been encouraged at a time when spending on welfare in the decade prior to the Financial Crisis had actually decreased (Berry 2018: 183).

Other perceived sources of the deficit, as might be imagined, were the EU, which was seen a 'black hole' absorbing endless money (184), and a 'bloated' public sector where people are paid for not doing any work (185). However, as Berry notes, the 'power and longevity' of the belief that migrants and asylum seekers were a significant drain on public resources – in large part because of the regularity with which the media frame them as an economic threat – meant it remained second on the list of Leave voters' reasons for leaving the EU when polled in 2016 (216). The spike in nationalist and ethno-nationalist sentiment around the time of the EU referendum is also understandable from the perspective of another dominant theme in Berry's findings. This is the false belief, again ably cultivated by the UK's dominant right-wing press, that the Labour government who were in power during the Financial Crisis had not only greatly expanded public spending but had done so by putting migrants ahead of British citizens in relation to housing and education and even driving lessons (219).

He also notes how, in the letters pages of newspapers, this preferential treatment of migrants would often be juxtaposed with a failure to support military veterans. There was, then, a heady mix of xenophobia and jingoism. However, Berry reminds us 'there are many stories that could be told about the public sector, welfare spending and migration but the narratives in parts of the press focus on a relentlessly one-sided negative framing of these issues' (220). He continues, 'the lack of any contextual information – for instance, the total level of benefit fraud within the system or the proportion of welfare spending that is claimed by migrant workers – means that readers are left with a distorted picture of how the welfare state operates' (221). It is, then, no surprise so many people were primed for austerity and so readily scapegoated 'foreigners'.

As this scapegoating continued and intensified, the radical right were themselves using critiques of the 'globalist' corporate class to offer people the change they were seeking. Trump strategist and Alt-Right champion, Steve Bannon, has taken an expectedly populist tone in many speeches, waxing lyrical over the entrepreneurial capacities of the average American degraded by the interests of an international corporate class. In his speech to CPAC in 2017, and in language that curiously evokes the writings of Carl Schmitt discussed in Chapter 5, Bannon valorizes the personality and economic vitality of a nation dulled by what he calls the 'administrative state', a term used by Schmitt in his 1932 critique of the liberal Weimar Republic (2004: 5). In Bannon's speech at the Vatican in 2014, hosted by *Dignitatis Humane* mentioned in Chapter 1, he also referred to this administrative state of international neoliberalism as 'the party of Davos', refining this further in a speech in Hungary in 2018 where he described this party as 'the scien tific-managerial-engineering-financial elite and all their apparatchiks'. As a nationalist and promoter of racist and white supremacist rhetoric, it can be assumed this is also something of an anti-Semitic dog-whistle about a Jewish-run world government.

However, what is at stake here is very important. While neoliberalism over the course of the last forty years has done its best to roll back the state, dismantle public services and undermine the welfare state, many countries, especially those in the EU have managed to hold onto features of the post-war consensus and protect some aspects of public service, infrastructure and welfare, albeit significantly diminished. What is currently taking place, then, is an internecine struggle among the ruling class – or what Leslie Sklair has called the transnational capitalist class (2001) – between those with an international view and who tolerate some of the post-war compromises as the best means of accumulating wealth and those who advocate a form of naked, nationalist capitalism devoid of any 'socialist' compromise. For Tamsin Shaw (2019), there is a class of billionaires who want to rid themselves of any government (read democratic) oversight whatsoever and use the state entirely for the purposes of amassing wealth. Shaw writes: 'Russia has pioneered this new form of "state capitalism", in which the state absorbs risk for the companies of certain loyal oligarchs, allowing them to reap enormous profits' (np).

For our purposes here, this is all veiled beneath romantic rhetoric of national rebirth, paternalistic platitudes about defending the people from the elite and mythical evocations of former greatness. This nationalist appeal, though, is nearly always couched in ethno-nationalist terms because, for the nationalists, the globalizing elite are necessarily unconcerned by 'national culture' (invariably in the United States, the United Kingdom and Europe, a euphemism for white culture) and are therefore prepared to enable its undermining by foreigners. This is the change they offer. Although they promise much, they will do absolutely nothing that will significantly improve the material well-being of workers and their families. What they do enable, though, is the chance for those weakened, stressed out, threatened and undermined by our economic system to feel momentarily emboldened by the malice they can direct at foreigners, migrants, refugees, Mexicans, Muslims, feminists, leftists, liberals, resisters and remainers.

In the UK, in particular, the decade of austerity with its evocation of post-war rationing and accompanying sense of solidarity and sacrifice works especially well as a breeding ground for nationalist sentiment and revival. David Kynaston (2010), author of *Austerity Britain 1945-1951*, wrote in *The Guardian*: 'We have a society accustomed to the pursuit of prosperity and individual gratification, often resentful of immigrants, and possessing a perilously skin-deep attachment to democracy. There may be real trouble ahead if our rulers get it wrong.' However, the problem, as I see it, is that our rulers are actually getting it right. The mobilizing of anxieties caused by economic precarity and redirecting them towards migrants, asylum seekers and foreigners is working as a means of distracting people from the real issues with our economic system. What many of them (the opportunists rather than the died-in-the-wool fascists) are getting wrong is the belief they will be able to put the far-right genie back in the bottle once they've let it out.

Privilege or social precarity

The complex precarity, outlined so far, has been further intensified by democratic challenges to the dominant Western identities of patriarchal masculinity, whiteness, heterosexuality and Christianity that have traditionally advantaged specific social groups. This challenge has taken the form of important political advances gained by second- and third-wave feminisms, black civil rights and the various forms of anti-racism, the pride of the LGBTQ community and the cultural advances brought about by the shift towards multiculturalism, but these are currently facing a pronounced reactionary backlash. While rooted in much older legislation that ended slavery and extended the franchise, the success of these challenges to traditional forms of social dominance can be seen in a variety of race relations and sex discrimination legislation in every democratic country in the second half of the twentieth century. This continued into the twenty-first century with widespread legislation relating to gay marriage, including the 2015 US Supreme Court *Obergefell v. Hodges* ruling that made same-sex marriage a basic right of all American citizens under the Fourteenth Amendment of the Constitution. However, social change does not happen at the speed of a legislator's pen. Consequently, progressive legal developments are in no way sufficient to deal with the types of marginalization, exclusion and even violence that non-dominant groups continue to face in society today.

Research continues to show a sharp difference in the US prison population for African Americans. In 2017, they represented 12 per cent of the country's adult population but 33 per cent of the country's inmates (Gramlich 2019). Rather disturbingly, the bias is so culturally engrained that just discussing these disparities can trigger the discrimination that causes the disparities in the first place (Hetey and Eberhardt 2018). Staying in the United States, another report showed that African American men were 2.5 times more likely to be shot by police than whites (Mock 2019). In 2016 the wealth gap based on race in the United States equated to the white median income being ten times greater than the income of African American households (Umoh 2019), while another report presents a much higher figure of twenty times greater (Sahm 2020). These gaps also apply to access to housing, health and educational outcomes and are repeated across numerous societies, including my own country of New Zealand (Marriot and Sim 2014). We also know that members of the LGBTQ community are exposed to disproportionate levels of violence. In the UK, a recent study showed the rate had doubled since 2014 (Marsh, Mohdin and McIntyre 2019). In terms of sexual violence, women continue to be disproportionately subjected to it; and yet another recent study finds that while reports of rape and assault have increased, the rate of prosecution in the UK is actually decreasing (Bindel 2019). There is also the very well documented gender pay gap that continues to entrench discrimination. A great deal of dedicated work is therefore still required.

There is, however, a widespread perception that these forms of 'identity politics' have made greater inroads than is the case. As J. C. Alexander notes, 'even the full force of conservative state power has utterly failed to put a stop to cultural liberalism, to the steady march of social incorporation, from industrial workers in the 1930s and Jews in the 1950s, to blacks, Hispanics, Asians, women, immigrants, and non-conforming sexualities in the long half century from the 1960s until today' (2019: 140). This is in part because these challenges have slowly been seen as a new marketing opportunity. Here, while people from minorities and historically suppressed communities have very particular experiences that challenge the dominant world view, neoliberalism was happy to try and subsume them within the logic of consumer choice central to its concept of the 'free market'. Capitalism thus discovered new groups to sell to and new resources to exploit in the never-ending search for shareholder value.

This commodification transformed the radical and universal demand for equality and freedom into a form of discrete, segmented, consumer-based 'identities' that could be marketed to. Here, any political challenge, such as those posed by feminism and radical civil rights movements was transformed in a way that deflected their militancy and put their energies to work in the service of power. We can see this in phrases like 'the gay dollar' or 'pink money' used to refer to the spending power of the gay community. It is also evident in the commercialization of black politics through the corporate appropriation of hip-hop culture or the exoticization of ethnicities offered as a palette for commodified 'lifestyles'. So, in spite of their radical challenge, power was able to reform itself around them. However, these political movements were always so much more than these marketing opportunities, and as they continued to make headway in societies whose laws and founding constitutions had promised greater representation, they did begin to impact the social privilege previously held by traditionally dominant groups.

So, in a world that was witnessing the gradual social advancement of minorities, something that really only became visible over the course of this short millennium with the improving inclusion of minority groups in our entertainment media, we also saw a decrease in the social advantage of those who up to this point had been first in the queue for jobs, education, housing, health and representations of their culture. Consequently, and in large part as an attempt to thwart further progress, the view that the causes of women's rights and black civil rights have been 'successful' has led to claims that we now live in a post-feminist or past-racial world; that gender and racial equality are now facts of life. Such a view is, of course, a highly blinkered, if not an utterly absurd one because it fails to see the realities of the very real, ongoing discrimination mentioned earlier. It completely ignores the injustices that began both the Black Lives Matter (BLM) and #MeToo movements.[1] Hence, over the last ten years, the need to continue the struggle for equality has focused on the blindness to privilege, understood as the unacknowledged social advantage beneath which a range of discriminations persist. The fourth type of precarity that this book addresses is, therefore, the loss of social privilege that many people could depend on as their first line of defence in times of difficulty. In this chapter I will endeavour to explain what privilege is, how it can be shown to still exist and why challenging it poses a threat to the particular identity targeted for recruitment by far-right politics, namely, the straight, white, Christian man and his domestic arrangements.

Defining privilege

Ordinarily, privilege, as both social position and cultural disposition, withdraws into the background of our lives such that it seems to not exist at all. This aligns very closely with the discussion of the familiarity of the world in Chapter 4. Paraphrasing Alison Bailey (1998: 104–19), privilege is not recognized by those who are privileged because an important aspect of privilege in the contemporary sense is to *hide itself*. When I was young, the term 'privilege' wasn't used the way it is now. My parents told me about privileged people, but the term was generally reserved for the very wealthy; but privilege as it is used today refers to any form of social advantage that arises from being a member of a socially dominant group or, like me, a member of several socially dominant groups (white, male, straight, fully abled, middle class and Christian). Peggy McIntosh famously described it as 'like an invisible weightless backpack of special provisions, maps, passports, codebooks, visas, clothes, tools and blank checks' (1989: np). So, privilege gives us access, clearance, protection, support and capacities, but the nature of privilege is that these remain invisible to us.

As we usually understand it, privilege relates to a special right that is granted to one person, group or entity and not to others. It has been used in a range of social settings, from schools to prisons to courts to encourage good behaviour, compliance and loyalty. The bestowal of privilege is the way a monarch or other head of state might show favour or reward. It is a way of establishing advantage for and loyalty from a particularly trustworthy servant or ally. The whole point of a privilege is that it is awarded to some and not to others. Division, separation and difference are essential to all privileges. Given that privilege is a form of preferential treatment, privileges are intrinsically connected to the creation of social hierarchy in which certain people are given opportunities that set them above others. Privilege, in this conventional sense, is also a form of immunity, an inoculation against the trials and tribulations that others might face.

The etymology of privilege comes from the Latin words for private (*privium*) and law (*lex* or *leg*). It is specifically not something public, but personal, particular and exceptional. It is a personal relation to the law defined as either advantage or exemption. We see this meaning most clearly in the 'executive privilege' in the United States that protects the executive branch from public disclosure of information or the 'parliamentary privilege' in the United Kingdom that protects politicians from civil or criminal liability during the course of their official legislative duties. This allows them to say things in the course of a debate for which an ordinary member of the public might be charged and prosecuted under laws pertaining to slander. There is also the *privilege de blanc* that permits a woman to wear a white dress during an audience with the pope. This privilege awarded to members of Catholic nobility, such as the Grand Duchess Joséphine-Charlotte of Luxembourg or Queen Paola of Belgium, allows them to break the usual tradition of wearing black. This privilege is especially interesting for its brazen display of exceptionality, hierarchy, inequality and the visual marking of difference. It puts on show the preferential treatment that is privilege. It is an extravagant display that some people are of more value or more important than others.

The granting of privilege is therefore closely connected to power; and yet this power is often disavowed or unacknowledged. Consequently, the most socially damaging effects of privilege are first of all the denial that it exists, or only exists in extreme cases, and secondly, that what is an exceptional experience is taken to be a general rule. It is then applied to instances where it is inappropriate or thoroughly unrepresentative. This can be seen in a white person's claim that their country isn't racist. They don't experience it, so they assume – or rather declare – that no one does. Politics, and society more broadly, are unfortunately full of powerful and privileged people making decisions about the lives of others based on their own partial experiences that they assume to be some form of universal truth. However, unlike legal and official privileges, social privilege cannot be simply revoked and can only be undone through continual self-reflection in the context of broad socio-economic transformation. Privilege as it is spoken about today cannot just be turned on or off. It is the texture of social life, the complex pattern of power, exemption, advantage and preference, interwoven with inequality, marginalization and discrimination. Consequently, if privilege is to be seriously challenged, the entire fabric of society needs to be changed. Precisely what the 'Alt-Right' and other defenders of 'Western civilization' understood as a patriarchal, white European heritage are trying to stop.

Privilege, then, is closely linked to power, but this also means it has a direct link to *authority*. This is an important distinction to make because while power can be expressed as either strength or force, when it is most effective, it has a sense of legitimacy and authority and is said to be 'hegemonic'. This term was developed by Antonio Gramsci to explain the creation of consent and leadership within a political system (1971: 57). It was a theoretical response to Karl Marx who had claimed the inherent contradictions of capitalism, especially the one between capital and labour, would eventually spell the demise of the system. Gramsci was therefore looking to explain why this hadn't happened. He concluded the reason lay in people giving their consent to authority, and consent being 'formed through everyday experience illuminated by "common sense", i.e. by the traditional popular conception of the world' (1971: 199). In other words, if repeated often enough, people see a collection of often 'fragmentary' and 'incoherent' bits of 'folklore' (419), developed to suit the most powerful in society, as a completely consistent and natural way of doing things. In this way, privilege is closely linked to *authorship* and the *authorial voice*. It's about what stories get told, who gets to tell them and how widely and regularly they are circulated. These stories range from the art consecrated in our galleries and museums, to the literature that forms the canon, or from the events that become our recorded history, to the reporting that shapes our current affairs.

Who speaks and what gets told are therefore crucial. This is why history is such a battleground, and I don't mean history as the record of wars. The writing of history itself is a battle – a cultural battle – over whose stories are privileged. Amids all the physical violence that takes place in Palestine, for example, it is storytelling that remains the most urgent problem. The Palestinian-American theorist, Edward Said (1984), wrote a compelling essay called 'Permission to Narrate' that encapsulated the primacy of stories even in a land so scarred by violence against person and property. In that essay he made the observation that the greatest disadvantage for Palestinians is that while they are there in the country, their story is not (30) and 'has never been officially admitted' (33). After the UN vote in 1947 that partitioned Palestine and led to the creation of the state of Israel in 1948, popular history and mainstream media have given primacy to the narrative that the land has always belonged to Israel, such that the Palestinian narrative of also belonging to that land either doesn't get heard or is seen as an attempt to usurp the Israeli story that was there first. Without an alternative story to make sense of their displacement, struggle and resistance it will always be seen as aggression.

This leads to one other very important point. History as the form of institutionalized storytelling is crucial to the common sense way we think about the present and the future. As a consequence, history is a specific form of legitimating authority. This means history isn't just an account of the past but a particular construction of it that plays an important role in establishing what is right and proper in the present. The logic states: 'this is how it has been, so this is how it should be now.' It is what Raymond Williams, called 'the selective tradition' (2006: 32–40). History, in essence, is the selection and interpretation of the past based on the present we wish to preserve, with a view to the future we want to project. Of course, the 'we' here is the group or groups of people with the most privileged access to storytelling and also with the greatest investment in things remaining the same. For example, the conservative nature of British culture is preserved in part by the writing of British history as continuity, stability and the benign extension of civilization. Those in power want a compliant population susceptible to the maintenance of legitimate authority still dominated by a vision of beneficent white, male, Christian mission no matter how much it might present itself as multicultural and inclusive. To do this, British history is written as a story of unbroken monarchy, the wars that protected that heritage and, in turn, supported the development of the greatest trading nation on earth. As a consequence, we are happy to wave little flags at an equally diminutive monarch and publicly fund her position.

There are, of course, numerous histories of Britain that could be written, which includes one primarily focused on rebellion, refusal and dissent. British history is filled with instances of revolt and non-compliance from Boudica to Emeline Pankhurst, from the Peasants' Revolt to the Notting Hill and Toxteth riots, from Mary Shelley to Alan Turing. Still, wherever possible, these instances of rebellion and non-conformity are recuperated to support the story of the long development of liberal democracy in order that their radical or disruptive potential is dampened down. If we were to write the history of Britain or any other country as a history of legitimate dissent against entrenched privilege, we would make opposition and dissent more acceptable in the present and revolution more likely in the future, but this is precisely what power and privilege guard against. Stories are potentially dangerous things that need careful policing and shepherding.

This is why an essential part of cultural and political activism is the recovery of histories that were lost beneath the constant drone of the dominant account of canonical authors or were actively suppressed as illegitimate, invalid, unworthy or potentially seditious. It is simply not the case that there weren't women scientists (Swaby 2015), writers, sculptors or painters, that there weren't stories that told the incredible lives of people of colour (Painter 2006) or written accounts that set out alternative experiences of gender and sexuality (Houlbrook 2005). These stories have always been there but struggled to be seen or heard in a society privileging the voices of white, straight men. For women, people of colour, gay and trans people, the working class, communities broken by the creation of nations and their arbitrary borders, for first peoples made derelict by colonialism, there have to be stories that speak positively and affirmatively about their experiences if they are to imagine a future for themselves not limited by those with the power to set the record (Dunbar-Ortiz 2014).

'Women's History Month' and 'Black History Month' create these spaces but also clearly show how much this storytelling remains the exception to the rest of the schedule of programmes or calendar of events. The United States and many other countries have 'Black History Month' because the other eleven have traditionally privileged a view of the past written by white European colonists, and the effects of that history writing cannot be challenged without specific time being given to the active recovery and reconstruction of evidence supporting alternative views of the past that have lain hidden and been marginalized. These are cultural pockets where different voices are allowed to speak, author their own history and, with that, have a significant impact on both present and future experience. They are of such importance in the fight against privilege that those who are out to protect it will do anything to shut them down. Among the Alt-Right/Lite and their conservative allies, anyone attempting to think outside the limits set by privilege is dismissed and ridiculed as 'PC' or 'woke'.

This defensive attitude can also be seen in the faux language of universality and fairness that is often used to protect privilege. Of note here was a proposed piece of legislation (House Bill 2120) introduced by Arizona Representative, Bob Thorpe, that would ban courses, activities and events at universities designed primarily for a specific ethnic group or that 'promote social justice towards a race'. This is in addition to a law passed in 2011 that prevented public schools in the state doing the same. This was presented as a law intending to stop the expression of 'resentment towards a race' and thereby claimed to be rooted in social equity; and yet it is clearly intended to do the very opposite and preserve existing structures of privilege by making it illegal to address them by paying particular attention to specific histories.

Given that universities are really just large repositories of stories and actively manage their dissemination, the nature of such a law is clear.

Thus, another key feature of privilege, as it relates to power and positions of social dominance, is that it assumes *neutrality* or *objectivity*, which also gives us one way of understanding why people might be privilege blind. On this topic, Richard Dyer's *White* is especially helpful because he starts by pointing out that twenty years ago 'white' had never been questioned or studied because race is traditionally something only applied to non-white people (1997: 1). Today there are, of course, plenty of examples of white people asserting the unique and superior qualities of the white race, but outside of explicitly racial politics, being white is and always has been particularly unremarkable. In other words, people of colour are 'marked, raced, whereas the white man has attained the position of being without properties, unmarked, universal, just human' (38).

For example, I am old enough to remember that when people of colour were first given the chance to speak on TV or radio they were primarily asked to speak for the community, people or issue they were supposed to represent.[2] In my lifetime I have therefore seen the beginning of a shift from white people talking about and for people of colour, to people of colour speaking for themselves. This was a significant and positive change, but for many years people from 'minorities' were only called upon to speak about 'minority' issues. A black man or woman would be called on to contribute to a discussion, but only because they were asked to speak about racism or racial discrimination. In other words, they were viewed as speaking from (and, indeed, only able to legitimately speak from) a specific position. Over the years, this has changed again, and we have gradually seen a diverse range of commentators speaking about matters of general interest. This is progress for a number of reasons, but in terms of privilege it is incredibly significant because white men and white people more broadly have assumed that only we can speak from this position of generality, as if we float above the world like gods.

Greater diversity or better representation in our media is unsettling to the Alt-Right/Lite and other Identitarian conservatives because it disrupts the assumed naturalness of their unremarkable universality. This explains the response of some white people to a film like *Black Panther*, which was not only explicit about its politics but also used a largely black cast to deliver it. For some white people, this was a cause of anxiety because it functioned as a significant moment of defamiliarization, interrupting the ideological steps that usually link white, normal and natural in a totally unproblematic way. This is akin to what Samuel Gaertner et al. (2005) call 'aversive racism' or the tension whereby people who ordinarily deny personal prejudice nevertheless still encounter unconscious negative feelings with regard to people of colour. This also returns us to the link between privilege and authority because while aversive racists might be happy to see a black man or woman in a film, indeed they may even think it is good, there are very specific limits that they set to the appropriateness of black representation. On this, Barbara Perry notes: 'From the dominant, white perspective, there are appropriate ways for subaltern groups to construct their race or gender or sexuality, ways that do not impinge on white male power. The problem arises when members of these groups resist – or are seen to resist – these externally applied criteria and opt to construct themselves according to their own images and ideals' (Perry 2001: 2).

The main point to take from this, however, is that despite the evidence of persistent inequalities relating to gender, ethnicity, sexuality and disability in terms of pay, housing, violence, incarceration, education and health, because white people, and specifically white men, regard themselves in neutral terms they cannot see what is specific or particularly advantaged about their own experience. Without the specific characteristics that are attributed to women, people of colour or members of the LGBTQ community, white men cannot see what it is that gives us any advantage. As Dyer notes: 'Having no content, we can't see that we have anything that accounts for our position of privilege and power' (1997: 9) and, in turn, 'white people unable to see their particularity, cannot take account of other people's' (9). This is the main reason the category 'white' has received so little attention. It is assumed to be natural and therefore transparent.

By contrast, colonialism wasn't just the physical confiscating of land and the subjugation of non-white people; it was the careful, deliberate and systematic construction of characteristics, marked by 'blackness' or 'brownness', that were attributable to the subjugated people's 'nature', such that the confiscation and subjugation were seen as legitimate. The colonized were presented as backward, primitive, savage, enfeebled, stupid, ignorant and in numerous other ways lacking the essential qualities of the colonizers. The image of the 'black', 'Indian', 'native' and 'oriental' are ideas created by white people and carefully set out in art, literature, science and other forms of storytelling comprehensively documented in Edward Said's *Orientalism* (1978).[3] This clearly disadvantages people of colour who have to overcome a range of deep-rooted cultural prejudices that white people don't face. This experience is an important factor in the long counter-history of stories about the meaning of 'black'. It is an effort to resist the process of 'othering' set out so clearly by Frantz Fanon in *Black Skin, White Masks*. In that book he famously recounts what he calls 'third-person consciousness' (1986: 110), revealed in the moment a white French child sees him and shouts to his mother that he's scared by the sight of a black man. Fanon writes about the feeling of having the image of his own body handed back to him but in an alien and distorted form. The child's vision was pre-loaded with the images of discrimination and prejudice.[4] The child did not see what Fanon sees but something else, strange and threatening.

Privilege is not having this happen to you but also assuming this doesn't happen to others. By extension we can say that a central feature of privilege is saying something isn't relevant, isn't true or isn't a problem because it isn't a problem for us. This is explained really well by Robin Diangelo in response to a woman in a workshop who claimed she didn't see 'race'. Diangelo was co-leading the workshop with a colleague who replied, 'Then how will you see racism?' Diangelo continues:

> He then explained to her that he was black, he was confident that she could see this, and that race meant that he had a very different experience in life than she did. If she were ever going to understand or challenge racism, she would need to acknowledge this difference. Pretending that she did not notice that he was black was not helpful to him in any way, as it denied his reality – indeed, it refused his reality – and kept hers insular and unchallenged. This pretense that she did not notice his race assumed that he was 'just like her', and in doing so, she projected her reality onto him. (2018: 42)

Michael Kimmel encapsulates this invisibility and the unacknowledged advantage of privilege in his use of the Chinese proverb that states: 'the fish are the last to discover the ocean' (2005: 5). You'd think we ought to be able to see the cultural, social, political and economic conditions that help sustain us, but as, I've noted already, our world appears so 'normal' and 'natural' that it disappears or withdraws into the background of everyday life. This is why the stories that might give us an understanding of how privilege is finely tuned across various areas of social life are extremely important. Checking your privilege is a difficult transition for us, white, straight, middle class, able-bodied men to have to take, which is one reason we push back or simply refuse to budge. We are unacknowledged narcissists that love being the centre of everything; and yet, we're being asked to support a Copernican revolution. It hardly needs saying that this experience is one that generates a profound sense of anxiety.

We can see traces of this if we return to the issue of what is considered *normal*. The word is derived from the Latin *norma*, which referred to a measuring device known as the carpenter's square but primarily means precept, rule or law. The norm is a very powerful social tool because it establishes what is acceptable and proper. Those who have the privilege of being normal also have the power to set the rules regarding which ways of living are moral and ethical, and by extension right and natural. The acceptable, the proper, the moral, the ethical, the right, the natural, this is how we understand what is normal, and this is the domain of privilege. This means that in the struggles that take place over how we think we should live, the privileged are in possession of the heavy artillery. In this capacity we can say that the realm of the privileged is the 'normative' because it sets itself up as the measure and model for acceptable behaviour. Through the establishment and maintenance of rules, privilege ensures its particular way of being in the world is *the* way of being in the world. These norms have also been established for such a long time that their prejudices are deeply entrenched and very hard to expose, let alone disarm.

The power of what is normal is therefore masked by its sheer normality. The norm is absolutely not exceptional. It is usual, quotidian, mundane and even boring. This is why people have difficulty criticizing it. They often think of it not in terms of establishing rules of behaviour but simply what average people commonly and naturally do. There is, then, an unperceived slippage from value to fact; and yet, think of its opposite and the dark heart of normality is immediately revealed. The 'abnormal' is something, which at the very best we treat with suspicion; but, in most cases, the abnormal is targeted for policing, disciplining, punishing, abusing, killing, stigmatizing, excluding, banishing, suppressing, restraining, incarcerating, mocking, correcting or curing. Also, as Michel Foucault (1999) showed us, the institutions of the abnormal are the clinic, the hospital, the asylum, the prison and the camp. The abnormal is also deemed the diseased, the perverted and the monstrous. The abnormal is the horror we cast out. Unnatural and ungodly, the abnormal is open to all manner of supposedly legitimate violence. So, instead of thinking about privilege as some really unremarkable realm of normality, think about its capacity for producing monsters based on nothing but its own sense of entitlement to do so.

As a consequence of continually casting out monsters and purging the abnormal, privilege (and its fantasy) is able to bask in the light of its own glory. Denying any difference it does not condone, privilege creates the world in its own image. This means privilege is the assurance that the world remains a perfectly reflective surface upon which we see an ideal image of ourselves, free of refraction or distortion. Another way of saying this is that privilege is never seeing yourself represented in a way that doesn't agree with the image you already have of yourself. To be privileged is to be assured that wherever you go and whatever media you interact with, you will see yourself reproduced. At worst, you will see an image of what you aspire to be. Like Narcissus, we stare at our perfectly reproduced image until we die, having tasked numerous agencies to remove anyone that might interrupt or disturb our self-love. The problem today is that some of those people trying to disturb the peace are getting through, and the Alt-Right/Lite think they need putting back in their place.

Challenging privilege

In January 2020 an episode on the BBC current affairs programme, *Question Time*, encapsulated the complex issues surrounding privilege. The programme's format has a panel of politicians, journalists and notable members of the public who answer questions from a live audience. For this episode, one of the panel members was Laurence Fox, an actor of minor celebrity from a family of successful actors that includes father, James, and uncle, Edward. One of the issues they were asked to discuss was the treatment the Royal Family member, Meghan Markle, received in the press, which many believed to have been motivated by racism. The key to this segment of the programme was the exchange between Fox and audience member Rachel Boyle, an academic from Edge Hill University who researches race and racism and its effects on education and is herself a woman of colour. 'The problem', she said, 'is that Meghan has agreed to be Harry's wife, and the press have torn her to pieces. Let's be really clear about what this is. Let's call it by its name. It's racism. She's a black woman and she has been torn to pieces.' Fox's response was immediate denial, saying that Britain is 'the most tolerant, lovely country in Europe', before continuing: 'It's so easy to throw the card of racism at everybody and it's really starting to get boring now.'

So, the first response from Fox was to deny racism is an issue but also reject the idea that a woman of colour who professionally researches the matter might be a more reliable authority. His second response was to refuse the offer to reflect and simply condemn her concerns as 'boring'. As I have already noted, privilege assumes the right to decide and privilege declares what might or might not be of interest or relevant. Fox encapsulated this arrogance. Hence, Boyle's next remark was perfectly correct. 'What worries me about your comment' she replied, 'is you are a white privileged male who has no experience in this.' Outraged that someone might suggest he is speaking from a particular position, let alone a privileged one, Fox immediately countered, saying, 'I can't help what I am, I was born like this, it's an immutable characteristic, so to call me a white privileged male is to be racist: you're being racist.' Here, in a discussion about how even a wealthy woman of colour might still be subject to racism, Fox centres himself as a victimized white man and shuts down the conversation. In this exchange, he not only utterly confirmed Boyle's charge of white male privilege but also demonstrated he had no idea what privilege means.

Privilege is absolutely not a biological condition but a social one that privileges, in the case of racism, certain biological characteristics. The accusation of white male privilege is a request to consider how you might be blind to the fact that the experiences of women and people of colour might be different from your own. It isn't automatically a charge of racism in and of itself. Instead, the injunction to 'check your privilege' is a call to reflect on the matter and through such reflection demonstrate you are in fact not racist or can commit to challenging racism. Fox abjectly and embarrassingly failed to do this. However, he did discover that being a minor Alt-Lite celebrity got him attention and he toured a few TV studios condemning 'diversity' – in particular attacking Sam Mendes film *1917* for including Sikh soldiers alongside British soldiers before acknowledging, in the truest style of white male privilege, that he didn't know what he was talking about. Shortly after, news stories circulated claiming he had left Twitter and pictured him in a resigned pose playing his guitar with a sad face.

Rachel Boyle's challenge of Laurence Fox questioned his assumed authority, his affected neutrality or objectivity and his conception of the world. Such challenges regularly produce hostile responses, but these responses are most profound when challenges to privilege – as they ultimately always do – challenge the myth that our society is *meritocratic* and those at the top deserve to be there. By myth, I don't mean something from the realm of legend and fantasy – although the idea that our society is meritocratic is certainly a fantastic one – I mean myth in Roland Barthes's sense of a deep-rooted and well-established ideology that helps us make sense of who we are. Myth, here, is a form of 'depoliticised speech' that takes something historical and created and gives it 'a natural justification, [. . .] making contingency appear eternal' (Barthes 1972: 142). Again, it becomes common sense, and as such it fades into the background as an uninterrogated assumption. The meritocratic myth encourages us to believe our society is egalitarian, when in reality it supports and supposedly justifies rampant inequality. Simply put, merit is to the class system what karma is to the caste system. This, of course, also applies to racial and gender hierarchies as much as it does to class because the primary function of meritocratic discourse is to present injustice as justice. Meritocracy regularly summons up ideals of fairness and a so-called level playing field, when in reality it is used to legitimize the products of social advantage as things that have been gained simply through talent or hard work.

The etymology of merit comes from the Latin *merere* meaning to earn or deserve, which is in turn the root of the Greek *meros*, meaning a share, portion or allotment. This provides the basic formula of meritocracy that what you deserve equals what you get. We are told, then, that in a meritocracy people get what they deserve, and what they deserve is what they supposedly earn through virtues like courage, diligence, application, commitment, dedication, resilience and ingenuity. Crucially, the ideology of merit will rarely be used to ask if we are doing enough to enable as many as possible to succeed or to question why some are able to get ahead and others aren't. Quite the contrary, when meritocracy is evoked, it is used to claim equality and fairness already exist, and that those who have succeeded have done so out of some natural ability that sets them apart. Rather than bring these people down, we are told, we must celebrate their special qualities or innate talent and, therefore, their right to what they have. So, rather than advocate for the equality that true meritocracy demands, we celebrate the natural differences and distinctions it supposedly reveals and take these to be the ideal instead. In this way, while meritocracy in political discourse is often presented as a philosophy that advocates for the many, it is in reality a myth that protects the few. In other words, we deploy the language of meritocracy not to ensure those without get something but to justify what those with everything have already got.

Meritocracy is therefore highly aristocratic. This becomes even more evident when we understand that the etymology of merit additionally gives us the root of the Greek word *moros*, meaning fate or destiny, and hence *moirai*, the three goddesses we also know as The Fates. According to the logic of the meritocrats, a society is fair if it enables people with predisposed, inherent and natural abilities to rise to the top. In other words, we should create a society that allows the naturally talented to secure their destiny, and because they argue the naturally talented do rise to the top, their merited success reinforces the fairness of a differentiated, class-based society that allows the best to 'shine'. As with the Greek concept of *moros*, the proponents of meritocracy believe that what someone deserves is already written in the stars due to the blessing of some God-given or genetic ability. This is no different from Socrates's justification of aristocracy in *The Republic*, where people are born with either a gold, silver or bronze soul that determines in advance their social station.

In Greek, *aristos* means the best; hence, aristocracy is asserted to be the rule of the best, and it is their destiny or lot in life to do so. Challenging privilege is therefore crucial for creating the real, substantial democracy we have so far failed to build. Our society has remained riddled with the hierarchies of early stages of history. Despite boastful claims about equality, we still live in a world riven with aristocratic advantage. Fully aware of this, we sit and watch shows like *Downton Abbey*, the modern equivalent of the medieval Great Chain of Being and bathe in the ideological comfort of a supposedly legitimate, paternal and truly caring elite who maintain perfect, virtuous order. It is also worth noting that the variety of groups aligned under the banner of the radical right are deeply opposed to any challenge to meritocracy precisely because it directly challenges aristocracy, and aristocratic assumptions of superiority and supremacy remain essential to their claims about the legitimacy of their social and political privilege. For example, the paleoconservative, Paul Gottfried, who first coined the term 'alternative right' 'ardently believed that inequality is the natural state of things and that efforts to overcome it amounted to a kind of tyranny' (Neiwert 2017: 237).

Contrary to the idea that merit is inherent and therefore permanent, Sartre, in *Anti-Semite and Jew*, argued 'merit has to be sought, just like truth; it is discovered with difficulty; one must deserve it. Once acquired, it is perpetually in question: a false step, an error, and it flies away. Without respite, from the beginning of our lives to the end, we are responsible for what merit we enjoy.' Then, commenting on the anti-Semite's assumption of racial superiority, he writes: 'Now the anti-Semite flees responsibility as he flees his own consciousness, and choosing for his personality the permanence of rock, he chooses for his morality a scale of petrified values' (19). The advantage here is that 'there is nothing I have to do to merit my superiority, and neither can I lose it. It is given once and for all. It is a thing' (18). For the white supremacist, then, they deserve everything simply for being white.

Ultimately, this aristocratic assumption within the discourse of meritocracy actually means we commit fewer resources to egalitarian projects and more to structures of distinction, such that children from an early age are divided into different ability 'streams'. Here, it just so happens that the most privileged kids tend to be the most 'talented' and have the brightest futures, and the most socially disadvantaged are those 'sadly' destined to a life of menial and precarious labour. The privileged therefore love the idea that we live in a meritocracy because we like to think we are where we are because we earned it. We love to recount how we deserve what we've got, but privilege is the very opposite of merit defined as something deserved or earned. Privilege is rather what Alison Bailey called 'unearned assets' (1998: 107). Thus, when us alpha-privileged folk recount our epic stories of everyday heroism, we forget the bit about how the position from which our story started was way beyond all the really treacherous terrain and brutal monsters that await those who start out on the journey from a lot further back. It's like we joined the marathon for the last mile, but we still take the tape, the medal, the shiny thermal blanket and the revitalizing drink. Then, while gasping for air and with sweat pouring off our titanic brows, we look straight to camera and let everyone know how our bodies were screaming at us to stop, but our noble spirit just refused to give up.

The sleight of hand played by the myth of meritocracy, then, is the belief that we have attained social status or economic success based on our own very special and personal talent; and it is here that we arrive at the most sacred part of our identity. We build our sense of self from a wide constellation of things that includes our taste in music, choice of football team, diet, national and regional pride, religious faith, job status and area of work, income, place of residence, hobbies and places travelled, but in all of this there is some sense of contingency. What grounds or anchors us, what is absolute, is that whoever I am and whatever I have achieved it is because I have earned it. This becomes the kernel of our sense of self. It is the essence of the 'good boy', the 'clever boy' my mother told me I was. It is the person that Jesus loves; the bit that I was told will go to heaven when I'm dead. It's the superhero beneath the National Health glasses, the fearless action man I imagined myself to be when I was seven. It is an internalized, ideal image of the special person we think we are. Deep inside us, then, is this little statue, a shiny, perfect, sacred object set on a pedestal in our little Temple of Holy Talent, and talk of privilege rather than merit, social advantage rather than just deserts, threatens to break down the doors of the temple and smash that little statue to pieces. It is not surprising, then, that challenges from 'libtards' and 'social justice warriors' are met with hostility and even violence from those expecting a chufty badge simply for being white. Threatening the inner sanctum and dislodging the little idol sends us tumbling into the abyss.

However, when calling meritocracy a myth, I initially said it doesn't refer to the realm of fantasy; but, in the psychoanalytic sense of the term, it does. According to the philosopher Slavoj Žižek, it is the fantasy of this perfect, idealized self that structures and 'coordinates' (2005: 304) every aspect of our reality. In a similar vein to the analysis in Chapter 4, the world of meanings, values and references, or what Žižek calls the symbolic, provides us with a place and an identity, beneath which there is no prior essence or substance. The important psychological and ideological function of fantasy is to fill in this absence, lack or void with a projection of self that substantiates our self and our world, and gives it a sense of reality (Žižek 2006: 57). Žižek goes further and suggests that this projection of an innate quality that we confidently declare has been there all along, lets us imagine we were present at our own conception.

This supposedly natural quality allows us to '"jump into the past" and appear as [our] own cause' (2002: 211), to call ourselves self-starters who don't and never did need anything from society. It thereby makes nonsense of any talk of advantage. This fantasy, then, is at the very heart of who us privileged folk think we are. It determines our sense of self and our view of others. It also governs our perceptions of threat because if we lose this idealized self-image, or even if it is tarnished by some unfounded gossip about privilege, we are left with very little to substantiate our world and we will project all manner of violent intent against the perpetrators of such sacrilege – something ably demonstrated by Laurence Fox. In the critique of privilege, whether that is claims about the advantages of masculinity, whiteness or any other socially dominant position, all roads lead to this little temple.

Privilege is therefore about authority, legitimacy, presumed neutrality, normality and merit. It is both the unmarked and unpositioned but also the distinct and the special. The critique of privilege, therefore, undoes all these one by one and can have the most devastating effect on the place we have taken and the status we have assumed. Given that this critique emerges out of struggles against elitism, sexism, homophobia, racism and xenophobia, it is a direct challenge to the straight, white, Christian man and his household. It should therefore be no surprise that the fascist ideologies that reaffirm white supremacy, aristocracy, heterosexuality, virile masculinity, Christian mission and ethno-nationalism are finding particular favour at the moment.

However, this raises two significant problems. The first is that the backlash against social progress is very strong, exacerbated by the current economic system that negatively affects a very broad swathe of the population. It makes those at the bottom increasingly more vulnerable, but it also places an ever-growing burden on the middle classes whose lives have become increasingly precarious. In these conditions, a form of politics claiming it can counter any loss of advantage or even more significantly claiming it can give it back is going to appear very attractive. Second, resistance to the rise of the Alt-Right demands a continued critique of privilege, which in turn requires the support of those who are most economically vulnerable. In other words, it requires people who seemingly have little material means to understand how they might still be advantaged in some way.

This therefore necessitates one final observation about privilege. Although class remains extremely important, the critique of privilege as it is currently used emerges from a much more diversified sense of politics understood to be intersectional (Pease 2010: 17). This is a term coined by Kimberlé Crenshaw to refer to the way that contemporary politics takes place within a context where a range of issues relating to class, gender, race, ethnicity, sexuality and disability intersect. What is important here is to dispel, for example, 'assumptions that race and gender are essentially separate categories' (Crenshaw 1991: 1244) or that any one category might take precedence over another. In particular, this was a challenge to a particular form of white feminism that failed to understand how gender and 'race' intersected for black women and how their lived experience was radically different from that of the white (invariably middle class) feminists. Thinking in intersectional terms means that while you might be disadvantaged as a woman, you may still be privileged in terms of your race and class. As Pease notes, 'an intersectional model recognises that different oppressions are distinct, but acknowledges that they are interrelated and mutually reinforcing' (2010: 18); while this opens up a more sophisticated way to think about structural oppression, it also explains the inherent difficulty in identity politics. Because identity is based on a number of different positions (race, ethnicity, gender, sexuality, class, religion and nation), 'different members of oppressed people may be pulled in different directions' (Pease 2010: 20), as is the case with white working-class men turning away for class-based politics to white, ethno-nationalism. On the subject of class, then, what some people find hard to accept is that if you are materially less well off or even relatively poor, if you are a white man, you still hold a privileged position in relation to race and gender, or rather won't experience the additional disadvantages faced by women or people of colour on low income.

This understanding of privilege is of the utmost importance if a politics is to be built that opposes the violent, discriminatory and divisive politics of the far-right in favour of a more universal politics that reaffirms equality and freedom. To do this, though, it is imperative that we understand domination, supremacy and privilege as the primary problem and resolve to understand the particularity of all its manifestations across class, race, gender, sexuality, generation, disability and religion. In 2001 Elizabeth Shüssler Fiorenza suggested using the term 'kyriarchy' to refer to the array of socially dominant positions. Rather than simply the rule of the father (patriarchy), Fiorenza was trying to capture and challenge the rule of the master (*kyrios* in Greek) across various social domains. I am, as yet, unsure how effective the term is, but it does point to the reality that it is domination through assumed superiority that is the problem. Consequently, if we are to continue to advocate for progressive politics, we absolutely must deal with the economic inequality that increasingly plagues our society and makes people especially susceptible to false promises of empowerment from hate-mongers. Part of the problem with doing that, however, is the subject of Chapter 8 where the epistemological precarity of our 'post-truth' age makes it even more difficult to separate fact from fiction in the attempt to build the much needed alternative socio-economic system.

8

Truth or epistemological precarity

One of the most significant factors in the current social and political climate is the turn towards 'post-truth'. The contemporaneity of this term is suggested by the fact the Oxford Dictionary voted it their international word of the year in 2016, the same year the dissembling, fabricating and falsifying Donald Trump became president of the United States. At the start of the next year, Trump, or more specifically his most vociferous surrogate, Kellyanne Conway, introduced us to post-truth's close relative, 'alternative facts', when she claimed that White House Press secretary Sean Spicer's false claims about the size of Trump's inauguration crowd were, in fact, true if judged by some fabled data they had spontaneously imagined. Media talk of a small crowd then introduced us to the third term of the post-truth triumvirate, 'fake news'. Of course, we were never introduced to what the 'alternative facts' were that countered the 'fake news', the phrases simply introduced the idea that the White House was from now on going to live in its own cognitive and perceptual universe, and it was the story of this other realm that it was going to tell.

This multiplication of realities coupled with the glut of information and the unregulated media through which that information spreads is another element in the constellation of precarity that defines the early twenty-first century. Such epistemological precarity, however, needs to be understood in a number of ways. First, it manifests as an uncertainty about what to believe and who to trust and is therefore highly corrosive of the social fabric; second, the destabilization of evidence-based argument decreases our ability to counter the circulation of information threatening the life of democracy (and, indeed, the planet) and third, misinformation is being actively used by powerful people as a means of distraction, obfuscation and confusion. In the words of Steve Bannon, the aim is to 'flood the zone with shit' (Balkissoon 2018).

However, while the specific characteristics of the current scenario make it new, it is wrong to treat this as an entirely novel phenomenon. The present assault on veracity is a variation and perhaps an intensification of methods that are as old as politics itself. After all, few would consider propaganda as the harbinger of truth; just as few would argue that propaganda is alien to liberal, capitalist democracies. Nor are people naïve enough to think that powerful corporate agendas are secured through absolute honesty and full disclosure. We also seem to have become comfortable with the now-common refrain that the first casualty of war is the truth – an expression reportedly coined by US senator Hiram W. Johnson in 1918. More recently, the phrase 'economical with the truth', attributed to the British politician Sir Robert Armstrong in 1986, was useful enough to find other willing adopters; but, as Margaret Canovan (1990) has shown, this thrifty approach to the truth has a pedigree going back at least to the eighteenth century and Edmund Burke's own advocacy of an 'economy of truth' as a necessary means to prevent social disorder. This variation on the conservative conception of the 'noble lie' is of quite a different order to Bannon's desire to 'flood the zone with shit', but understanding the history of either economizing with truth or blocking it with an excess of effluent information is crucial if we are to understand the current challenge and the dangers it poses.

Having said that, what *is* perhaps new is the technology through which the current maelstrom of disinformation travels, as is the supposed leader of the free world adopting mantras from the dictator's playbook by calling the press 'the enemy of the people'. To unpack the cluster of issues that are deepening our epistemological precarity, it will be necessary to offer a brief overview of the history of post-truth, which will include the discrediting of or wilful abuse of expertise, before addressing the political economy of traditional media and the nature of our attention economy in an age of 'info-glut' (Andrejevic 2013). In such a situation, as Julian Baggini has argued, the problem 'is not the absence of truth, but its overabundance' (2017: 14).

A pre-history of post-truth

The concept of a post-truth age contains a set of ideas, practices and dispositions that need to be carefully worked out. First of all, as Baggini (2017) has noted, post-truth does not mean people any longer believe in, value or seek the truth. For him, the opposite is the case. For many, it is still 'essential to living well' (2), and they 'remain outraged by lies' (6). However, he does believe there is something specific to our current time that makes truth especially elusive but suggests rather than being a permanent feature of our lives we might consider it a temporary moment, a kind of 'cultural convulsion born of despair' (9). The source of this despair stems from a variety of problems pertaining to knowledge, information and media, but it is crucial for a proper understanding of our epistemological precarity, so it will need careful exposition. In doing this, it is also worth bearing in mind

Baggini's protest that 'the claim we live in a post-truth world is the most pernicious untruth of them all. It serves the interest of those who have the most to fear from truth' (10). As already noted, he rightly argues that the truth remains important to people, so our critical assessment should avoid any cynical resignation to the condition because that will only help those seeking to weaponize the problem.

As Baggini has carefully argued, one of the difficulties in defining what *post-truth* is arises from a preceding problem establishing what *truth* is. In his introduction to the question, *A Short History of Truth*, he discusses a number of ways we think about what is true. These include eternal truths, or the word of a divine creator; authoritative truths, or the word of discipline-based experts; esoteric truths, or the hidden knowledge known to only the enlightened; reasoned truths, or the necessary connection of concepts; empirical truths, or the correspondence between an idea and an object or an event; creative truths, or making something so through a performative utterance (as in 'I declare this bridge open); relative truths, or truth based on perspective and environment; powerful truths, or truth promoted by vested interests; moral truth, or the belief in what is right and just and holistic truth, or ideas that are dependent on other ideas to create a secure theory. For our purposes here, while all of these versions of truth bear on our current predicament, it is perhaps the jettisoning of empirical truth that is the most disturbing element. As Lee McIntyre (2018) argues in another useful, if problematic book, post-truth primarily represents the abandonment of objective facts. In this sense 'truth has been eclipsed' (5), subverted or become irrelevant.

The type of subversion that is happening today, however, has a pre-history in the commercial manipulation of scientific evidence. Corporations were able to exploit a weakness in scientific method that is paradoxically also its strength. As Baggini explains, 'the strength of empirical truth resides in the fact that it is always open to scrutiny, revision and rejection' (2017: 56). This is in keeping with Popper's famous definition of science as something that is falsifiable. On this topic, McIntyre concurs that scientific truth is never absolute, but always dependent on new data. A scientific theory is therefore a 'strongly warranted belief based on justification given the evidence' (2018: 19). In part this goes back to the problem of induction set out in David Hume's *Treatise on Human Nature* published in 1739. Induction is a way of knowing the world that moves from observable events to theories about those events, and according to Hume, the problem is twofold because we cannot assume a future event will be just like a past event or that the next event will have the same effect as the previous one. Theories based on previous events, no matter how many times they have been observed cannot say with absolute certainty that the next event will continue to 'prove' the theory correct, no matter how likely or probable it is. Scientific method provides very workable theories, but they are always dependent upon the next piece of data.

In the 1960s, this chink in the certainty of science was ruthlessly exploited first by companies producing sugar and then tobacco companies to undermine the science that linked both products to health issues. As Baggini notes, during the Second World War, the American Medical Association was already identifying sugar as a problem. To counter this information the Sugar Research Foundation was set up in 1943, and by the 1960s, it was found to have 'paid three Harvard scientists to downplay the association between sugar consumption and heart disease and point the finger at saturated fat instead' (2017: 79). This technique then became an art form when the tobacco industry did everything it could to promote the idea that the link between smoking and cancer was inconclusive, a matter set out in detail in *Merchants of Doubt* by Naomi Oreskes and Eric Conway. The ploy by the tobacco industry was to use the inherent uncertainty of science to keep repeating that the link between smoking and increased rates of mortality were not proven or were not conclusive. For Robert N. Proctor, this is an example of *agnogenesis* or 'manufactured ignorance' (2008: 11).[1] He says that 'the industry's standards for proof are so high that nothing in this world could satisfy them' (17–18). Here, we enter the strange situation where the tobacco industry is using science to effectively demand it be unscientific in its declaration of absolute certainty. Proctor goes on to note that 'the industry eventually recognized itself as a manufacturer of two separate, but codependent products: cigarettes and *doubt*' (17). This is, of course, the technique adopted by the fossil fuel industry in relation to the science of climate change, a practice especially associated with the Heartland Institute (McIntyre 2018: 27). Here, 'calls for precision play out as prevarication' (Proctor 2008: 20). In the end, Proctor asks us to remember that 'ignorance has a history and is always unevenly distributed' (26).

Such a cynical use of counter-evidence, however, does not dismiss the belief that there can be alternative facts. As a cultural studies scholar, I was trained to always look for facts that told a different history of colonialism, the role of women, the experiences of people of colour, the culture of the working class or unknown accounts of gay and lesbian lives, but as Baggini argues, these are not alternative facts, 'just *additional* facts we might have missed, or genuine facts that replace bogus facts' (2017: 76). I agree but would rather state this a little more strongly and say these are additional facts that have been wilfully ignored or are actively suppressed facts that replace dominant facts. However, when Kellyanne Conway spoke of 'alternative facts' she wasn't speaking as a cultural historian looking to share suppressed stories. Nor, as McIntyre notes, was she simply operating within the discourse of PR or in the mode of a spin doctor where facts are 'shaded, selected, and presented within a political context that favors one interpretation over another' (2018: 6). Rather, she was taking documented and objective facts (the known number of attendees at two presidential inaugurations) and using them to support a reality that did not exist. As Colleen McQuillen pointed out to me, such statements are not alternative facts, they are *counterfactual*. As McIntyre continues, 'when our intent is to manipulate someone into believing something *that we know to be untrue*, we have graduated from the mere "interpretation" of facts into their falsification' (8).

McIntyre goes on to summarize what he believes defines the current manifestation of post-truth. 'In its purest form', he writes, 'post-truth is when one thinks that the crowd's reaction actually *does* change the facts about a lie' (9). By this logic, every lie told on the campaign trail is transformed into a fact if it gets you elected. This is a new form of magic or political alchemy. It is, then, not surprising that in working such miracles of transubstantiation many of Trump's supporters treat him as the messiah. Coupled with this idea that belief is now the guarantor of truth, McIntyre notes a second feature of today's post-truth, namely, the rejection of 'the idea that *some things are true irrespective of how we feel about them*' (11). There has, of course, always been a relationship between truth and affect. This is registered in the common idiom that 'the truth is hard to swallow'. Most often the truth is a corrective to belief and therefore produces a sense of disorientation, disappointment or sadness, but today truth is solely measured by positive affect: if you like it and if it confirms or helps realize your world, then it is true. Ultimately, this leads to McIntyre's third feature of contemporary post-truth, which is a challenge not just to the idea of *knowing* reality but to the existence of reality itself' (10).

This is exemplified in a conspiracy theory called 'QAnon' that has become synonymous with Trump. While Trump himself is more than happy to promote an array of conspiracy theories (including Birtherism, Spygate, the Great Replacement, climate change as a Chinese hoax, voter fraud, the Seth Rich murder, Uranium One and the Clinton Body Count, to name just a few), QAnon is a new jigsaw puzzle in which all the parts relate to the Trump administration. It was started on the social media site 4Chan in October 2017, when someone called 'Q' – a moniker chosen because Q designates the level of clearance needed to see top secret information in the US Department of Energy – started dropping material about a deep state plan for a coup. This also included the Trump administration's strategy to expose a child trafficking ring run by liberal actors and politicians while also faking collusion with Russia to employ Robert Mueller to take down the plotters. Other than these details, it remains consistent with earlier far-right conspiracies in that it is anti-Semitic in its construction of the enemy as a globalist elite called 'The Cabal' and that this cabal will bring about the usual apocalyptic scenario that in this narrative is called 'The Storm'. However, what *is* interesting about this conspiracy theory is how it seems to perfectly reflect our post-truth moment. Rather than being a complete story, each of Q's 'drops' are picked up and interpreted by members of the movement who weave their own elements of the story and feed those back into the network as part of the ever-emerging reality, or as Ethan Zuckerman (2019) prefers to call it 'the Unreal'.

For Zukerman, the mentality of the conspiracy theorist – and of QAnon members in particular, who compete to offer the best new morsel of (un)reality – fits with the current zeitgeist because 'the conflict between Trump's reality and that of the mainstream media leads to the sense that we are no longer arguing a partisan battle over the interpretation of a common set of facts, but over facts from our own realities that both represent and lead inexorably to our own view point' (np). Zuckerman is a little lax with his use of facts here, which I think is especially unhelpful, but the crux of the matter is that the politics of the unreal is not an argument over something that is shared but a competition over which reality can be successfully asserted. In Zuckerman's words, the task is not 'to persuade someone of your interpretation of the facts, but to recruit them to your own reality' (np). In many respects, Trump's rallies function in this way. Unlike 'imaginary stations' such as Disneyland that Jean Baudrillard (1983) provocatively claimed have the function of adding a certain reality to the rest of America, Trump's rallies are oases of his alternative reality, where the diehard and newly baptized cognoscenti confirm the rest of America is fake.

Most importantly, in relation to the politics of post-truth, Zuckerman suggests that even if you aren't recruited to the reality being presented or persuaded by the interpretation of 'facts' being offered, 'a plurality of unreality [. . .] encourages the listener to doubt everything' (np). And just as Baggini argued that believing we really are in a post-truth age only benefits those who want to weaponize it, Zuckerman concurs, arguing 'those who benefit from the stasis caused by imposed doubt are those who are already in positions of power. Those who suffer the most are those who have been excluded from power. In that sense, unreality and the doubt it generates is an inherently conservative force' (np). This, together with the vulgar theatricality of Trump's various mediated performances, also brings to mind Peter Pomerantsev's (2015) work on Putin's 'political technologist' (78), Vladislav Surkov. Surkov is the 'grand vizier of the Kremlin court' (85) whose portfolios include 'ideology, media, political parties, religion, modernization, innovation, foreign relations and [. . .] modern art' (76). His function is to stage manage Kremlin politics like an avant-garde piece of performance art culminating in an election that includes an opposition of 'almost comical leaders' who are 'designed and funded in such a way as to actually strengthen the Kremlin' by making Putin seem like 'the only sane candidate' (49).

According to Pomerantsev, 'Surkov has directed Russian society like one great reality show' (77). It is total political control practised as a form of continual shapeshifting:

> The brilliance of this new type of authoritarianism is that instead of simply oppressing opposition [. . .] it climbs inside all ideologies and movements exploiting and rendering them absurd. One moment Surkov would fund civic forums and human rights NGOs, the next he would quietly support nationalist movements that accuse the NGOs of being tools of the West. With a flourish he sponsored lavish arts festivals for the most provocative modern artists in Moscow, then supported Orthodox fundamentalists, dressed all in black, and carrying crosses, who in turn attacked the modern art exhibitions. The Kremlin's idea is to own all forms of political discourse, to not let any independent movements develop outside of its walls. Its Moscow can feel like an oligarchy in the morning and a democracy in the afternoon, a monarchy for dinner and a totalitarian state by bedtime. (79)

This is further modelled through the state TV channel *Russia Today* that doesn't offer a counter-model to the West, like in the days of the Cold War, but is 'more about slipping inside its language to play and taunt it from the inside' (57).

Although the pantomime tribalism of Trump rallies lacks the subtlety of Surkov's detailed stage direction, they do have their own burlesque artistry aimed at sowing doubt and producing a sense of the unreal. The rallies are, of course, only one node in a wider disinformation project where the use of social media communication perhaps comes closer to Surkov's methods of misdirection and sleight of hand. This is a matter to which I will return below, but in terms of post-truth's pre-history the intended outcome is not very different from the aim of propaganda in the 1930s and 1940s that Hannah Arendt famously analysed. In *The Origins of Totalitarianism* she wrote: 'The most striking difference between ancient and modern sophists is that the ancients were satisfied with a passing victory of the argument at the expense of truth, *whereas the moderns want a more lasting victory at the expense of reality* [my italics]' (1968: 9). Later, in that same work, she writes in a manner that very much speaks to the function of the Trump rally in which all that was previously solid melts into air. On the ability and willingness to rewrite both the near and distant past and convince a crowd of the new reality, she had this to say:

> To this aversion [. . .] for official historiography, to its conviction that history, which was a forgery anyway, might as well be the playground of crackpots, must be added the terrible, demoralizing fascination in the possibility that gigantic lies and monstrous falsehoods can eventually be established as unquestionable facts, that man may be free to change his own past at will, and that the difference between truth and falsehood may cease to be objective and become a mere matter of power and cleverness, of pressure and infinite repetition. Not Stalin's and Hitler's skill in the art of lying but the fact that they were able to organize the masses into a collective unit to back up their lies with impressive magnificence, exerted the fascination. Simple forgeries from the viewpoint of scholarship appeared to receive the sanction of history itself when the whole marching reality of the movements stood behind them and pretended to draw from them the necessary inspiration for action. (333)

What is most disturbing in this quote is not the power of propaganda to brow beat a populace into submission, but the idea that people will 'back up' the propagandist, as if there is a desire to succumb to the unreality. What is most unsettling, then, about post-truth is that when coupled with the ontological precarity discussed in Chapter 4 it becomes especially effective. As people feel their world is under threat or their life is losing its way in the face of other interpretations about how we should live and what is meaningful, there is a desire to hold on to and even amplify (give 'magnificence' to) the message that re-substantiates our world and makes it feel real.

McIntyre reports how this need for confirmation is an interesting feature of psychological experiments designed to examine how and when people alter or adapt what they know. Working with a basic premise of human psychology, one developed by Freud to explain the phenomena of repression and projection, it is understood that we always try to maintain psychic equilibrium. If something disturbs the balance, we try to remove it from our conscious mind (repression) or express it outwards (projection) at some offending object. This has an epistemological component in that 'when a person's beliefs are threatened by an "inconvenient fact", sometimes it is preferable to challenge the fact' (McIntyre 2018: 13). This also relates to something called 'The backfire effect' where 'the presentation of refutatory evidence caused some subjects to increase the strength of their mistaken beliefs' (48). This is what Neiwert believes defines the entire 'Alt-America universe' where 'established facts supported by concrete real-world evidence are [. . .] interpreted as further evidence of the conspiracy and its efforts to hide "the truth"' (2017: 35). The backfire effect is therefore especially evident when a threatened belief endangers the wider collapse of a person's world.

This desire to compensate for a lost belief or a threatened world is one of the most insightful aspects of Jacques Ellul's great work on propaganda, which he argues serves the purpose of giving an individual a sense of identity. In other words, it compensates for what in Chapter 4 I called our referential dependency. 'For propaganda to *succeed*', he writes, 'it must correspond to a need for propaganda on the individual's part. [. . . T]here is a citizen who craves propaganda from the bottom of his being and a propagandist who responds to this craving' (1973: 121; emphasis in original). For Ellul, the rapid changes and developments encountered during the twentieth century (and this is perhaps even more the case in the first two decades of the twenty-first) left people in need of 'outside help to be able to face [this condition . . . and] ward off certain attacks and reduce certain tensions' (138). Modern life, for Ellul, is marked by its production of alienation, and the absence of 'apparent meaning' (143). What he called 'modern man' is also 'the lonely man' (147); although this is frustratingly gendered and a little heavy on the rhetoric, he argued modern man is 'a victim of emptiness [. . . and] in search of only one thing – something to fill the void' (147).

I quote this because it echoes the need Heidegger felt we all had for a meaningful life. Without it, Heidegger argues, we are uncoupled from our world, which causes profound anxiety. Despite his language, Ellul had a lot of respect for 'the average man who tries to keep informed, [but] a world emerges that is astonishingly incoherent, absurd, and irrational, [and] which changes rapidly and constantly for reasons he cannot understand' (145). In our own time, it is interesting to think of this in relation to the disposability of consumer culture, the never-ending novelty of our commodified world, the surfeit of information, the processes of globalization, the diversity of multiculturalism and the demographic shifts that have all happened since Ellul's book was first published. In relation to the specifically closed and authoritarian world view of the Alt-Right, Neiwert argues it 'creates a certain kind of cognitive dissonance, a feeling of unreality, because it runs smack into the complex nature of the modern world and attempts to impose its simplified, black-and-white explanation of reality onto a reality that contradicts and undermines it at every turn' (2017: 44).

Propaganda as a prophylactic against incoherence also shows how close it is to the function of the conspiracy theory. As the world fractures and splinters and its seeming simplicity is lost among an array of conflicting worldviews, opinions and events, Zuckerman proposes that the 'core appeal' of the conspiracy theory 'is its sense of a master narrative, an explanation for otherwise disturbing and confusing events that assures believers that they understand the big picture in ways non-believers do not. The master narrative gives believers a sense of control over uncontrollable events' (np). It might be argued, then, that with an increase in our sense of precarity comes a commensurate susceptibility to propaganda. In other words, we are psychologically and ontologically predisposed to the unreality of post-truth.

Traditional and new media

New media, especially the social networking sites, micro-blogs and social news aggregation sites we collectively call social media, are regularly blamed for increasing the spread of the Alt-Right/Lite and intensifying our epistemological precarity by distributing fake news, but our traditional media must also carry a portion of the blame. Much of that is indirect and connected with developments in the organization of capitalism and the ways in which our economy has become increasingly dependent on information, a matter I will return to shortly. However, it is more directly responsible in the way its own bias made it unfit to counter the precarity outlined in earlier chapters, especially around the War on Terror and the Financial Crisis. While I do not have the room to rehearse the many studies on the problematic relationship between the 'commodity form of journalism' (Hirst 2017: 86) – privatized, corporate and profit-seeking – and the functioning of democracy (Schiller 1989; McChesney 2015), it is worth noting just a few examples of the way that mainstream media are regularly co-opted by powerful political and economic interests.

I have already spoken about the ways the media failed to adequately report the causes of the Financial Crisis and the problems brought about by decades of deregulation in Chapter 6. However, this was very much in keeping with the media's widespread and early adoption of neoliberal rhetoric around free markets, competition and choice and the part they played in the cultural deification of entrepreneurs. It was also evident in their consolidation of meanings around value and wealth creation that perfectly matched the rhetoric coming from the corporate sector. The media also helped promote the anti-welfare sentiment that has evolved over time into a cottage industry of TV programmes devoted to 'poverty porn', where shows like *Benefits Street* and *Wife Swap* encourage us to indulge a prurient (Hester 2014) interest in poor people and help support as self-evident the view they are inherently lazy or feckless (Jensen 2014).

The partiality rather than objectivity of the media has also been well documented in areas such as war and conflict reporting (Kuypers 2006; Kellner 2016). As with the media parroting of neoliberal rhetoric, the first Gulf War also saw the media quickly adopt new military jargon. We were supposed to believe this somehow better reflected the reality of war fighting when in fact the new jargon, such as 'collateral damage' and 'friendly fire' were euphemisms designed to mask what was really happening. By the time the second Gulf War came round, the media were already using 'enhanced interrogation' instead of 'torture', 'extraordinary rendition' instead of 'kidnap', 'targeted killing' instead of 'assassination' and 'enemy combatant' instead of 'name-given-to-the-enemy-so-they-have-no-legal-protection-under-the-Geneva-Convention'. Rather than interrogating, they mimicked.

In terms of our current situation, however, the most blatant example of contemporary bias is the media's treatment of white supremacist terror. Of course, throughout the War on Terror, the media made a significant contribution to the rise in Islamophobia (Ogan et al. 2014), and the exaggeration of that threat has continued to dominate security concerns today, even when the most immediate threat comes from neo-Nazis. A murderer whose neo-Nazi ideology lead them to kill tends to be reported as a 'lone wolf' with 'mental health issues', while a murderer whose interpretation of Islam lead them to kill is always presented as a representative of a faith conceived as a 'death cult' for whom other members of that faith must apologize. Even when Canadian prime minister Justin Trudeau denounced as terrorism the attack that killed six people and injured nineteen more in Quebec City mosque on 29 January 2017, the media preferred to repeat the 'lone wolf' trope and portray Alexandre Bissonnette as a quiet man with an interest in chess.

By the time white supremacist Tobias Rathjen killed nine in two bars in the German town of Hanau in February 2020, it seemed we were beginning to overcome our reluctance to name what this is, and yet the media hysteria that would have followed an Islamist attack of this scale did not manifest, and the story quickly disappeared from the news. This is one way in which McIntyre's book on post-truth is problematic. He seems to think any claim about structural bias in commercial media is a problem. He writes, 'if one believes that all media are biased, perhaps it makes less difference to choose an information source that is biased in one's favour' (2018: 86–7); but our fear of post-truth should not prevent us from challenging the *fact* that in countless instances mainstream media can be shown to be captured by the discourses of power. Without this, we simply submit ourselves to another version of the noble lie where veracity is supplanted by the need to maintain social order.

This problem is, of course, more pronounced on social media where the traditional media's commitment to fact checking, albeit compromised, is completely absent. In *Anti-Social*, Andrew Marantz argues that the early social media entrepreneurs saw themselves as disruptors: 'metamedia insurgents' aiming to 'catalyze cultural conflict' (2019: 19). They espoused the neoliberal dogma that reduced measurement of the good to popularity or success in the market. Mark Zuckerberg, for example, claimed that 'the best stuff spreads, whether it's the best news article, or the best song, or the best product' (in Marantz 2019: 48). While this is a great example of the way the human capacity for technical ingenuity always outstrips our capacity for moral reflection, it nevertheless became the adopted idiocy that dominated almost every consideration of social media's value. For Peter Thiel, who is on the board of Facebook and was also one of the exclusive invitees to Cassandra Fairbanks's 'DeploraBall', the new technology was a form of 'disintermediation' (Marantz 2019: 49) where the traditional intermediary role between politicians and people formerly held by newspapers and broadcasters was broken. It is easy to see how this opening up of the intermediary function could be seen as democratic and yet the completely unregulated nature of social media and the direct access it provides to billions of people has produced the opposite effect. As Marantz notes, these disruptors turned out to be 'deft propagandists who, having recognized that social media was creating an unprecedented power vacuum, had set out to exploit it' (64).

The internet had already disrupted the power of traditional media, and it is well known how much the fall in revenue as a result of online blogs, magazines and news sites affected journalism, but this has a further significant side effect. As Neiwert explains: 'While the constraints on information imposed by the top-down mass media pyramid […] had seemingly been lifted, one of their important by-functions had vanished as well: the ability to filter out bad information, false of badly distorted "facts"' (2017: 215). Bad information, he continues, 'pollutes and toxifies people's worldviews, their interpretations and understandings of news and events as they occur, as well as their interactions with others' (218). In keeping with Zuckerman's analysis of unreality, Neiwert adds: 'Facts can be falsified or distorted or spun to support a constructed reality that, as more false information is accreted, spins an epistemological bubble that both resembles the real world but is also largely detached from it, except insofar as the people inside it are able to share their illusions with like-minded others' (218–19). For Marantz, such a situation gave Alt-Right/Lite disrupters an opportunity to move what they call the 'Overton window' – a metaphor developed 'in the 1990s by a libertarian think tank [the Mackinac Center for Public Policy] to explain how cultural vocabularies fluctuate over time' (2019: 54). As Marantz explains, ideas in the centre of the window 'are so mainstream they are taken for granted', with the most extreme ideas being outside the window and therefore unthinkable. However, the theory also proposes the idea that 'unthinkability is a temporary condition' (54). The success of the Alt-Right/Lite in this regard is perhaps best seen in the return of (pseudo-) scientific racism and eugenics (Saini 2019).

However, before commenting further on the ways social media have contributed to our epistemological precarity, it is important to set out a systemic problem pertaining to our society's reliance on information. For some time now, the centrality of the internet to our media environment but also to the global economy has encouraged us to speak of an information society. This not only refers to the significance of instant access to information (about anything) via the ubiquity of internet search engines, but it also refers to the role of 'big data' archives and algorithmic sorting in the collection of information on user activity that also enables the creation of predictive models about future behaviour. As such, it also registers the way capitalism has become increasingly dependent on that information, such that data itself becomes one of its leading 'products', competing with oil as the system's primary asset. Information continues to allow companies to fine-tune production and distribution, as it has done since the 1980s, but it now also allows them to recommend and directly target specific consumers with what it is believed they want. In our information society, the algorithms supposedly know us better than we know ourselves.

The need for machine sorting stems from what Mark Andrejevic (2013) has called the 'infoglut'. Infoglut, he argues, is a situation where 'we have all become intelligence analysts sorting through more data than we can absorb' (3), but it is not just the 'the tsunami of information' (4) that is the problem, it is 'the narrative recycling, the multiplication of alternative narratives, and the reflexive documentation of the story behind the story' (13). Part of the problem for our mainstream media is that this situation compounds a lack of trust in traditional sources because it brings with it the 'demise of symbolic efficiency' (12) or the ability for any authorial voice to secure what is true or even what is the case (real, actual).

Ordinarily, a challenge to authority is seen as a challenge to power, but like Baggini and McIntyre, Andrejevic believes this actually gives those with power the ability to retain it. Being able to manipulate 'symbolic efficiency' amid the infoglut was very much part of the neoconservative approach to disinformation around the War on Terror and the invasion of Iraq when Donald Rumsfeld actively deployed the informational fog around weapons of mass destruction with his infamous analysis of known knowns, known unknowns and unknown unknowns. As Andrejevic notes, it also gave some sense of legitimacy to George W. Bush's refusal to consider experts and go with his 'gut'. The proliferation of information and attempts to interpret it seems to demand we cut through the clutter by using our intuition, thereby anticipating the move towards the unreal or the reduction of truth to how we feel about it.[2]

The importance of mining information and data to the current formation of capitalism introduces the second systemic issue, which is the scarcity of attention. Quoting Thomas Davenport and John Beck, Christian Marazzi recounts their observation that the 'width of the telecommunications band is not a problem, the problem is the width of the human band' (2008: 64).[3] He goes on to explain how 'the technological revolution has certainly enlarged social access to information enormously, but the limitless growth in the supply of information conflicts with the *limited* human demand' (64). In conjunction with the infoglut, we also have what Marazzi calls '*infostress*' (65) because we cannot *attend* to it all. The problem for corporations, then, is not only to capture data but to also capture the attention that will deliver either further data (or a sale). Attention, therefore, as Marazzi notes, 'has *diminishing* returns. [. . .] It is a *scarce* and extremely *perishable good*' (66; emphasis in original). Marazzi would even go so far as to say this introduces a new contradiction and limit to capitalism. In addition to the contradictions between labour and capital and finite resources and infinite growth, we now have the 'disproportion between information supply and attention demand' (68). Grabbing attention is therefore absolutely essential in the current media environment.

Just as Bush made an appeal to his gut to cut through the informational clutter, competition for attention online has led to a similar focus on feeling and emotion or what Kayla Keener calls the 'manipulation of collective affects' (2019: 143). According to Marantz, the method adopted by Eli Pariser, the founder of the liberal news site, *Upworthy*, became the model adopted as the industry standard across the internet. *Upworthy* is a content aggregation site that recycles stories from across the web, but it simply repackages existing stories with catchier headlines. These were aimed at triggering high-arousal emotions or the 'activating emotions [. . .] that lead to measurable behaviours' (2019: 79). Activating emotions include joy, anger, outrage, fear, anxiety and hate. They are believed to draw attention and encourage sharing, which in turn draws more attention. Emerson Spartz, owner of *Dose* and *Memestache* is also a notable contributor to this method of attracting website visits. In an interview with Marantz, he explained how he would post the same article with lots of different headlines and the Dose algorithm would decide which one was most effective (94). He operates under the same maximum that what is popular is good and explains how the method is all about 'maximizing traffic' (95).

This is also the origin of media content now referred to as 'click bait': stories intended to shock, scandalize or scare people into paying attention. Unfortunately, while this model has come to dominate new media, it has also infected our traditional media. Under commercial pressure from the loss of readers and with the need to continue to generate an income, 'click bait' has increasingly become the go-to strategy with traditional broadcasters and established newspapers. You will often find it in especially concentrated form at the bottom of a webpage where a nine-panel grid of click bait stories – collectively known as the 'chum box', after the bucket containing bits of dead fish that anglers throw into the water to draw the attention of bigger fish – offers readers the temptation of ever escalating scandal and shock. Here, 'the attention market's slide into raw Darwinism' (Marantz 2019: 112) becomes a significant contributor to our epistemological precarity. In the first instance it not only undermines the traditional functions of journalism by making more sober, reasoned and long-form discussions of topics less viable, but it also helps circulate and even legitimize opinion that gains attention simply for being scandalous – a phenomenon the Alt-Right/Lite have taken complete advantage of.

Disinformation, flooding and free speech

The problem is accentuated by the traditional media's increased dependence on the social media through which most people now get their news. For example, McIntyre (2018: 94) notes a Pew poll completed in 2016 that showed 71 per cent of Americans got their news from Facebook. Here, it is not just the systemic problem of content searching out attention by any means necessary but that the algorithms managing the feeds on social media are also written to search out and maximize what they call 'engagement'. Just as the Google algorithm, PageRank, presents search results based on 'relevance', measured in links to and from a site; the Facebook algorithm, EdgeRank, has always managed users feeds to prioritize posts from people they interact with more often. In other words, in the quest to get your attention, Facebook will give you more of what you attended to in the past. This is what Eli Pariser (2011) and others have referred to as a 'filter bubble' in which we increasingly see only what we have previously liked.

This also exacerbates another major informational problem on the internet whereby the technology that was introduced as the means to connect us in diverse and unexpected ways has actually done the opposite and is increasingly breaking us down into groups of like-minded individuals using the internet and social media to reinforce their interpretation of the world. Where it *is* connecting us, the 'elimination of spatial boundaries allows online communities "to draw in otherwise isolated movement participants"' (Neiwert 2017: 259). In 2018, Facebook's algorithm was further modified to recognize and promote what it calls 'meaningful interactions', or posts that are receiving comments, and it doesn't take much to work out that what is often gaining significant attention on Facebook is not necessarily the most reasoned, thought-out, fact-based or academically rigorous content. According to Marantz, what is true for Facebook is also true for Twitter, whose algorithm has 'overrepresented controversy' (2019: 160).

With all aspects of our media ecosystem comprised by the need for engagement and where engagement is driven by triggering the activating emotions, it is clear how an Alt-Right 'pipeline' (Wendling 2018: 206) could be set up that moved content from the margins of 4Chan, 8Chan and Reddit, via Twitter and Facebook, to the mainstream evening news, especially when the most powerful man in the world is prepared to heighten engagement through his own tweets. Furthermore, the Alt-Right has become especially adept at triggering this engagement. A very good example is the 'It's okay to be white' meme (Hawley 2018: 112), which works by not only offering the Alt-Right community a new slogan with which to disrupt social media but produces even more engagement by provoking a liberal or left-wing backlash. Again, the shock jock mode that increasingly plagues mainstream media currently desperate for traffic works in a similar way. Here, engagement is actually increased by those wanting to counter the sentiment expressed in the purposefully outrageous headline or sentiment expressed by a shock jock and distributed via social media. In other words, the attempt to argue against it only puts it in front of more people, which in turn encourages the airing of more outrageous opinion. The conditions of post-truth thereby produce a positive feedback loop that only increases the privileging of affect over reason, scandal over truth and unreality over fact.

'Fake news' is a phenomenon formed out of all of these issues. According to Siva Vaidhyanathan, Craig Silverman had been tracking fake news for BuzzFeed since 2014 (2018: 184). Despite attempts from conservative commentators to downplay his work, the Trump transition team adopted the phrase in early 2017, only to utterly transform the phrase's meaning. What had been an important engagement with online disinformation quickly became Trump's preferred term to 'deride news stories and outlets he does not like' (Hirst 2017: 83). Fake news works primarily because of our desire for information that confirms our own beliefs (biases and prejudices) and has a capacity to travel because people like to post it as part of their online identity performance. All posting on social media involves some form of self-presentation, and circulating specific news stories says a lot about an individual and marks them as a member of a specific community. In the search for epistemological confirmation, users are attracted to stories that reinforce a particular attitude be that conservative, liberal or left.

Fake news stories will also often take the form of click bait and can therefore quickly drive engagement and be extremely profitable. An early story about fake news involved Macedonian teens writing fabricated stories designed to attract US conservatives and Trump supporters in particular. They had a peculiar talent for hitting all the right buttons and sat and watched the cash roll in as US advertisers bought up spots on their website. At this point, it seemed to be just East European teens who'd found a novel way to fund their lifestyle, but then the news broke about a potential concerted effort by Russian troll farms to write and post fake news with a view to directly impacting the 2016 US election. It turns out, though, that the Macedonia example wasn't just a spontaneous outbreak of malevolent entrepreneurialism but was also part of a concerted political campaign. As Craig Silverman et al. (2018) revealed in a *BuzzFeed* article, the troll farm was launched by Macedonian media attorney, Trajche Arsov, who also had connections to US conservatives running for office in Nevada. At the time of publication, Macedonian security services were also looking into links with Russia, a connection that haunted the Trump presidency with claims of election interference.

As I've already noted, disinformation is not new, but 'its alarming amplification' by Facebook was (Vaidhyanathan 2018: 185). Facebook is effectively the biggest media company in the world. While it might like to hide behind the idea it is merely a platform that allows others to post media content, it nevertheless has the greatest reach of any media company so far. Traditionally, securing an audience has been about broadcasting to as many people as possible, while narrowcasting was linked to niche communication to a very small audience. In the age of social media and Facebook, in particular, we have fully entered the age of the mass narrowcast first suggested with the introduction of multichannel cable TV. Not only does the data collected on users allow advertisers, politicians and troll farms to mass target specific groups, the problem is compounded on social media sites like Twitter by what the Knight First Amendment Institute at Columbia University call 'machine-amplified distortions of public discourse'. In other words, the problem is compounded by the use of automated accounts or 'bots' that continually and automatically spread the disinformation.

The report that alerted the world to what was going on was the breaking of the Cambridge Analytica scandal, brought into the public eye through the brilliant work of Carol Cadwalladr (2017). Her work exposed how a small and little known data agency was mining information from Facebook users in order to enable directed political campaigning. For Vaidhyanathan, this epitomized Facebook's role in the 'erosion of democratic practice and norms in the United States and elsewhere' (2018: 175). The problem, as he explains, was the use of 'dark-post ads' (177) where the advertisers or promoters have greater privacy than the users (178). Without knowing who is pushing the disinformation, he argues, it destroys public discourse because there is no ability to counter falsehoods, no right of reply nor criticism because of anonymity. All of this takes place on a medium without regulation. As Facebook has become increasingly synonymous with anti-democratic politics, Zuckerberg has been slowly forced to consider regulation as some form of reputation management, and in February 2020 was suggesting a new type of regulation that was somewhere between that which applied to newspapers and broadcasters and that which applied to telecommunication companies. Whatever happens, though, something clearly needs to be done because, as Vaidhyanathan notes, 'if you wanted to design a media system to support authoritarian leaders and antidemocratic movements, you could not do much better than Facebook' (186).

This is where we get to the crux of our epistemological precarity. Contrary to the long-held belief that the internet would bring greater freedom, Vaidhyanathan is explicit about how the internet and social media especially are perfect tools for authoritarian control. He explains how social media can be used to organize counter-movements to any protest groups, how the state can frame debate by having greater resources to commit to its message, how they can use social media as forums for citizens to harmlessly vent and express themselves and how they can use social media to coordinate pro-regime rallies. Of all of these, it is perhaps the resources that a state can commit to its propaganda/disinformation campaign that is the most significant and returns us to Bannon's injunction to 'flood the zone with shit'.

In such a scenario, we have what Pomerantsev calls 'censorship through noise' (2019: 44). Here, authoritarian leaders control the field of communication and messaging with a deluge of their own information that drowns out any opposing or critical voice. Vaidhyanathan (2018: 190–5) shows how this was especially effective in India, the Philippines, Cambodia and Myanmar where authoritarian leaders had the added advantage of a population captured by Facebook's Free Basics service, a supposedly philanthropic service that reduced the digital divide by enabling free internet access via Facebook but effectively channelled the population's media access through one platform. In the instance of the Philippines, Facebook actually deployed a team to teach Duterte's campaign staff how to use the service, and troll farms were developed along the lines of Russia's infamous Internet Research Agency to bombard the populace with regime favourable information.

All of this has profound implications for how we think about media regulation and how we understand the changing nature of propaganda and disinformation practices that contribute so significantly to our epistemological precarity. Traditional media have been captured by commodity form journalism that makes charismatic figures like Donald Trump primetime, stock-price-friendly viewing. The economic pressures of for-profit reporting also make click bait evermore enticing. As a consequence, they are less able to do the democracy preserving work they ought to be doing. In such a situation, it does mean there is a real need to regulate which opinions are given a platform, and what qualifies as desirable or permissible speech. In a world dominated by 'infoglut' and 'infostress' in which the attention of '*listeners*' is the primary focus, Tim Wu argues the First Amendment of the US Constitution may now be obsolete. This is because it 'presupposes an information-poor world, and it focuses exclusively on the protection of *speakers* from *government*' (2018: 548; my italics) when it was assumed the government was 'the main threat to the "marketplace of ideas"' (554). This has now radically changed because, as I have already noted, modern censorship is about deploying a flood of information. It is not about blocking who can speak but overloading the channels so that listeners predominantly hear one message.

In the days of the early twentieth century, when the First Amendment came into its own, aside from the government, the fabled 'marketplace of ideas' was also dominated by just a few media moguls and the circulation of information and opinion was an expensive business. Today, the internet and social media have changed all that. As Wu notes, 'the fundamental challenge comes not from cheap speech itself, but that its cheapness makes it easier to weaponize as a tool of speech control. The unfortunate truth is that cheap speech may be used to attack, harass, and silence as much as it is to enlighten' (549). In such a situation, Marantz asks the question: 'Does free speech mean literally anyone can say anything? Or is it actually more conducive to the free exchange of ideas if we create a platform where women and people of color can say what they want without thousands of people screaming, "Fuck you, light yourself on fire, I know where you live"' (214)? In an age when the *proliferation* of speech is contributing to our epistemological precarity we clearly need a rethink because no one anticipated '*speech itself being used as a censorial weapon*' (Wu 2018: 557; my italics). In such a situation, if free speech is to be considered our first and last line of democratic defence against the rise of the far-right, I would reiterate that we are in a great deal of trouble.

Coda

My argument in the previous chapters has been that the constellation of precarities that define our time makes us especially vulnerable to a politics promising immediate empowerment through the designation of a maligned object. The permission to spite, abuse, blame and hate the foreigner, the migrant or the culturally different has been a significant unifying tactic for millennia. We only really departed from this script eighty years ago when the full horror of such politics became apparent, and the heart of modern, enlightened Europe became the home of the most appalling genocide. However, what makes our current situation more acute, and something I haven't mentioned yet, is that the familiarity of the world we built after the catastrophe of the 1930s and 1940s makes us prone to amnesia. As I explained in Chapter 7, this happens at an individual level where a person with every social advantage is given no reason to reflect upon their privilege, but it can also happen at a social level where people are born into a range of progressive benefits unavailable to previous generations (civil rights, peace, healthcare, welfare, labour protections) that they assume are somehow natural and inevitable. Unfortunately, we lose sight of how precious, how historically fragile these things are and how hard we had to fight for them. It also comes at a time when the long path to democracy has ended in a shift towards plutocracy and corporate oligarchy that threatens to eliminate every check, every balance and every element of accountability and transparency we had painstakingly attached to the exercise of power.

For modern Britain, as I noted in Chapter 3, the Second World War still dominates the social imagination. In particular, it is a vision of 1940 when the small island nation stood 'alone' against the might of Nazi Germany. It was also the year we are said to have turned defeat into victory, when hundreds of little boats set off to Dunkirk to rescue thousands of stranded British troops. This event, in turn, became the epitome of British 'spirit' or 'pluck' that is continually evoked at the first sign of any crisis. It also came to symbolize the courage of the little man, defiant against all the odds in the face of foreign tyranny. In the run-up to Brexit, and in the chaotic aftermath of that potentially world-historical vote, the imagery and rhetoric of Dunkirk, plus the White Cliffs of Dover and our intrepid Spitfire pilots (not the Polish ones, of course) were used to drum up jingoistic support for severing ties with the country's largest trading partner. Consequently, British nationalists continue to return to 1940 as some kind of crowning jewel of the nation's greatness, in part because it works for those in power as a galvanizing myth of unity when they are spending so much time actively dismantling any sense of democratic equality or social solidarity.

Here, British people placed under extreme pressure by the ideology of austerity can still appeal to their Britishness as some immediate route to empowerment. A similar phenomenon is evident is the United States and the mythologizing of its past greatness. In his essay, 'The Future of an Illusion', Sigmund Freud called this 'narcissistic satisfaction'. While talking about how the Roman plebeian takes comfort from at least being Roman, he offers us a psychological account that perfectly sums up the support for Brexit and Trump and explains why this form of identification is so politically useful for those at the top:

> The satisfaction can be shared in not only by the favoured classes, which enjoy the benefits of the culture, but also by the suppressed ones since the right to despise the people outside it compensates them for the wrongs they suffer within their own unit. No doubt one is a wretched plebeian, harassed by debts and military service; but, to make up for it, one is a Roman citizen, one has one's share in the task of ruling other nations and dictating their laws. (Freud 1991: 192–3)

While people might be materially and politically disempowered, they gain compensatory strength and status from simply identifying with a culture or nation that has (or has historically had) power over others.

The war was, of course, also important in the UK for the creation of the welfare state and the National Health Service. While these were also part of a long-fought struggle by the UK labour movement over the preceding half-century, the war was the catalyst for the necessary change of both government and national mood that enabled their introduction. It also flies in the face of the argument that the UK, now battened down under the special measures of austerity, cannot afford social security and public services. When these institutions were set up, the country was economically on its knees. We just choose to organize ourselves differently these days because we are seemingly obliged to ever increase shareholder value.

The war also led to renewed efforts to establish robust institutions to promote peace. It is, of course, not beyond the bounds of historical truth to argue that the period of war actually stretched from 1914 to 1945, with a temporary armistice of twenty years in the middle. After such a tumultuous and violent first half of the twentieth century, it is unsurprising that nations would make a concrete effort to work towards a lasting peace. The League of

Nations was replaced by the United Nations in 1945 (although the League didn't cease operations until 1946), and there were progressive attempts to draw European nations together in a bid for greater cooperation and stability. Three generations of Britons have now grown up in a country that has progressively attempted to build institutions of peace in Europe, establishing an age of friendship that has lasted for almost eighty years. The danger is that the privilege of living in such an age – and if we look at other parts of the world, we can certainly see why it is a privilege – has meant that people either believe these things simply appeared automatically, growing as naturally and inevitably as an oak tree grows from an acorn, or they believe that we no longer need to support these institutions and processes because the age of peace and stability has somehow rendered them unnecessary.

Those on the political right who are looking to demolish these protections are less worried by what we might revert to because their social Darwinism believes disease and warfare strengthen both body and mind, and that the dog-eat-dog competition brought on by destitution is good for the spirit and the particular animus they call 'entrepreneurialism'. This was exemplified in a tweet posted on 15 December 2018 by Anthony Middleton, a former British soldier with some current celebrity as an explorer. He commented on the predicted chaos of a 'No Deal' Brexit saying: 'A "no deal" for our country would actually be a blessing in disguise. It would force us into hardship and suffering which would unite & bring us together, bringing back British values and loyalty and a sense of community! Extreme change is needed!' Aside from being a profoundly privileged statement that completely fails to acknowledge the extreme suffering that was already the reality of many British people struggling, dying or committing suicide because of austerity, this attitude is not, of course, peculiar to Middleton. The sentiment can be found in the columns of any British tabloid and is central to the myth of 1940.

It also brings to mind the attitude of intellectuals across Europe in the run-up to the First World War, which it was believed would deliver salvation for the people of Europe from the ennui and alienation of modernity. In *Redemption by War* Roland N. Stromberg writes: 'The war had psychic explanations, but these are not of the order of hidden springs of malevolence; they included, rather, a powerful thirst for identity, community, purpose – positive and, in themselves, worthy goals, perverted and miscredited but not poisoned at the springs' (1982: 191). He goes on to argue that these 'positive' goals suggest we need to find a 'moral substitute' (191) for war rather than destroy its roots. Some will no doubt suggest that Brexit was such a substitute, but where Stromberg is fundamentally wrong is that these goals of identity and community – the limitlessness of the good infinite – can be separated from the projection of evil – the limitlessness of the bad infinite – against which we must test ourselves. As I argued in Chapter 2, they are in fact mutually implicated in each other. Brexit will be a fleeting compensation but will not satisfy the narcissism at the heart of that project. If Britain stays on its current trajectory, once the EU ceases to satisfy in the role of malevolent agent, politicians will move onto some other object for their malice.

Although much of this mythologizing of 1940 is nothing more than the jingoistic fluff that drives newspaper sales, it is being accompanied by a return to a martial sense of virtue among the Alt-Right and their more traditional conservative allies. In keeping with the Alt-Right's celebration of machismo and virility, social media are awash with right-wing influencers offering stories, often fabricated, about the trials of Spartan boys and other classical figures who were forced into extreme feats of endurance to prove their manhood. Alongside this, others call for a return to something like the heroic society set out by Alasdair MacIntyre (1981) in *After Virtue* where in order to belong to a real community – a true *patria* rather than an anonymizing society (254) – individuals are required 'to face a particular kind of pattern of harms and dangers' (125). I cannot broach the long and complex philosophical argument here, but it is worth noting that modern society has been a regular target for Conservatives precisely because it has tended to advance equality but also because it has undone 'the unity of a human life [understood as] the unity of a narrative quest' (MacIntyre 1981: 219). As I noted in Chapter 1, it is therefore equated with artificial interference into natural patterns of justice and morality.

If neo-nationalist governments do take us into a new age of belligerently competitive nationalism this cultural shift towards martial virtue and national cohesion through sacrifice would no doubt be amplified. Its resurgence should therefore be troubling.

To placate any sense of looming danger, we will be told that capitalism loves peace and that trade opposes conflict. While this is true in some regard, it is only a partial biography. The long history of capitalism and its imperial adventures demonstrates the close link between capitalism, conflict and violence – even if that violence is hidden by the victor's pen. More recently, the neo-imperial turn in capitalism, hidden beneath the veil of liberal interventionism, shows the close link between war and capitalist opportunity. This is what Naomi Klein (2007) has called 'disaster capitalism', first modelled by Milton Friedman under the dictatorial rule of Augusto Pinochet in Chile but given its contemporary form by George W. Bush and the neoconservatives under the guise of the War on Terror. Here, in the space of a few years the handing out of thousands of security contracts to private companies turned homeland security into an industry and a '$200 billion sector' (13). The super wealthy that now guide our politics also know their wealth makes them largely immune to the worst effects of this 'state of nature' and that they have a vast human shield of poor people who will be disproportionately affected by this new age of belligerence.

A similar point about amnesia can be made in relation to our democratic institutions. Like the peace of international cooperation and integration and the security of social welfare, we have grown accustomed to our democratic rights and freedoms. We act as if they have always been there and will continue to exist even if we pay no mind to how we might preserve them. We expect to be able to talk and meet freely and to have a free press. We expect our universities will continue to act as 'critic and conscience' and for our institutions of government to operate according to the principle of the separation of powers, even if we may not know exactly what that means. Nevertheless, we assume our government won't be able to indiscriminately imprison us or confiscate our property; and yet we seem to have forgotten where these rights came from. We have forgotten the very long and complex struggles that brought them into being while also losing sight of the fact that these rights need constant tending if they are to remain alive.

Over recent years democracy as an ideal and a practice has been greatly undermined. Not only has the corporate influence, if not control of politicians, increased unchecked, in addition, we have seen the erosion of democratic rights under the auspices of the War on Terror which governments have claimed requires greater surveillance and the weakening of civil and human rights. At the same time, a particular version of freedom has become dominant, especially on the political right. This is one fuelled by decades of instant consumerist gratification and the neoliberal dogma of 'free choice', but it has also appeared in relation to free speech debates and efforts to break the spread of the pandemic. Here, the democratic conception of freedom rooted in relations of mutual support within a society dominated by the rule of law has been supplanted by an absolutist understanding of freedom without limit that refuses to recognize any social obligation. So, we have what I think is a perfect political storm. Those in power are pursuing economic and social policies that increase precarity for the majority of the population. As a diversionary tactic, they use the anger and hostility resulting from that increased sense of precarity to target the scapegoats of the foreigner and the poor who are presented as being responsible for our growing sense of disempowerment. At the same time, the privilege of living in a peaceful and secure country makes us feel we no longer need the institutions that gave us that security in the first place, and we can let them wither on the vine. What makes this situation even more troubling is that the dual perils of terrorist threat and financial crisis have encouraged submission to the idea that we need strong leaders who are prepared to make the difficult decisions required by the state of emergency and that we ourselves have no time for the luxuries of criticism or compassion.

All the while, the array of ethno-nationalists that are drawing ever closer to the political mainstream pat each other on the back for their part in the demise of the liberal order and eradication of the last vestiges of 'socialism', but an international alliance of nationalists is an oxymoron and will no doubt fall apart as soon as one group gets in the way of another. This is the reason I started to write this book, because the backlash against a politics advancing the lives of the vulnerable, disenfranchised, minority or traditionally repressed groups is no accident. It is part of a concerted effort by the radical right to reassert a social hierarchy with the white, straight, Christian man returned to his throne as patriarch, overseeing an exclusionary politics premised on genetic superiority and divine entitlement. Even if this is not the avowed position of some Conservatives, they are still happy to let this genie out of the bottle in an attempt to distract from their own flagrant attempts to enrich themselves. They arrogantly think they can control this venting of racism, misogyny and violent, persecutory hatred, but that is misguided. As Staub rather soberingly argued, 'hate does not remain under the leaders' control' (2005: 61).

If the immanent threat of right-wing authoritarianism supplanting democracy sounds alarmist, all I can say is that looking around me, seeing what has happened over recent years, I do feel the need to take that little red hammer and break the glass. Aside from some tiki torches, I may not be seeing flames, but I'm certainly seeing a lot of smoke. And, to be honest, I'd rather shout out a warning and be wrong than think everything will turn out just fine and be wrong. There has been a lot of talk about the robustness of democratic institutions, but they are nothing more than the laws we create, which are as potentially ephemeral as the speech and action that maintain them. They are consequently rather fragile, especially, as I've noted, when we seem to have accepted the need for strong, charismatic leaders in a time of emergency. Watching US Republicans build a North Korea-style cult of personality around Trump should have been a warning. At the time, many Americans understandably looked back at the Obama administration and mourned what the country had lost. The first black president was an extraordinary event, and he did wonders for America's standing in the world so damaged by George W. Bush, but simply letting the normal service of neoliberalism resume is not an option. Even if this most recent spawning of belligerent, exclusionary nationalism passes like a bad case of streptococcus, we can only decrease the chances of its return by changing our attitude to the diversity of experiences, beliefs, desires, needs and hopes that make up the complex tapestry of human life on earth, but this requires restructuring our society and the economy that underpins it. To this effect, we need to engage what my colleague, Avril Bell, calls the 'relational imaginary' (2014: 199).

Re-imagining the economy comes first. This means we need to move beyond the idiotism (Curtis 2013) that has dominated economic thought for the last half-century and build social economies rather than ones run for the personal gain of a few – and by idiotism, I mean the dogmatic prioritizing of the private (*idios* in Greek) over the public (*demos*). As 'free market' capitalism struggled to exit the crisis of 2008, capitalism began to remodel itself on an earlier, more belligerent form ideologically tied to the preservation of 'national character'. As I have repeatedly said, the idea of the nation functions as a security blanket, and stories of cultural superiority compensate for our sense of precarity. In so doing, the structural problems that led to the crisis – and became so plainly visible again during the pandemic – were displaced onto internal and external enemies such as migrants, refugees and the poor who were represented as the real threat to our 'way of life', which in turn could only be secured through a form of national cleansing and renewal.

Challenging the return of divisive, competitive nationalism requires economists to step up and offer alternative visions of how we might organize ourselves, especially given the very real need to respond to climate change. If we are to reduce the anxiety that prevents us from seeing and supporting the legitimate demands of socially and economically subordinated groups, if we are to build bridges that overcome very dangerous divisions and if we are to sustain our planetary ecosystem, we need to radically rethink the mode of production and commit to equitably share the fruits of our collective economic productivity. In the first instance we need to recommit ourselves to the principles or welfare and public assets and services that will support us while we make a transition to greater social and economic equality. In this task the identity politics of minority or subordinate groups help us bear witness to the ongoing social and material inequities in our society, and the call to check our privilege is the appeal for us to see these injustices that are hidden in plain sight. Secondly, these specific and local forms of politics remain crucial for understanding particular experiences and histories, but we also need to resist the move towards separatism and division that gives shape to the identity politics of the Alt-Right/Lite. To this effect we need to enact forms of what Gilroy calls 'conviviality', which he defines as 'the processes of cohabitation and interaction' (2005: xv). The local therefore also needs to work with a conception of the 'trans-local' (72). Indeed, the challenge of climate change will increasingly demand a sense for planetary connection and consciousness.

Fortunately, I have a great deal of hope, even belief that this call will be heard. Not only is the politics of the Alt-Right a politics of the dead, the dying and the decadent, representing every conceivable regressive ideology from colonialism to eugenics, patriarchy to pollution, there seems to be a growing movement among younger members of society that sees the principles of the political left based on mutuality, collectivism, commonality and sustainability as the way forward. Fortunately, then, in opposition to the necropolitics of the Alt-Right there is something different on offer. The difficulty, however, is that such a politics is based on something akin to love. Rather than the immediately empowering emotion of hate, this politics asks that we take a *risk*. It asks us not to judge or condemn, but be kind and have compassion; it asks us to see our potential vulnerability in the real disadvantages of others but also our welfare in the diverse connections that maintain us. It demands we build ever-increasing circles of solidarity and support.

This means that alongside the material restructuring of our economy we also need to rebuild our *conscience*. I would say social conscience, but that is a tautology because conscience – or *con-science* – literally means joint knowledge. Conscience is knowledge of others created with others. Christian doctrine has introverted and individualized this, reducing conscience to a voice in our heads, which is then popularized as the version of ourselves that tries to encourage us to do better; but conscience is nothing if not a profound awareness of and concern for others. It may indeed be something that is felt personally, but conscience proper is more like a sense for and understanding of the reciprocal relations that manifest in the knowledge and know-how that help us thrive as well as our shared potential for suffering. We can see it in the 'strong majority attitudes' that Nadine Strossen (2018: 131) argues *ought* to curb the need to legislate against hate speech, but such attitudes have grown fainter and fainter. As Erwin Staub argues, 'unless witnesses or bystanders powerfully communicate that [certain] behaviour is unacceptable [. . .] people justify what they have done by seeing their actions as a rightful response to the victim's actions or character' (2005: 59). Slow hate works by disengaging this behaviour. As a consequence, the racism that has always haunted our societies has been given a new lease of life. Indeed, it is possible to argue that with the election of Trump and the Brexit vote 'strong majority attitudes' have been developing that enable persecutory, hostile and hateful politics to gain a stronger purchase on our political life. As Sartre would say, 'the temperature of the community' (1976: 20) has changed.

However, during the pandemic of 2020 the reaffirmation of the original collective meaning of conscience came to the fore. It became apparent that there really is such a thing as society, and we became much more aware of others around us, not as a threat or a danger, but as contributing members of the complex social and economic webs that sustain each of us. To this effect, it brought into relief something that is normally hidden in the hustle and bustle of busy, individualized lives and is another way to think about relational imaginaries. It revealed what Geoffrey Hosking calls 'unreflective trust' (2010: 26). Trust, he argues, is how collectives 'maximize cooperation, security and mutual self-knowledge' (23) to minimize disasters. Most of this goes entirely unnoticed when society is functioning normally but is revealed at a time of crisis.

To understand this important layer of social dependence, he asks us to think about travelling by air; 'Which of us before boarding an aircraft' he enquires,

> demands to see the pilot's qualification to fly it, or checks every rivet, joint and fuel duct in it? Or even the competence of the engineers responsible for maintaining and repairing those parts? Obviously we do not. Yet our lives depend on the impeccable working order of every one of those parts, and on the skill and conscientiousness of the engineers.

He continues: 'The fact is we take them on trust because everyone else does so and because aeroplanes very seldom crash. Besides, to do otherwise would require us to have time and skills we don't possess. We don't "decide" to board an aircraft – we just do it' (24–5). In doing this, we trust 'symbolic systems: the sciences of aeronautics, mechanics, metallurgy' (25). We trust institutions of regulation and oversight, of teaching and training. We trust corporations to put safety before profit, and we trust the media to accurately report the risk of flying. 'Trust', he concludes, 'especially unreflective trust is part of the deep grammar of any society. It generates the templates within which people relate to each other, and within which they think and feel about how to face the future' (27). These are society's 'invisible bonds' (27); and it is these bonds we must once again acknowledge and celebrate. They have not gone away, we have simply been encouraged during neoliberalism's four-decade long assault on the social contract to blind ourselves to them.

Bringing into relief this network of social relations and dependencies is one way we can undo the atomizing of society under neoliberalism. In the four-decade long assault on commonality, collectivity and interdependence, the dogma has stipulated we are all separate, self-sufficient individuals, while pathologizing those who don't make the grade. In conjunction with this need to roll back the ideology of atomization, we also need to challenge the rhetoric of purity. For the Alt-Right/Lite and their traditional conservative allies, the only solidarity they will recognize is one based on sameness or an identity of non-contamination. The conviviality mentioned earlier would therefore embrace the interpenetration of our lives, as well as our histories, cultures and identities. This is not to say there are, nor can be, no distinct cultures. After all, every culture does its multi-culture differently. It is rather to recognize that each culture and every identity emerges from webs of connectivity, influence and heritage, of language, ritual and passage. In this, what is especially interesting for me is how those who are demonized and despised by the radical right, namely, people of colour and groups who have been subject to slavery and colonization or who have been displaced by colonialism's ongoing legacy, offer us an important path to understanding this aspect of the relational imaginary we so urgently need to re-engage.

For example, Günter Lenz speaking about W. E. B. Du Bois's conception of 'double consciousness' argues it is 'a dynamic, bi-(or multi-)cultural mode of inquiry of African American experience, culture, thinking, and discourse' (2012: 68). In other words, much like Fanon's experience of 'third-person consciousness' where he had his self-image presented to him in an alien form by a child afraid of a black man, the experience of African Americans and other historically or newly displaced people of colour can give us an insight into the dynamics of identity. This is especially the case for those who have negotiated the need to assimilate while attending to (practising, preserving, discovering, reinterpreting) their own culture. Lenz continues by quoting Bernard Bell who argues 'African American double consciousness thus signifies a biracial, bicultural state of being in the world, an existential site of socialized cultural ambivalence and emancipatory possibilities of personal and social transformation' (68). In a similar vein, Lenz quotes another scholar, Nahum Chandler, who 'argues that Du Bois "never ceased to affirm this heterogeneity as *also* a good, a resource, in general," a discourse on "impurity" that "opens a powerful critical reflection upon its own historical production"' (68). Lenz concludes, very much in the mode of the relational imaginary, by proposing that Du Bois's 'African American exploratory discourses are modes of a *radical cosmopolitanism*' in the sense of 'an open, trans- (and post-)national, diasporic discourse that acknowledges and negotiates intercultural multiplicity, heterogeneous interests and positions, and hybrid publics' (88). From this perspective, the identities formed in the wake of slavery, transportation, colonialism and migration become a kind of 'new, transgressive cosmopolitanism' (89).

This is neither the neoliberal cosmopolitanism of airport lounges and ethnically branded lifestyles nor is it the liberal cosmopolitanism that Gilroy notes quickly morphs into Bush and Blair's 'armoured cosmopolitanism' premised on 'messianic civilizationalism' (2005: 60). Speaking of the radical cosmopolitanism he believed writers like Du Bois articulated, and which

I think we sorely need as a counter to the separatism of far-right identity politics, Gilroy writes:

> The black thinkers of the Western hemisphere have sometimes been alive to the destiny involved in understanding their own position in planetary terms that confound conventional distinctions between nationalism and cosmopolitanism. The anti-racism that inherited a worldly vision from pan-Africanism and passed it on to the anti-colonial movements did not descend to the present through the temperate landscape of liberal pieties. It came via disreputable abolitionism and translocal, multicultural, and anti-imperial activism that was allied with the insurrectionary practice of those who, though legally held in bondage, were subject to the larger immoralities of a race-friendly system of dominance. (57)

In keeping with the need for an equitable economic system, he also argues this means 'articulating cosmopolitan hope upward from below' (67). It is a cosmopolitanism born out of struggles against disenfranchisement in all its forms and attaches itself to the 'civic and ethical value [. . .] that can be cultivated when mundane encounters with difference become rewarding' (67). Ultimately, for Gilroy, it calls for a planetary consciousness and 'relies on a reimagining of the world which is as extensive and profound as any of the revolutionary changes in perception and representation of space and matter that preceded it' (75).

In this challenge, is there anything the far-right and white supremacy have to tell us? Ironically, I think there is, and it adds an important element to Flahault's analysis of the fantasy of malice previously discussed. At the end of Ghassan Hage's book *Alter-Politics*, he closes with a discussion of the different ways we conceive our relations with other beings that I think is crucial for the relational imaginaries we need to engage. First of all, he talks about the relations designated by sovereignty. This he describes as an 'order of domestication' (2015: 191); an order where everything and everyone has its proper place. It is also an order of delineation between self and other and friend and enemy and is very much the order the far-right espouses, at least in theory. Next is the order of 'reciprocity' that understands relationships in terms of exchange. In the drive towards separatism, Hage notes, racists 'try to remove [themselves] from the reciprocal mode of existence' (191). Finally, he argues, there is mutualism, which 'highlights a mode of existence where people (and animals, plants, objects and so on) exist in each other. "He is from us and in us," the Lebanese say to emphasise that someone is strongly connected to them. Mutualism is this sense that others are "in us" rather than just outside us' (188–9). He references the work of Lucien Lévy-Bruhl who talked of mutualism as 'a mode of living where we sense ourselves and others as *participating* in each other's existence' (189). Here, boundaries are non-distinct, even non-existent.

However, despite desiring and even claiming to be sovereign domesticators (builders of walls), the racists, white supremacists and ethno-nationalists of the radical right are in fact mutualists. Hage explains the phenomenon as follows:

> the mutualist order of existence involves a sense of inter-penetration of existence whereby the other is seen as participating in our very existence and vice versa. In exemplifying this I used the positive example of the life force of others enhancing our own life force. Yet one of the vilest expressions of racism emanates from a negative experience of this mutuality, an experience akin to forms of black magic and sorcery: seeing in the existence of the other the malefic forces that are diminishing rather than enhancing one's own life force. This is indeed one of the most unpleasant and visceral forms that racism takes. Here, the racist conceives of the other [. . .] as sucking one's life and soul away from them, leaving them drained. (191)

Ultimately, and despite their protestations, the radical right shows just how intertwined we all are and proves the mutualist perspective as true. Our task in the engagement of the relational imaginaries needed to move us in a progressive direction is to embrace and activate positive mutualism. In doing this, we stand some chance of understanding the source of our hate and redirecting it for genuine and revolutionary democratic purposes.

Notes

Introduction

1 Alan Taylor (2017) offers a short visual introduction to American Nazis and the German American Bund in the Atlantic. One event featured is the massive German American Bund rally at Madison Square Garden in 1939, which was advertised as a 'Pro-American Rally' and a 'Mass Demonstration for True Americanism'. Miller's explanation is, thus, a further white supremacist dog whistle.

2 Article 7 of the EU Citizens Rights Directive actually gave significant powers to member states to remove migrants should they not prove they are able to support themselves.

Chapter 1

1 Another good essay that works as a checklist for the ascendancy of the far-right today is Umberto Eco's 'Ur-Fascism or Eternal Fascism' (1995). All of his fourteen points can be seen in different combinations across the range of neo-nationalist politics today. Most notable are point 1 that notes 'Ur-Fascism is the cult of tradition'; point 2 that it is anti-modern; point 6 that it 'derives from individual or social frustration'; point 7 that at its root 'there is the obsession with a plot, possibly an international one'; point 8 that stipulates 'followers must feel humiliated by the ostentatious wealth and force of their enemies'; point 10 that it 'can only advocate a popular elitism'; point 11 stating that 'everybody is educated to become a hero' and heroism stems from sacrifice; point 12 that 'the Ur-Fascist transfers his will to power to sexual matters. This is the origin of machismo' – a phenomenon currently rampant in far-right politics today; point 13 that the Leader is the interpreter of the people and the person who will take down '"rotten" parliamentary governments' and point 14 that 'Ur-Fascism speaks Newspeak', making 'use of an impoverished vocabulary, and an elementary syntax, in order to limit the instruments for complex and critical reasoning'.

2 Eileen G'Sell (2016) wrote a very good piece for Salon on this trend but also addressed the longer historical linking between the fashion industry and Nazism.

3 Another really important group was Tom Posey's Civilian Military Assistance that sourced mercenaries for activity in Africa and Central America. This was also part of an organized defence of white supremacy

around the world that saw 2,300 US mercenaries defend white supremacy in Rhodesia between 1965 and 1980 (Belew 2018: 79) and included both CIA-funded operations in Nicaragua and Operation Red Dog in 1981 that planned to overthrow the Dominican government (85).

4   The press release was still available to read on 28 June 2020 at https://ww w.dhs.gov/news/2018/02/15/we-must-secure-border-and-build-wall-ma ke-america-safe-again. Comparisons to the white power movement's slogan have been described as conspiratorial by the department.

5   At the time of writing, it is not clear what will happen to Anglin and The Daily Stormer. As, in July 2019, he was ordered by a court to pay $14 million in damages for unleashing a troll storm on Tanya Gersch, a Jewish woman from Montana who tried to make Richard Spencer's mother sell her building in Whitefish, Montana. For an account of the event, see Neiwert (2017: 333–4).

6   An interesting exposé of one of the groups that organized the 'Unite the Right' rally, American Vanguard, and their subdivision into Patriot Front was provided by Ray Miller-Still (2020) in the *Renton Reporter*.

7   The post can be found here: https://voxday.blogspot.com/2016/08/what-alt-right-is.html

8   These have been documented by the Southern Poverty Law Center: https://www.splcenter.org/fighting-hate/extremist-files/individual/mike-cernovich

9   A version of this can also be found in Russia where the derogatory term 'churok' is 'the insulting name given to anyone from the Caucasus or Central Asia. The paranoia that men from the "south" will take away white women has grown into something of a Russian obsession' (Pomerantsev 2015: 73).

10 In a blog post in which he tries to step back from his association with the 'incel' community, Peterson writes: 'It's been a truism among anthropologists and biologically-oriented psychologists for decades that all human societies face two primary tasks: regulation of female reproduction (so the babies don't die, you see) and male aggression (so that everyone doesn't die). The social enforcement of monogamy happens to be an effective means of addressing both issues, as most societies have come to realize (pair-bonded marriages constituting, as they do, a human universal)' (2018: np). The rather old data he relies on also reproduces the idea that a woman's sexuality is an economic resource and stems from an age in which marriage was regarded in terms of economic exchange (Ley 2018).

11 Hawley also claims 'the Alt-Right does not seriously engage with public policy' (2019: 26) while also spending time talking about the importance of the think tank the National Policy Institute (132), and the funding they receive from multi-millionaire donor William Regenery II, founder of the Charles Martel Society in 2001 and publisher of Occidental Quarterly (130).

12 He said this during his Margaret Thatcher memorial lecture in 2013, which can be found here: https://www.cps.org.uk/files/factsheets/original/131128 144200-Thatcherlecturev2.pdf. Accessed 28 March 2020.

Chapter 2

1 C. Fred Alford also discusses the relationship between love and hate. 'The lie of hatred', he writes, 'is that it can connect a person with others as love does, without risking love's vulnerability and heartache. Hatred is not the opposite of love. Hatred is the imitation of love, love in the realm of malevolence' (2005: 241).

Chapter 3

1 There are other issues I have with Strossen's argument that I don't have room to deal with here, but they are worth noting. She does little to challenge a series of false equivalences such as the Nazi salute and the Black Power salute (2018: 55) or criticisms of homophobia and criticisms of religious belief (80). She also opts for a version of victim blaming arguing for 'proactive counselling and training about how to engage constructively with "hate speech" (165) while developing skills and outlooks that can help [. . .] minimize the potentially adverse psychic and emotional impact of such speech' (170), which sounds very much like advising women to dress differently to avoid being raped. She is also oddly selective in her sources depending on the aspect of her argument she is trying to make. So, she argues it is important 'to convey accurate, positive information about traditionally marginalized groups' (168–9) and that 'counterspeech by leaders in the pertinent community' (174) can be helpful, while going on to note how 'Social Science studies have shown that positive media depictions reduce prejudice' (169). However, when talking about harm she chose social science research showing 'the effects on audience behaviour are "weak"' (127). It goes without saying that a lawyer would see straight through this defence.
2 Report by the UN Security Council Counter-Terrorism Committee, April 2020 https://www.un.org/sc/ctc/news/2020/04/01/cted-launches-trends-alert-extreme-right-wing-terrorism/

Chapter 4

1 To get a sense of how the past persists in the present, it is also worth noting that the state of Mississippi didn't ratify the Amendment until 2013.
2 It is worth noting that in 2014 Andrew Anglin expressed a similar belief: 'My problem with blacks is that I have come to understand that their biological nature is incompatible with White Society . . . and that we will never have peace as long as they are among us, given that irrational outbursts of brutal violence are a part of their nature' (Neiwert 2017: 249).

3   Leading Alt-Right figures were publicly very pleased with the election of Donald Trump (Piggott 2016). Richard Spencer tweeted: 'For the first time in my adult life, I am really proud of my country because it feels like hope is finally making a comeback.' On the neo-Nazi website, *Daily Stormer*, Andrew Anglin wrote: 'Our Glorious Leader has ascended to God Emperor. Make no mistake about it: we did this. If it were not for us, it wouldn't have been possible. . . . [T]he White race is back in the game. And if we're playing, no one can beat us. The winning is not going to stop.'

4   Hannah Devlin (2018) has reported that recent DNA analysis of the skeletal remains of 'Cheddar Man', Britain's oldest known inhabitant, has revealed he had 'dark to black' skin.

Chapter 5

1   The Australian Member of Parliament, Stephen Anning, said in a statement dated 15 March 2019 'while this kind of violent vigilantism can never be justified, what it highlights is the growing fear within our community, both in Australia and New Zealand, of the increasing Muslim presence. [. . .] The real cause of bloodshed on New Zealand streets today is the immigration programme which allowed Muslim fanatics to migrate to New Zealand in the first place.'

2   A very good example of this elasticity is pastor Rick Wiles on his TruNews TV programme in June 2019 telling people that meatless burgers is a Satanic plot to change human DNA and stop people being born again.

3   These anxieties about dissolution, rooted in long-standing fears about immigration, are also not alien to the UK. In Enoch Powell's infamous 'rivers of blood' speech from 1968, he echoed the white nationalist's fear that their position of dominance would be removed. Quoting a constituent, he recalled the man telling him: 'I have three children, all of them been through grammar school and two of them married now, with family. I shan't be satisfied till I have seen them all settled overseas. In this country in 15 or 20 years' time the black man will have the whip hand over the white man.' Powell's oratory used images of desolation and a 'future defeated' – at one point saying the 'inflow' of immigrants was 'like watching a nation busily engaged in heaping up its own funeral pyre'. He concluded by dramatically invoking Sybil's prophecy, saying: 'As I look ahead, I am filled with foreboding. Like the Roman, I seem to see "the River Tiber foaming with much blood".'

4   Tamsin Shaw (2020) has written an excellent piece in the *New York Review of Books* on how Barr has become Trump's Carl Schmitt, using the primacy of the friend and enemy distinction in his Federalist Society address to argue for giving Trump 'unchecked executive privilege' and place the president above the law.

5   J. C. Alexander (2019) clearly sees this in the world view of Steve Bannon: 'Just as there is no room for supra-national governance, there is no space for

constitutionally authorized third parties to mediate conflicts on the domestic scene on behalf of the broader solidarity of a civil sphere. [. . .] Bannon reverses Clausewitz's observation about war being politics by another means. For him, politics is war by another means. No wonder he has vowed that "every day, every day, it's going to be a fight"" (143).

6 Neiwert accredits the first use of the term to Daniel Jonah Goldhagen (1996) who spoke of the 'eliminationist mind-set' that characterized Germans' thinking about the Jews in *Hitler's Willing Executioners: Ordinary Germans and the Holocaust*, but it was also attributed to the American Right in Hofstadter's 'Paranoid Style' essay for *Harper's Magazine*. He wrote: 'the paranoid [. . .] does not see social conflict as something to be mediated and compromised, in the manner of the working politician. [. . .] Since the enemy is thought of as being totally evil and totally unappeasable, he must be totally eliminated – if not from the world, at least from the theatre of operations to which the paranoid directs his attention' (1964: 5).

7 In 2017, *The Guardian*'s Ed Pilkington reported that Trump's hostility to Muslims only added to the phenomenon, with twenty-three bills in eighteen states being introduced that year. This brought the total from 201 to 217 in forty-three states.

8 A report from the International Consortium of Investigative Journalists, entitled *Solitary Voices* (Woodman et al. 2019), documents a third of cases reviewed placed immigrants with mental health issues in solitary confinement. Isolation was also used for gay and transgender inmates. Commenting on another camp at Dilley, Texas, Martin Garbus (2019) notes that while Dilley was set up by Obama it 'is run by CoreCivic, a company that contributed $250,000 to President Trump's inauguration'. Garbus goes on to describe conditions at Dilley: 'The agents take them in their wet clothes, at first, to the "hielera", the "icebox", a refrigerated building, a large processing center, where they had to try to sleep on the concrete floor or sit on concrete benches under mylar blankets, prodded by agents all night and day, deliberately kept awake. Bathroom breaks are frequently not granted, or not in time, so both women and children often soil themselves. [. . .] After the Hielera, they went to the "perrera", or "doghouse", a place where families were put in cages, cyclone fencing between them as though they were animals. But at least the chain link cages – dog kennels, really – were warmer, the mothers told me.'

9 At the same time, it was being reported that the Trump administration had chosen to hold a surplus of migrant children at a former Japanese internment camp in Oklahoma (Hennigan 2019).

Chapter 6

1 A particularly disturbing example of how financialization has become enmeshed in personal income is Mary O'Hara's (2014) discussion of the

extortionate rates offered by payday lenders. She notes how the archbishop of Canterbury was especially critical of the payday lenders Wonga for preying on the most economically vulnerable. To combat this he tried to set up a church-based credit union in 2013 only to find out the church's pension fund had investments in Wonga (88).

2   This was only possible if the cash ratio or reserve requirements of banks – which had traditionally been the safety cushion in times of crisis – were drastically cut. In 2006 the reserve requirement in the United States was cut to 10 per cent. This means that a bank can lend £1,000 pounds to another bank who can in turn lend £900 (keeping £100 pounds in reserve) to another bank who can in turn lend £810, etc. While this represents the genius of the banking system in that it can create £2,710 from £1,000 (and, of course, much more should the lending continue), this also means that £1,710 that is in circulation doesn't actually exist, that is, if everyone asked for the money back at the same time someone would be left carrying a large debt. If we add the shadow banking system to this (investment banks, hedge funds, structured investment vehicles, money markets and insurers, and which had become almost as large as the traditional banking sector over this period) and the fact that the reserve requirement here was cut to zero in the United States, it is clear that this was a recipe for disaster.

3   This was exacerbated by the financial sector adopting the 'Value at Risk' (VaR) model of assessment. VaR became the accepted statistical model for calculating the probability of deviations in risk which are represented by the Greek letter Σ, sigma. While proponents might note VaR worked in most cases, it completely failed to predict the risk that manifested in the 1998 Russian bond default and collapse of LTCM, which was viewed as a seven-sigma event. By the time the full crisis hit Lanchester recalls that David Viniar, the CEO of Goldman Sachs, was talking about twenty-five sigma events happening every few days, and wryly notes: 'Remember, what we're talking about here is a drop in house prices which caused people with bad credit to have trouble paying their mortgages. That was turned into something that was literally the most unlikely thing to have happened in the history of the universe' (140). The irony of Hayek's complaint regarding socialism's use of pseudo-scientific theory (2007: 173) is especially acute here.

4   It is also worth noting that the 2008 bail out had so little effect on the structure of the economy that during the coronavirus crisis the governments were 'extending loans to businesses at a time when private debt [was] already historically high. In the United States, total household debt just before the current crisis was $14.15 trillion, which is $1.5 trillion higher than it was in 2008 (in nominal terms)' (Mazzucato 2020).

5   As Harvey notes, new forms of accumulation by dispossession include patents and licencing on genetic material, intellectual property rights, biopiracy and the commodification of cultural creativity (2003: 48).

6 A good review of this is offered by Joseph Stiglitz (2020), former chief economist of the World Bank, who argues that stock prices are not a good indicator of the health of an economy. He writes: 'To get a good reading on a country's economic health, start by looking at the health of its citizens. If they are happy and prosperous, they will be healthy and live longer. Among developed countries, America sits at the bottom in this regard. US life expectancy, already relatively low, fell in each of the first two years of Trump's presidency, and in 2017, midlife mortality reached its highest rate since World War II. This is not a surprise, because no president has worked harder to make sure that more Americans lack health insurance. Millions have lost their coverage, and the uninsured rate has risen, in just two years, from 10.9% to 13.7%.'

Chapter 7

1 The movement began in 2013 after George Zimmerman was acquitted for killing Trayvon Martin and grew in 2014 with the police killings of Michael Brown and Eric Garner. Among the numerous other killings, the fatal shooting of Philando Castile in 2016, when his girlfriend used Facebook Live to broadcast the immediate aftermath, encapsulated the problem of epidermal privilege when carrying weapons.

2 Another feature of white privilege, Dyer (1997: 12) noted, is for representations of white people across an array of cultural forms to be flexible, multifarious and varied to the point of always being singular. The 'stereo' in stereotype literally means rigid. It is the cultural privilege if not prerogative of white people to be idiosyncratic and eccentric, whereas the representation of people of colour is often rooted in rigid, generic caricature.

3 Said describes 'Orientalism' as a 'discourse' that enters into an exchange with various types of power: 'power political (as with a colonial or imperial establishment), power intellectual (as with reigning sciences like comparative linguistics or anatomy, or any of the modern policy sciences), power cultural (as with orthodoxies and canons of taste, texts, values), power moral (as with ideas about what "we" do what "they" cannot do or understand as "we" do)' (1978: 12). It is a totalizing network of knowledge and representation that forms and disseminates a complex nexus of authority (19–20). Ultimately, Orientalism's combined power 'speaks the Arab Oriental, not vice versa' (321): it produces an object while denying a subject.

4 White supremacism is also engrained in English, which language associates 'white' with purity, innocence, the untainted, beneficence and spirituality, while 'black' has connotations of evil, foreboding, wicked, sinister, macabre, dirty, soiled, malevolence, disgrace, depressed and angry. To be a 'black' person inside a 'white' language places you at an immediate and distinct disadvantage.

Chapter 8

1 Proctor has coined a new term for the study of ignorance: agnotology. Ignorance is an important part of social life. It is an essential part of our understanding of privacy, while also being the crucial element that drives science forward. He proposes there are three areas of agnotology: ignorance as a native state (we don't know until we know), ignorance as the lost realm (decisions about actions cause us to lose things we remain ignorant of such as languages, plant or animal species) and ignorance as a strategic ploy. It is the latter that is most relevant to our current politics.

2 Another important feature of post-truth as neoconservative strategy was evident in the claim attributed to Karl Rove that reporters live 'the reality-based community [but] that's not the way the world really works anymore. [. . .] We're an empire now, and when we act, we create our own reality. And while you're studying that reality – judiciously, as you will – we'll act again, creating other new realities, which you can study, too' (Suskind 2004).

3 Discussion of the attention economy goes back to Herbert A. Simon's (1971) early organizational theory for an information society.

References

Agamben, G. (1998) *Homo Sacer: Sovereign Power and Bare Life*. Stanford, CA: Stanford University Press.

Ahmed, S. (2001) 'The Organisation of Hate', *Law and Critique*, 12, pp. 345–65.

Alexander, J. C. (2019) 'Raging Against the Enlightenment: The Ideology of Steven Bannon', *Politics of Meaning/Meaning of Politics: Cultural Sociology of the 2016 US Presidential Election*, edited by Jason L. Mast and Jeffrey C. Alexander. New York: Palgrave MacMillan.

Alford, C. F. (2005) 'Hate Is the Imitation of Love', *The Psychology of Hate*, edited by Robert J. Sternberg. Washington: American Psychological Association, pp. 235–54.

Americans for Tax Fairness. *Walmart on Tax Day: How Taxpayers Subsidizes America's Biggest Employer and Richest Family*. Accessed on 26 April 2019. https://americansfortaxfairness.org/files/Walmart-on-Tax-Day-Americans -for-Tax-Fairness-1.pdf

Anderson, C. (2017) *White Rage: The Unspoken Truth of Our Racial Divide*. New York: Bloomsbury.

Andrejevic, M. (2013) *Infoglut: How Too Much Information Is Changing the Way We Think and Know*. London: Routledge.

Arendt, H. (1968) *The Origins of Totalitarianism*. New York: Harcourt Inc.

Baggini, J. (2017) *A Short History of Truth: Consolations for a Post-Truth World*. London: Quercus Editions Ltd.

Bailey, A. (1998) 'Privilege: Expanding on Marilyn Frye's "Oppression"', *Journal of Social Philosophy*, 29(3), pp. 104–19.

Balkissoon, D. (2018) 'The New Yorker, the Economist and Steve Bannon's Squad of Useful Idiots', *The Globe and Mail*, 5 September.

Barthes, R. (1972) *Mythologies*. New York: The Noonday Press.

Bataille, G. (1992) *Theory of Religion*. New York: Zone Books.

Bataille, G. (1993) *The Accursed Share*, volumes 2 and 3. New York: Zone Books.

Baudrillard, J. (1983) *Simulations*. New York: Semiotext(e).

Baumeister, R. F. and D. A. Butz (2005) 'Roots of Hate, Violence and Evil', *The Psychology of Hate*, edited by Robert J. Sternberg. Washington: American Psychological Association, pp. 87–102.

Beck, A. T. and J. Pretzer (2005) 'A Cognitive Perspective on Hate and Violence', *The Psychology of Hate*, edited by Robert J. Sternberg. Washington: American Psychological Association, pp. 67–86.

Belew, K. (2018) *Bring the War Home: The White Power Movement and Paramilitary America*. Cambridge, MA: Harvard University Press.

Bell, A. (2014) *Relating Indigenous and Settler Identities: Beyond Domination*. Basingstoke: Palgrave MacMillan.

Bellah, R. N. (1967) 'Civil Religion in America', *Daedalus*, 96(1), pp. 1–21.

Bennett, K. and C. Takei (2018) 'Before Resigning, Jeff Sessions Handcuffed the Justice Department's Ability to Police the Police', *ACLU*, 9 November. https://www.aclu.org/blog/criminal-law-reform/reforming-police-practices/resigning-jeff-sessions-handcuffed-justice

Berkowitz, L. (2005) 'On Hate and Its Determinants: Some Affective and Cognitive Influences', *The Psychology of Hate*, edited by Robert J. Sternberg. Washington: American Psychological Association, pp. 155–84.

Berlant, L. (2006) 'Cruel Optimism', *Differences: A Journal of Feminist Cultural Studies*, 15(5), pp. 20–36.

Berry, M. (2018) *The Media, the Public and the Great Financial Crisis*. Basingstoke: Palgrave.

Beydoun, K. A. (2018) *American Islamophobia: Understanding the Roots and Rise of Fear*. Oakland: California University Press.

Billig, M. (1995) *Banal Nationalism*. London: Sage Publications.

Bindel, J. (2019) 'Rape Is Becoming Decriminalized: It Is a Shocking Betrayal of Vulnerable Women', *The Guardian*, 12 September.

Blackness, M., A. Charuvastra, A. Derryck, A. Fausto-Sterling, K. Lauzanne and E. Lee (2000) 'How Sexually Dimorphic Are We? Review and Synthesis', *American Journal of Human Biology*, 12(2), pp. 151–66.

Blee, K. (2004) 'Positioning Hate', *Journal of Hate Studies*, 3(1), pp. 95–106.

Blok, A. (1998) 'The Narcissism of Minor Differences', *European Journal of Social Theory*, 1(1), pp. 33–56.

Blyth, M. (2013) *Austerity: The History of a Dangerous Idea*. Oxford: Oxford University Press.

Bourdieu, P. (1984) *Distinction: A Social Critique of the Judgement of Taste*. Cambridge, MA: Harvard University Press.

Boyle, N. (2017) 'The Problem with the English: England Doesn't want to be Just Another Member of a Team', *The New European*, 17 January.

Braunstein, R. (2019) 'Muslims as Outsider, Enemies and Others: The 2016 Presidential Election and the Politics of Religious Exclusion', *Politics of Meaning/Meaning of Politics: Cultural Sociology of the 2016 US Presidential Election*, edited by Jason L. Mast and Jeffrey C. Alexander. New York: Palgrave MacMillan.

Brown, A. (2017) 'What Is Hate Speech? Part 1: The Myth of Hate', *Law and Philosophy*, 36, pp. 419–68.

Brown, R. (2017) *The Inequality Crisis: The Facts and What We Can Do about It*. Bristol: Policy Press, 2017.

Browning, C. R. (2018) 'The Suffocation of Democracy', *The New York Review of Books*, 25 October.

Cadwalladr, C. (2017) 'The Great British Brexit Robbery: How Our Democracy was Hijacked', *The Guardian*, 7 May.

Canovan, M. (1990) 'On Being Economical with the Truth: Some Liberal Reflections', *Political Studies*, 38(1), pp. 5–19.

Carron, C. (2018) 'Students Who Made Apparent Nazi Salute in Photo Won't be Punished', *The New York Times*, 24 November.

Chernus, I. (2006) *Monsters to Destroy: The Neoconservative War on Terror and Sin*. Boulder, CO: Paradigm Publishers.

Clarke, J. and J. Newman (2012) 'The Alchemy of Austerity', *Critical Social Policy*, 32(3), pp. 299–319.

Cohen, E. (2001) 'World War IV', *Wall Street Journal*, 20 November.

Crenshaw, K. (1991) 'Mapping the Margins: Intersectionality, Identity Politics, and Violence against Women of Color', *Stanford Law Review*, 43(6), pp. 1241–99.

Curtis, N. (2007) 'Tragedy and Politics', *Philosophy and Social Criticism*, 33(7), pp. 860–79.

Curtis, N. (2013) *Idiotism: Capitalism and the Privatization of Life*. London: Pluto Press.

Curtis, N. (2016) 'The Explication of the Social: Algorithms, Drones and (Counter-) Terror', *Journal of Sociology*, 52(3), pp. 522–36.

Curtis, N. (2019) '"Don't bother being nice": *Joker* and the Art of misogyny', *Ceasefire Magazine*, 5 November.

Dearden, L. (2019) 'Islamophobic Incidents Rose 375% after Boris Johnson Compared Muslim Women to Letterboxes, Figures Show', *Independent*, 2 September.

Denker, A. (2019) *Red State Christians: Understanding the Voters Who Elected Donald Trump*. Minneapolis, MN: Fortress Press.

Denning, S. (2018) 'How to Fix Stagnant Wages: Dump the World's Dumbest Idea', *Forbes*, 26 July.

Devlin, H. (2018) 'First Modern Britons had "dark to black" Skin, Cheddar Man DNA Analysis Reveals', *The Guardian*, 7 February.

Diangelo, R. (2018) *White Fragility: Why It's So Hard for White People to Talk about Racism*. Boston, MA: Beacon Press.

Douglas, M. (2001) *Purity and Danger: An Analysis of Concepts of Pollution and Taboo*. London: Routledge.

Dunbar-Ortiz, R. (2014) *An Indigenous Peoples' History of the United States*. Boston, MA: Beacon Press.

Dyer, R. (1997) *White*. London: Routledge.

Eaton, G. (2019) 'Jonathan Haidt Interview: "I'm Jewish but I want My Kids to Read *Mein Kampf*"', *New Statesman, America*, 2 January.

Eco, U. (1995) 'Ur-Fascism or Eternal Fascism', *The New York Review of Books*, 22 June.

Ellul, J. (1973) *Propaganda: The Formation of Men's Attitudes*. New York: Vintage Books.

Fanon, F. (1986) *Black Skin, White Masks*. London: Pluto Press.

Flahault, F. (2003) *Malice*. London: Verso Books.

Fortin, J. (2017) 'High School Students Kicked off Football Team After Protesting During National Anthem', *The New York Times*, 2 October.

Foster, J. B. and F. Magdoff (2009) *The Great Financial Crisis: Causes and Consequences*. New York: New York University Press.

Foucault, M. (1999) *Abnormal*. New York: Picador.

Freud, S. (1991) 'The Future of an Illusion', *Civilization, Society and Religion*, The Penguin Freud Library volume 12. London: Penguin Books.

Fronczak, J. (2018) 'The Fascist Game: Transnational Political Transmission and the Genesis of the U.S. Modern Right', *The Journal of American History*, 105(3), pp. 563–88.

Frum, D. and R. Perle (2003) *An End to Evil: How to Win the War on Terror*. New York: Random House.

Gaertner, S. L., J. F. Dovidio, J. Nier, G. Hodson and M. A. Houlette (2005) 'Aversive Racism: Bias Without Intent', *Handbook of Employment Discrimination Research*, edited by L. B. Neilsen and R. L. Nelson. New York: Springer, pp. 377–93.

Garbus, M. (2019) 'What I saw at the Dilley, Texas, Immigrant Dentention Center', *The Nation*, 26 March.

Gaylin, W. (2003) *Hate: The Psychological Descent into Violence*. New York: Public Affairs.

Gentleman, A. (2014) 'Vulnerable Man Starved to Death after Benefits Were Cut', *The Guardian*, 28 February.

Gerson, M. (1997) *The Neoconservative Vision: From the Cold War to the Culture Wars*. Lanham, MD: Madison Books.

Gerstein, J. (2018) 'Kavanaugh Signaled Sitting President Couldn't be Indicted', *Politico*, 7 November.

Ghosh, J. (2018) 'The Political Roots of Falling Wage Growth', *Project Syndicate*, 11 December.

Gilroy, P. (2005) *Postcolonial Melancholia*. New York: Columbia University Press.

Goldhagen, D. J. (1996) *Hitler's Willing Executioners: Ordinary Germans and the Holocaust*. New York: Alfred A. Knopf.

Gramlich, J. (2019) 'The Gap between the Number of Black and Whites in Prison Is Shrinking', *The Pew Center*, 30 April.

Gramsci, A. (1971) *Selections from the Prison Notebooks*. London: Lawrence and Wishart.

Green, T. H. (2015) *The Fear of Islam: An Introduction to Islamophobia in the West*. Minneapolis, MN: Fortress Press.

Grewal, M. (2018) 'How Trump Weaponized the Government's Refugee Resettlement Agency', *ACLU*, 28 November.

G'Sell, E. (2016) '"Dapper" and Dangerous: The Ugly History of Glamorizing White Nationalism', *Salon*, 4 December.

Hage, G. (2015) *Alter-Politics: Critical Anthropology and the Radical Imagination*. Melbourne: Melbourne University Press.

Hamm, M. S. (2009) 'From Klan to Skinheads: A Critical History of American Hate Groups', *Hate Crimes*, vol. 1, edited by Brian Levin. Westport, CT: Praeger Perspectives.

Hanson, R. (2018) 'Two Types of Envy', *Overcoming Bias*. http://www.overcomin
gbias.com/2018/04/two-types-of-envy.html

Hawley, G. (2019) *The Alt-Right: What Everyone Needs to Know*. Oxford: Oxford
University Press.

Haque, U. (2019) 'Is the Future Fascist?', *Eudamonia & Co.*, 5 June. https://ea
nd.co/is-the-future-fascist-e0a7ee69ed71

Harvey, D. (2003) *The New Imperialism*. Oxford: Oxford University Press.

Harvey, D. (2010) *The Enigma of Capital*. London: Profile Books.

Hayden, M. E. (2019) 'Stephen Miller's Affinity for White Nationalism Revealed
in Leaked Emails', *Southern Poverty Law Center*, 12 November.

Hayek, F. A. (2007) *The Road to Serfdom*. Chicago: University of Chicago Press.

Heidegger, M. (1962) *Being and Time*. Oxford: Basil Blackwell Ltd.

Heidegger, M. (1999) *Ontology—The Hermeneutics of Facticity*. Bloomington:
Indiana University Press.

Heidegger, M. (2001) *Phenomenological Interpretations of Aristotle*.
Bloomington: Indiana University Press.

Heinze, E. (2016) *Hate Speech and Democratic Citizenship*. Oxford: Oxford
University Press.

Helleiner, E. (1994) *States and the Reemergence of Global Finance: From Bretton
Woods to the 1990s*. Ithaca: Cornell University Press.

Hendrikse, R. (2018) 'Neo-illiberalism', *Geoforum*, 95, pp. 169–72.

Hennigan. W. J. (2019) 'Trump Administration to Hold Migrant Children at
Base That Served as WWII Japanese Internment Camp', *Time*, 11 June.

Hermsmeier, L. (2020) 'Germany's Post-Nazi Taboo against the Far Right Has
Been Shattered', *New York Times*, 7 February.

Hester, H. (2014) 'Weaponizing Prurience', *Narrating Poverty and Precarity in
Britain*, edited by Narbara Korte and Frédéric Regard. Boston: De Gruyter,
pp. 205–24.

Hetey, R. C. and J. L. Eberhardt (2018) 'The Numbers Don't Speak for
Themselves: Racial Disparities and the Persistence of Inequality in the
Criminal Justice System', *Current Directions in Psychological Science*, 27(3),
pp. 183–7.

Hirst, P. (2001) *War and Power in the 21st-Century*. Cambridge: Polity Press.

Hirst, P. (2017) 'Towards a Political Economy of Fake News', *The Political
Economy of Communication*, 5(2), pp. 82–94.

Hochlaf, D., H. Quilter-Pinner and T. Kibasi (2019) 'Ending the Blame Game:
The Case for a New Approach to Public Health and Prevention', *Institute for
Public Policy Research*. https://www.ippr.org/files/2019-06/public-health-a
nd-prevention-june19.pdf

Hofstadter, R. (1964) 'The Paranoid Style in American Politics', *Harpers
Magazine*. https://harpers.org/archive/1964/11/the-paranoid-style-in-am
erican-politics/

Hopkins, N. (2019) 'Grenfell: Toxic Contamination Found in Nearby Homes
and Soil', *The Guardian*, 28 March.

Hosenball, M. (2018) 'Steve Bannon Drafting Curriculum for Right-Wing Catholic Institute in Italy', *Reuters*, 14 September.

Hosking, G. (2010) *Trust: Money, Markets and Society*. London: Seagull Books.

Houlbrook, M. (2005) *Queer London: Perils and Pleasures in the Sexual Metropolis, 1918–1957*. Chicago: University of Chicago Press.

Jackson, L. B. (2018) *Islamophobia in Britain: The Making of a Muslim Enemy*. Basingstoke: Palgrave Macmillan.

Jackson, M. (2018) 'No One's Exercise of Free Speech Should Make Another Feel Less Free', *E-Tangata*, 6 May.

Jensen, M. C. and W. H. Meckling (1976) 'Theory of the Firm: Managerial Behaviour, Agency Costs and Ownership Structure', *Journal of Financial Economics*, 3, pp. 305–60.

Jensen, T. (2014) 'Welfare Commonsense, Poverty Porn and Doxsophy', *Sociological Research Online*, 19(3), pp. 277–83.

Johnson, S. and J. Kwak (2010) *13 Bankers: The Wall Street Takeover and the Next Financial Meltdown*. New York: Pantheon Books.

Katz, J. M. (2018) 'Not Every Concentration Camp is Auschwitz'. *Slate*, 20 June.

Kaufman, E. (2019) 'The "1619 Project" Gets Schooled', *Wall Street Journal*, 16 December 2019.

Keener, K. (2019) 'Alternative Facts and Fake news: Digital Mediation and the Affective Spread of Hate in the Era of Trump', *Journal of Hate Studies*, 14(1), pp. 137–51.

Kellner, D. (2016) *Media Spectacle and the Crisis of Democracy*. London: Routledge.

Kendzior, S. (2015) *The View From Flyover County: Dispatches from the Forgotten America*. New York: Flatiron Books.

Kimmel, M. (2005) *The History of Men: Essays in the History of American and British Masculinities*. Albany: State University of New York Press.

Klein, N. (2007) *The Shock Doctrine*. New York: Picador.

Krugman, P. (2009) *The Return of Depression Era Economics and the Crisis of 2008*. New York: W. W. Norton & Co.

Kuypers, J. I. (2006) *Bush's War: Press Bias and Framing the War on Terror*. Lanham, MD: Rowman & Littlefield.

Kynaston, D. (2007) *Austerity Britain: 1945–51*. London: Bloomsbury.

Kynaston, D. (2010) 'Austerity was a Hard Sell in the 40s: Today It's Harder Still', *The Guardian*, 21 June.

Lanchester, J. (2010) *Whoops! Why Everyone Owes Everyone and No One Can Pay*, London: Penguin Books.

Lapavitsas, C. (2011) 'Theorizing Financialization', *Work, Employment and Society*, 25(4), pp. 611–26.

Laughland, O. (2019) 'Outcry after Trump Officials Reveal Sixth Migrant Child Died in US Custody', *The Guardian*, 23 May.

Lee, M. J. (1993) *Consumer Culture Reborn: The Cultural Politics of Consumption*. London: Routledge.

Lenz, G. (2012) 'Radical Cosmopolitanism: W. E. B. Du Bois, Germany, and African American Pragmatist Visions for Twenty-First Century Europe', *Journal of Transnational American Studies*, 4(2), pp. 65–96.

Lerner, R. M., A. Bilalbegović Balsano, R. Banik and S. Naudeau (2005) 'The Diminution of Hate Through the Promotion of Positive Individual-Context Relations', *The Psychology of Hate*, edited by Robert J. Sternberg. Washington: American Psychological Association, pp. 103–20.

Levin, J. and G. Rabrenovic (2009) 'Hate as Cultural Justification for Violence', *Hate Crimes*, vol. 1, edited by Brian Levin. Westport, CT: Praeger Perspectives.

Ley, D. J. (2018) 'Monogamy and Violence', *Psychology Today*, 21 May.

López, V. (2018) 'Warehousing Immigrant Children in the Texas Desert', *ACLU*, 1 November.

MacIntyre, A. (1981) *After Virtue: A Study in Moral Theory*. London: Duckworth.

Macnab J. J. (2020) *The Seditionists: Inside the Explosive World of Anti-Government Extremism in America*. London: St. Martin's Press.

Mann, M. (2004) *Fascists*. Cambridge: Cambridge University Press.

Marantz, A. (2019) *Anti-Social: Online Extremists, Techno-Utopias, and the Hijacking of the American Conversation*. New York: Viking.

Marazzi, C. (2008) *Capital and Language: From the New Economy to the War Economy*. New York: Semiotext(e).

Marriot, L. and D. Sim (2014) 'Indicators of Poverty for Māori and Pacific People', *Victoria University of Wellington Working Papers in Public Finance*. https://www.wgtn.ac.nz/sacl/centres-and-chairs/cpf/publications/workin g-papers/WP09_2014_Indicators-of-Inequality.pdf.

Marsh, S., A. Modhin and N. McIntyre (2019) 'Homophobic and Transphobic Hate Crime Surges in England and Wales', *The Guardian*, 14 June.

Mazzucato, M. (2018) *The Value of Everything: Making and Taking in the Global Economy*. London: Allen Lane.

Mazzucato, M. (2020) 'Capitalism's Triple Crisis', *Project Syndicate*, 30 March.

McChesney, R. W. (2015) *Rich Media, Poor Democracy: Communication Politics in Dubious Times*. New York: The New Press.

McGahey, R. (2013) 'The Political Economy of Austerity in the United States', *Social Research*, 80(3), pp. 717–48.

McIntosh, P. (1989) 'White Privilege: Unpacking the Invisible Knapsack', *Racial Equity Tools*. https://www.racialequitytools.org/resourcefiles/mcintosh.pdf

McIntyre, L. (2018) *Post-Truth*. Cambridge, MA: MIT Press.

McKenzie, L. (2015) *Getting By: Estates, Class and Culture in Austerity Britain*. Bristol: Policy Press.

Meier, H. (1998) *The Lesson of Carl Schmitt: Four Chapters on the Distinction Between Political Theology and Political Philosophy*. Chicago: University of Chicago Press.

Meier, H. (2006) *Leo Strauss and the Theologico-Political Problem*. Cambridge: Cambridge University Press.

Melling, P. (1999) *Fundamentalism in America: Millennialism, Identity and Militant Religion*. Edinburgh: Edinburgh University Press.

Miller-Still, R. (2020) 'White Nationalism Comes to Renton', *Renton Reporter*, 13 January.

Misra, T. (2019) 'The Life and Death of an American Tent City', *Citylab*, 15 January.

Mock, B. (2019) 'What New Research Says about Race and Police Shootings', *Citylab*, 6 August.

Morgenson, G. and J. Rosner (2011) *Reckless Endangerment: How Outsized Ambition, Greed, and Corruption Led to Economic Armageddon*. New York: Times Books.

Neiwert, D. (2009) *The Eliminationists: How Hate Talk Radicalized the American Right*. London: Routledge.

Neiwert, D. (2017) *Alt-America: The Rise of the Radical Right in the Age of Trump*. London: Verso Books.

Nelson, F. (2016) 'The Return of Eugenics', *The Spectator*, 2 April.

Nixon, R. (2011) *Slow Violence and the Environmentalism of the Poor*. Cambridge, MA: Harvard University Press.

Nguyen, T. (2017) 'Steve Bannon has a Nazi problem', *Vanity Fair*, 12 September.

Northcott, M. (2004) *An Angel Directs the Storm Apocalyptic Religion and American Empire*. London: I. B. Tauris.

Norton, A. (2004) *Leo Straus and the Politics of American Empire*. Cambridge, MA: Yale University Press.

Ogan, C., L. Willnat, R. Pennington and M. Bashir (2014) 'The Rise of Anti-Muslim Prejudice: Media and Islamophobia in Europe and the United States', *International Communication Gazette*, 76(1), pp. 27–46.

O'Hara, M. (2014) *Austerity Bites: A Journey to the Sharp End of Cuts in the UK*. Bristol: Policy Press.

Opotow, S. (2005) 'Hate, Conflict and Moral Exclusion', *The Psychology of Hate*, edited by Robert J. Sternberg. Washington: American Psychological Association, pp. 121–54.

Ostry, J. D., P. Lougani and D. Furceri (2016) 'Neoliberalism: Oversold?', *Finance and Development*, 53(2), pp. 38–41.

Painter, N. I. (2006) *Creating Black Americans: African-American History and Its Meanings, 1619 to the Present*. Oxford: Oxford University Press.

Pariser, E. (2011) *The Filter Bubble: How the New Personalised Web Is Changing What We Read and How We Think*. London: Penguin Books.

Partnoy, F. (2017) 'What Is (Still) Wrong with Credit Ratings', *Harvard Law School Forum on Corporate Governance and Financial Regulation*, 31 May.

Pease, B. (2010) *Undoing Privilege: Unearned Advantage in a Divided World*. New York: Zed Books.

Perry, B. (2001) *In the Name of Hate: Understanding Hate Crimes*. London: Routledge.

Peterson, J. (2018) 'On the New York Times and "Enforced Monogamy"'. https://www.jordanbpeterson.com/media/on-the-new-york-times-and-enforced-monogamy/

Piggott, S. (2016) 'White Nationalists and the So-Called "alt-right" Celebrate Trump's Victory', *Southern Poverty Law Center*, 9 November.

Pilkington, E. (2017) 'Anti-Sharia Laws Proliferate as Trump Strikes Hostile Tone Towards Muslims', *The Guardian*, 30 December.

Podhoretz, N. (1980) *The Present Danger: "Do We Still Have the Will to Reverse the Decline of American Power?"*. New York: Simon & Shuster.

Podhoretz, N. (2002) 'How to Win World War IV', Commentary, February, pp. 19–29.

Pomerantsev, P. (2015) *Nothing Is True and Everything Is Possible: Adventures in Modern Russia*. London: Faber & Faber.

Pomerantsev, P. (2019) *This Is NOT Propaganda*. London: Faber & Faber.

Popper, K. (2002) *The Open Society and It's Enemies*. London: Routledge.

Post, J. M. (1999) 'The Psychopolitics of Hatred: Commentary on Ervin Staoub's Article', *Peace and Conflict: Journal of Peace Psychology*, 5, pp. 337–44.

Power, M. and T. Dalgleish (2016) *Cognition and Emotion: From Order to Disorder*, 3rd edn. London: Psychology Press.

Proctor, R. N. (2008) 'Agnotology: A Missing Term to Describe the Cultural Production of Ignorance (and Its Study)', *Agnotology: The Making and Unmaking of Ignorance*, edited by R. N. Proctor and L. Schiebinger. Stanford, CA: Stanford University Press.

Quiggin, J. (2010) *Zombie Economics: How Dead Ideas Still Walk Among Us*. Princeton: Princeton University Press.

Quinby, L. (1994) *Anti-Apocalypse: Exercises in Genealogical Criticism*. Minneapolis, MN: University of Minnesota Press.

Reber, A. S. and E. S. Reber (2002) *The Penguin Dictionary of Psychology*. New York: Penguin Books.

Royzman, E. B., C. McCauley and P. Rozin (2005) 'From Plato to Putnam: Four Ways to Think About Hate', *The Psychology of Hate*, edited by Robert J. Sternberg. Washington: American Psychological Association, pp. 3–36.

Rutherford, A. (2020) *How to Argue With a Racist: What Our Genes Do (and Don't) Say About Human Difference*. New York: The Experiment.

Sacchetti, M. (2019) 'Trump Administration Cancels English Classes, Soccer, Legal Aid for Unaccompanied Child Migrants in US Shelters', *Washington Post*, 5 June.

Sahm, C. (2020) 'Encouraging Banks to Serve the Credit Needs of Everyone', *Washington Center for Equitable Growth*, 3 February. https://equitablegro wth.org/encouraging-banks-to-serve-the-credit-needs-of-everyone/.

Said, E. (1978) *Orientalism*. London: Routledge & Keegan Paul Ltd.

Said, E. (1984) 'Permission to Narrate', *Journal of Palestine Studies*, 13(3), pp. 27–48.

Saini, A. (2019) *Superior: The Return of Race Science*. London: 4th Estate.

Sartre, J.-P. (1976) *Anti-Semite and Jew: An Exploration of the Etiology of Hate*. New York: Schocken Books.

Sayer, A. (2016) *Why We Can't Afford the Rich*. Bristol: The Policy Press.

Scahil, J. (2007) *Blackwater: The Rise of the Wold's Most Powerful Mercenary Army*. London: Serpant's Tail.

Scarry, E. (1985) *The Body in Pain: The Making and Unmaking of the World*. Oxford: Oxford University Press.

Schiller, H. I. (1989) *Culture Inc: The Corporate Takeover of Public Expression*. New York: Oxford University Press.

Schmitt, C. (1996) *The Concept of the Political*. Chicago: University of Chicago Press.

Schmitt, C. (2003) *The Nomos of the Earth*. New York: Telos Press Publishing.

Schmitt, C. (2004) *Legality and Legitimacy*. Durham, NC: Duke University Press.

Schmitt, C. (2005) *Political Theology: Four Chapters on the Concept of Sovereignty*. Chicago: University of Chicago Press.

Serwer, A (2020) 'The Coronavirus Was an Emergency Until Trump Found Out Who Was Dying', *The Atlantic*, 8 May.

Shaw, T. (2019) 'The Oligarch Threat', *The New York Review of Books*, 27 August.

Shaw, T. (2020) 'William Barr: The Carl Schmitt of Our Time', *The New York Review of Books*, 15 January.

Sheehan, T. (1981) 'Myth and Violence: The Fascism and Julius Evola and Alain de Benoist', *Social Research*, 48(1), pp. 45–73.

Shüssler Fiorenza, E. (2001) *Wisdom Ways: Introducing Feminist Biblical Interpretation*. Maryknoll, NY: Orbis Books.

Silverman, C., J. L. Feder, S. Cvetkovska and A. Belford (2018) 'Macedonia's pro-Trump fake news industry had American Links, and is under investigation for possible Russia ties', *BuzzFeed News*, 18 July.

Simon, H. (1971) 'Designing Organizations for an Information-Rich World', *Computers, Communication and Public Interest*, edited by M. Greenberger. Baltimore, MD: The Johns Hopkins University Press.

Sinclair, T. J. (2005) *The New Masters of Capital: American Bond Rating Agencies and the Politics of Creditworthiness*. Ithaca: Cornell University Press.

Sklair, L. (2000) *The Transnational Capitalist Class*. Oxford: Blackwell Publishers.

Southwood, I. (2011) *Non-Stop Inertia*. London: Zero Books.

Standing, G. (2016) *The Corruption of Capitalism: Why Rentiers Thrive and Work Does Not Pay*. Hull: Biteback.

Stanley, T. (2012) 'Belgium's Heart of Darkness', *History Today*, 62(10), np.

Staub, E. (2005) 'The Origins and Evolution of Hate, With Notes on Prevention', *The Psychology of Hate*, edited by Robert J. Sternberg. Washington: American Psychological Association, pp. 51–66.

Sternberg, R. J. (2005) 'Understanding and Combating Hate', *The Psychology of Hate*, edited by Robert J. Sternberg. Washington: American Psychological Association, pp. 37–50.

Stiglitz, J. E. (2020) 'The Truth About the Trump Economy', *Project Syndicate*, 17 January.

Stolburg, S. G. (2018) 'White House Withholds 100,000 Pages of Judge Brett Kavanaugh's Records', *The New York Times*, 1 September.

Stout, L. (2012) *The Shareholder Value Myth: How Putting Shareholders First Harms Investors, Corporations and the Public*. San Francisco, CA: Berrett-Koehler Publishers, Inc.

Stromberg, R. N. (1982) *Redemption by War: The Intellectuals and 1914*. Lawrence: Regents of Kansas Press.

Strossen, N. (2018) *Hate: Why We Should Resist It With Free Speech, Not Censorship*. Oxford: Oxford University Press.

Suskind, R. (2004) 'Faith, Certainty and the Presidency of George W. Bush', *The New York Times*, 17 October.

Swaby, R. (2015) *Headstrong: 52 Women Who Changed Science—and the World*. New York: Broadway Books.

Taylor, A. (2017) 'American Nazis in the 1930s—The German American Bund', *The Atlantic*, 5 June.

Taylor, F. W. (2006) *Principles of Scientific Management*. New York: Cosimo Classics.

Thompson, A. (nd) 'The Smith Act of 1940 (1940)', *The First Amendment Encyclopedia*. https://mtsu.edu/first-amendment/article/1048/smith-act-of-1940

Thompson, I. (2018) 'Will Angela Merkel's Exit begin the Bannonization of Europe?', *Vanity Fair*, 29 October.

Tracy, A. (2018) '"We Are At a Turning Point": Counter-Terrorism Experts Are saying Trump Is Inspiring a Terrifying New Era of Right-Wing Violence', *Vanity Fair*, 2 November.

Umoh, R. (2019) 'How Closing the Racial Wealth Gap Helps the Economy', *Forbes*, 15 August.

Vaidhyanathan, S. (2018) *Anti-Social Media: How Facebook Disconnects Us and Undermines Democracy*. New York: Oxford University Press.

Varoufakis, Y. (2018) *Austerity*. London: Penguin.

Venn, C. (2018) *After Capital*. London: Sage Publications.

Waldron, J. (2012) *The Harm in Hate Speech*. Cambridge, MA: Harvard University Press.

Watkins, J., W. Wulaningsih, C. Da Zhou, D. C. Marshall, G. D. C Sylianteng, P. G. Dela Rosa, V. A. Miguel, R. Raine, L. P. King and M. Maruthappu (2017) 'Effects of Health and Social Care Spending Constraints on Mortality in England: A Time Trend Analysis', *BMJ Open*, 7(11), e017722. https://bmjopen.bmj.com/content/7/11/e017722

Wendling, M. (2018) *Alt-Right: From 4-Chan to the White House*. London: Pluto Press.

Wilkerson, I. (2010) *The Warmth of Other Suns: The Epic Story of America's Great Migration*. New York: Random House.

Williams, R. (2006) 'The Analysis of Culture', *Cultural Theory and Popular Culture: A Reader*, edited by John Storey, London: Pearson, pp. 32–40.

Wilson, S., S. Hall and J. Treadwell (2017) *The Rise of the Right: English Nationalism and the Transformation of Working-Class Politics*. Bristol: Policy Press.

Woodman, S., K. Kehoe, M. Saleh and H. Rappleye (2019) 'Thousands of Immigrants Suffer in US Solitary Confinement', *International Consortium of Investigative Journalists*, 21 May.

Wu, T. (2018) 'Is the First Amendment Obsolete?', *Michigan Law Review*, 117(3), pp. 547–81.

Zanona, M. (2017) 'Trump Cuts Funds to fight Anti-Right Wing Violence', *The Hill*, 14 August.

Zempi, I. and I. Awan (2016) *Islamophobia: Lived Experiences of Online and Offline Victimisation*. Bristol: Policy Press.

Žižek, S. (2002) *For They Know Not What They Do: Enjoyment as a Political Factor*. London: Verso Books.

Žižek, S. (2005) *Interrogating the Real*. London: Continuum.

Žižek, S. (2006) *How to Read Lacan*. London: Granta Publications.

Zuckerman, E. (2019) 'QAnon and the Emergence of the Unreal', *Journal of Design and Science* (6). https://doi.org/10.21428/7808da6b.6b8a82b9

Index

affect   39, 143, 152
Agamben, Giorgio   100, 101, 102
Ahmed, Sara   35, 37, 38, 42, 43,
    52, 76
Alamo Drafthouse   79–80
Alexander, J. C.   30–1, 97, 122,
    174
Alford, C. F.   38, 44–5, 46, 71, 173
Al-Qaeda   87, 88
alternative facts   13, 59, 139, 142–3
Alt-Lite   23–5, 27, 133
Alt-Right   3, 6–9, 18–27, 47, 63, 72,
    82, 88, 89, 95, 97, 119, 125,
    127, 128, 132, 137, 147, 161,
    164–6, 172, 174
    and Barak Obama   70
    and ethnic cleansing   18
    and feminism   23–4, 77
    and free speech   56
    and globalism   93, 119
    and identity politics   23
    and masculinity   23, 25–6, 38,
        77, 79
    and media   148, 150–1, 153–4
    origin of term   7
    and paranoid style   9
    and psychology   48
    and race   19–20, 23
    and traditional
        conservatism   27–31
    and white supremacy   19–22, 30
Americans for Tax Fairness   115–16
Anderson, Carol   20, 80–3
Andrejevic, Mark   140, 151
Anglin, Andrew   21, 22, 35, 172,
    173, 174
anxiety   7, 10, 37, 49, 72, 74, 76, 77,
    79, 80, 83–4, 102, 128, 130,
    147, 152, 164

Antifa   64–5
anti-racism   2, 33, 121, 168
anti-Semitism   31, 36, 46, 72, 88,
    93, 94, 119, 144
apocalypse   13, 89, 93, 99
    and postmillennialism   92
    and premillennialism   90, 92–3
    and the restrainer   96–7
    and white power   93–4
Arendt, Hannah   32, 48, 145
Atkinson, Rowan   54–8
austerity   4, 13, 103, 109–14, 116,
    118, 120, 159

Baggini, Julian   140, 141, 142, 144
Bailey, Alison   123, 135
Bannon, Steve   2–6, 30–3, 62–3,
    97, 119, 139, 140, 156,
    174–5
    Bannonization   30
Barr, William   64, 94, 174
Barthes, Roland   133
Bataille, Georges   46–7
Baudrillard, Jean   144
Beam, Louis   20–1, 24
Belew, Kathleen   20–1, 24, 70, 80,
    87, 93–4, 99, 172
Bell, Avril   164
Berlant, Lauren   4
Berry, Mike   116–18
Beydoun, K. A.   98
Biedermann   1, 6, 17, 57, 61, 65
    syndrome   28, 54
Billig, Michael   18
Black, Don   21, 70
Black Lives Matter (BLM)   7, 14, 28,
    33, 62, 123
Black Panther   128
Blee, Kathleen   43